Studien zur Geschichte des Völkerrechts

Edited by

Prof. Dr. Jochen von Bernstorff
Prof. Dr. Bardo Fassbender
Prof. Dr. Anne Peters
Prof. Dr. Miloš Vec

Founded by

Prof. Dr. Michael Stolleis (1941–2021)

Volume 45

Henri de Waele | Christian J. Tams [Eds.]

Realising The Hope of Ages?

Novel Perspectives on the Permanent Court of International Justice

Nomos

The Deutsche Nationalbibliothek lists this publication in the Deutsche Nationalbibliografie; detailed bibliographic data are available on the Internet at http://dnb.d-nb.de

ISBN 978-3-7560-3298-3 (Print)
978-3-7489-6074-4 (ePDF)

Onlineversion
Nomos eLibrary

1st Edition 2025

Preface

This volume contains a series of papers originally presented at an international workshop at Radboud University Nijmegen, The Netherlands, on 17 and 18 June 2022, subsequently revised and expanded for publication. The workshop's main intention was to celebrate the centenary of the 'booting-up phase' of the Permanent Court of International Justice. Entitled 'The Hope of Ages is in the Process of Realization', borrowing from James Brown Scott's contemporary assessment, it consciously sought to reconnect with the spirit of optimism accompanying the establishment of the first World Court.

Originally scheduled to take place in mid-2020, the COVID-19 pandemic required us to postpone the event by two years, so that on the eventual date, we rather commemorated the PCIJ's first plenary session instead of the official legal moment of the PCIJ's creation. The impact of this postponement on the quality of the presentations and discussions was, fortunately, absolutely nil. Some of the erstwhile presenters alas proved unable to contribute to the present volume, requiring us to make inquiries elsewhere, producing last-minute additions fitting most handsomely within our overall *thématique*. The title of the volume maintains the optimistic spirit of the workshop. The question mark is important, though; it deliberately leaves open the possibility of a more sober appraisal.

The editors would like to thank the steering board of the Radboud-Glasgow Collaboration Fund for the benevolent review of our initial grant application in 2019, and their terrific confidence and patience as the project shaped up further. They moreover wish to express their heartfelt gratitude to Ms. Lin Kluck, student-assistant at the Department of International and European Law of Radboud University Nijmegen, for excellent research assistance and editing work, and to Dr. Athene Richford at the School of Law of the University of Glasgow, whose help proved invaluable in the preparation of the original workshop. Above all, thanks are due to all contributors for their willingness to offer novel perspectives on the PCIJ, and their patience throughout the editorial process.

Lastly, we are very much pleased the editors of the *Studien zur Geschichte des Völkerrechts* have deemed this work worthy of inclusion in their series.

Nijmegen/Glasgow, November 2024

Henri de Waele
Christian J. Tams

Foreword

The World Court recently reached its centenary. Starting in 1922 as the Permanent Court of International Justice, it was in 1946 succeeded by the International Court of Justice, the principal judicial organ of the then-newly established United Nations. The pandemic somehow prevented the Court from celebrating its important anniversary, a milestone in the development of peaceful settlement of international disputes. It is therefore gratifying that two academic institutions, Radboud University Nijmegen and the University of Glasgow, joined forces and decided to initiate a dedicated project themselves. In June 2022, the two driving forces behind it, Professors Henri de Waele and Christian Tams, convened an international workshop at the Faculty of Law in Nijmegen, marking this epochal turning point in the history of international law development. The present volume consists of updated and revised contributions of scholars from various countries, presented at the conference.

In hindsight, it is remarkable how the ten-member Advisory Committee of Jurists, constituted by the Council of League of Nations in order to assist in implementing the task set out in Article 14 of the Covenant, succeeded just in the course of some five weeks, sitting in the Peace Palace in The Hague, in preparing a draft Statute of the future Court. This was an extraordinary achievement deserving full admiration, as the Statute has withstood the test of time and continues to serve, with minor modifications, as the main instrument guiding the judicial activities of the present International Court of Justice. According to Article 92 of the Charter of the United Nations, the Statute of the International Court of Justice is based upon the Statute of the Permanent Court of International Justice. The ten 'wise men' were able to agree on such delicate issues as the method of electing the judges of the Court, which, in the past, in particular during the Second Peace Conference in The Hague in 1907, were the main stumbling blocks in efforts to create a permanent judicial body. True, their proposal to endow the new Court with compulsory jurisdiction was not endorsed by the Council and the Assembly of the League of Nations. It was met with opposition by some major powers which were not ready to submit to the jurisdiction of the Court without their consent in a specific case or in a specific legal instrument. They were not ready then, and still, a century later, they are not ready today. The leading international law historian Arthur Eyffinger, in his contribution 'The Hope of Ages', puts the quest for a World Court into an interesting historical narrative. At the conference, he presented the first volume of his trilogy on the History of the World Court, a magnificent volume covering the period 1870–1920.

The Advisory Committee of Jurists was an extraordinary group of lawyers dedicated to pursuing the idea of creating a truly international court of justice. In his contribution, Sean Morris provides short biographical sketches of the main protagonists, focusing on what he calls "legal internationalism" as a science.

Undoubtedly, the Netherlands played an important role on the road to the establishment of the World Court, in its best Grotian tradition and as a host of the two Peace Conferences in The Hague, in 1899 and 1907 respectively. Where the introductory chapter already sets the scene, the country's specific role is the subject of the contribution by Karin van Leeuwen, highlighting the activities of Dr. Bernard Loder, the Dutch Member of the Advisory Committee of Jurists and the first President of the Permanent Court of International Justice (1922-1924).

The creation of the Court was not an enterprise of exclusively Western States and their jurists. Among the ten Members of the Advisory Committee we find two distinguished lawyers who contributed to the debates: Brazilian Raul Fernandes and Japan's Mineichirō Adachi, the latter becoming, in 1931, the fourth President of the Permanent Court. Raul Fernandes, during the discussion in the League of Nations, when the proposal for compulsory jurisdiction of the new Court was met with opposition, came up with a compromise formula according to which, in addition to a State becoming a party to the Statute, a declaration would be required by which that State would accept the jurisdiction of the Court as compulsory. This system remains in force today. The role of these two lawyers and of their countries — Brazil and Japan — in the negotiations in the League's organs, when they considered the draft Statute, is the subject of the contributions by Lucas Lima and Itai Apter.

The Permanent Court of International Justice was a success from its very inception. It was unknown how busy it might become. This explains why only its President and the Registrar were (and still are, as far as the ICJ is concerned) required to reside in The Hague, where the Court would meet for ordinary sessions (of some three months) and, when necessary, for extraordinary sessions. The system of sessions, in view of the increasing workload of the Permanent Court, was later, in 1936, abandoned, while the régime for Members of the Court to opt for non-resident status remains applicable even today.

What kept the Permanent Court busy from its inception were requests for advisory opinions. In the span of nine years, it received 27 such requests, mostly from the Council of the League of Nations. What a contrast with the Security Council of the United Nations, which, during the 80 years of its activities, requested the International Court of Justice for an advisory opinion only once, in 1970, on the *Legal Consequences for States of the Continued Presence of South Africa in Namibia (South West Africa) Notwithstanding Security Council Resolution 276 (1970)*. The very first contentious case, the *Wimbledon* case, was bought before the Permanent Court in 1923. The twenties were the foundational period for the World Court. It started to develop its jurisprudence, as well as its working methods, being ably assisted by a small Registry led by the energetic Åke Hammarskjöld, appointed at the age of 28, as its first Registrar. Åke Hammarskjöld, whose younger brother Dag became in 1953 the Secretary-General of the United Nations, occasionally published, under pennames — Paul de Vineuil or Michel de la Grotte — articles in leading international law journals of that time, commenting on some of the Court's decisions. In 1936, he was elected as Member of the Permanent Court at the young age of 43, but unfortunately, prematurely passed away less than one year later.

Three contributions are devoted to this foundational period in the activities of the Permanent Court. Sean Morris focuses on the concept of international law in the early advisory opinions. Momchil Milanov analyses how the court dealt with preliminary objections to its jurisdiction *ratione materiae*, in particular in the *Mavrommatis* case and in the saga of the *Chorzów Factory* cases. These were not only leading cases of that time but constitute jurisprudence invoked frequently by the parties before the present Court and are occasionally relied on by the latter in its decisions. Antoine Ollivier focuses on the development of the working methods of the Permanent Court and its quite efficient case-management. It has to be acknowledged that they still exert impact on today's conduct of business by the present-day Court.

In parallel with interstate litigation before the Permanent Court of International Justice, another form of third-party settlement of international claims by private persons against States rapidly developed, namely before the Mixed Arbitral Tribunals established pursuant to the post-World War I peace treaties. Michel Erpelding, who has recently and extensively published on the activities of these tribunals, briefly describes, in his contribution included in this volume, the relationship between the Permanent Court and the Mixed Tribunals. He refers to the observation by the Permanent Court in the *Certain German Interests* case that "the Mixed Arbitral Tribunals and the Permanent Court of International Justice [were] not courts of the same character". According to him, it appears that there was almost no dialogue between these institutions. However, there were some personal ties between them, as two members of the Permanent Court served, for some time, as members of the Mixed Arbitral Tribunals—and five members of the tribunals were appointed as "national judges", the term having been replaced (since 1929) by the term "judge *ad hoc*" in cases before the Permanent Court.

Overall, one may conclude that the establishment of the Permanent Court of International Justice and its activities, since its inception until early 1940, when they were cut short by the invasion of the Netherlands by Germany, were a success story. Through its judgments and advisory opinions, and through the elaboration and revisions of its Rules, the Permanent Court laid solid foundations for judicial settlement of inter-State disputes. Remarkably, the International Court of Justice was able to pursue its own activities on these solid foundations and to rely on its jurisprudence. And even today, an important part of that jurisprudence has not lost its relevance.

This volume is a valuable contribution to a better appreciation of this foundational period in the development of the judicial settlement of disputes between States. I therefore recommend it to all those interested in international law and its historical development.

Peter Tomka

Judge and former President
of the International Court of Justice

Table of Contents

About the Authors

Itai Apter is Ph.D. Candidate at the University of Haifa

Henri de Waele is Professor of International and European Law at Radboud University Nijmegen and the University of Antwerp

Michel Erpelding is Research Group Leader at the Max Planck Institute for Legal History and Legal Theory in Frankfurt-am-Main and Associate Member of the Institut de recherche en droit international et européen de la Sorbonne, Université Paris 1 Panthéon-Sorbonne

Arthur Eyffinger is Director of the JUDICAP Research Centre and former Head Librarian of the International Court of Justice (1988-2003)

Karin van Leeuwen is Assistant Professor of European Political History at Maastricht University

Lucas Carlos Lima is Professor of International Law at the Universidade Federal de Minas Gerais in Belo Horizonte

Momchil Milanov is Associate Legal Officer at the International Court of Justice

P. Sean Morris is Visiting Scholar in Law at the Faculty of Law of the University of Finland

Antoine Ollivier is Deputy Registrar of the International Tribunal for the Law of the Sea

Christian J. Tams is Professor of International Law at the University of Glasgow and at Sorbonne Law School in Paris

About the Authors

Introduction – Life and Times of a World Court

Henri de Waele

A. Introduction

By now, it has become a trite observation to state that international law scholarship has undergone a 'turn to history'. The literature on the discipline's past is burgeoning, with numerous different epochs receiving an attention that at times seems long overdue.[1] While academics are thus agreeably catching up, methodological turf wars have ensued on the most appropriate lenses to apply, and on who may be considered best qualified to undertake the most accurate inquiries.[2] So far, these battles remain undecided, with only few researchers in the legal field displaying a willingness to yield to those trained as historians. The current volume, largely composed of studies conducted by lawyers, serves as a further demonstration of that reticence. At the same time, the contributing authors draw from the ever-expanding range of sources, collecting insights from beyond their 'native' domains where necessary.

The aftermath of the First World War, the interbellum, and the 1920s in particular have not suffered from a lack of scholarly interest.[3] In that era,

---

1 Foundational have been Martti Koskenniemi, *The Gentle Civilizer of Nations* (Cambridge University Press, Cambridge 2001), albeit that the path was paved by Wilhelm Grewe, *Epochen der Völkerrechtsgeschichte* (Nomos, Baden-Baden 1984). See more recently e.g. Bardo Fassbender, Anne Peters and Simone Peter (eds), *The Oxford Handbook of the History of International Law* (Oxford University Press, Oxford 2012); Andreas von Arnauld (ed), *Völkerrechtsgeschichte(n): Narrative und Konzepte im Wandel* (Duncker & Humblot, Berlin 2017); Ignacio de la Rasilla y Moral, *International Law and History – Modern Interfaces* (Cambridge University Press, Cambridge 2021).

2 See e.g. Jacob Katz Cogan, 'Review of *The Oxford History of International Law*' (2014) 108 *American Journal of International Law*, 371; Lauren Benton, 'Beyond Anachronism: Histories of International Law and Global Legal Politics' (2019) 21 *Journal of the History of International Law*, 7; Natasha Wheatley, 'Law and the Time of Angels: International Law's Method Wars and the Affective Life of Disciplines' (2021) 60 *History & Theory*, 311.

3 Amongst many others: Susan Pedersen, *The Guardians – The League of Nations and the Crisis of Empire* (Oxford University Press, Oxford 2012); Marcus Payk, *Frieden durch Recht? Der Aufstieg des modernen Völkerrechts und der Friedensschluss nach*

the Permanent Court of International Justice (PCIJ) constitutes a logical focal point, forming a subject of enduring relevance in view of the riches it passed on to its successor, the International Court of Justice (ICJ).[4] At the same time, still today there would appear to be a series of 'known unknowns', or even 'unknown unknowns', with regard to the early years of the PCIJ, its establishment phase, and the first exercises of its jurisdiction. These lacunae invited a closer investigation by a selection of experts, the results of their endeavours being presented here.[5] Occasionally, the assembled chapters broach original topics, not meaning to produce the final word, but placing them in a belated limelight and happily inviting follow-up efforts. Some are more helpful in setting the scene, rehearsing readily accepted truths, yet not shying away from criticising or complementing conclusions reached by colleagues in the past. By the looks of it, existing works have centred on the Court's main output and general practice, relatively neglecting the pivotal (choices made during the) 'booting up' stage. Consequently, even though the PCIJ may be argued to have been examined *ad nauseam* already, this volume adds to the contemporary body of knowledge in multiple respects – not restricting itself to the installation phase, but also incorporating thought-provoking assessments of its actual operation. For the sake of clarity, we will proceed to flag up a number of the perceived gaps that are to be filled up in due course.

---

dem Ersten Weltkrieg (De Gruyter, Berlin 2018); Michel Erpelding, Burkhard Hess and Hélène Ruiz-Fabri (eds), *Peace through Law – The Versailles Peace Treaty and Dispute Settlement After World War I* (Nomos, Baden-Baden 2019); Christian J. Tams, 'Experiments Great and Small: Centenary Reflections on the League of Nations' (2019) 62 *German Yearbook of International Law*, 93; Henri de Waele, 'A New League of Extraordinary Gentlemen? The Professionalization of International Law Scholarship in the Netherlands, 1919–1940', (2020) 31 *European Journal of International Law*, 1005.

4 Ole Spiermann, *International Legal Argument in the Permanent Court of International Justice* (Cambridge University Press, Cambridge 2005); Philippe Couvreur, 'Regards sur la Cour permanente de justice internationale' in Mahmoud Cherif Bassiouni et al. (eds), *The Global Community Yearbook of International Law and Jurisprudence: Global Trends: Law, Policy & Justice – Essays in Honour of Professor Giuliana Ziccardi Capaldo* (Oxford University Press, Oxford 2013), 101; Christian J. Tams and Malgosia Fitzmaurice (eds), *Legacies of the Permanent Court of International Justice* (Brill Nijhoff, Boston/The Hague 2013).

5 The chapters mostly result from presentations delivered at a workshop entitled 'The Hope of Ages is in the Process of Realization', which took place on 17/18 June 2022 at Radboud University Nijmegen, the Netherlands.

B. Filling Gaps in the PCIJ's Historiography

In the first part of the book, concentrating on the Permanent Court's establishment, the ball is opened with a preliminary survey by Arthur Eyffinger. He begins by taking a step back, reflecting on the 'riddle of the quest', formulated as "mankind's highest pursuit of all, stubbornly upheld amidst the gore of centuries: to improve on the fate of man, attain sustainable peace and establish the Rule of Law in this world". Next, the essay offers a meticulous review of the constitutional parameters and overtures at the end of the 19th century, parsing the scattered ingredients that fed into the design, from the Treaty of Washington and the failed Prize Court to the First Hague Peace Conference and the Permanent Court of Arbitration. Eyffinger dwells extensively on the Advisory Committee of Justice (ACJ) and the drafting of the Statute, highlighting the reception of the latter document and concomitant discourse in the Council and Assembly of the League of Nations (LoN). He intriguingly expounds on the underexplored role of a sub-committee of the Assembly's Third Committee, which enacted a comprehensive overhaul of the findings of the ACJ, including the tabling of the *pis-aller* of the optional clause. In his generic appraisal, Eyffinger describes how the Court found itself perennially caught up in disputes that lacked wider moral, social or political implications, but that in fact the pettiness of the cases betrays the almost pathological sensitivities of the State-parties. The PCIJ certainly did play a prominent part in the less politicised domain of international governance, substantially assisting in the expanding and deepening of the world organization as such. At the end of the day however, at least as Eyffinger gives one pause to think, it was never likely to construe anything akin to a comprehensive judicial system, or a wholly refined trove of legal concepts.

Though there is no dearth of studies on the influence of particular countries on the development of the PCIJ, there are still enough stories and backgrounds here that deserve to be told. Also, from such exposés, the role of countless individuals regularly turns out to be more significant than has ordinarily been acknowledged. As the chapter by van Leeuwen underscores, the Netherlands is a case in point, where the tension between the nation's 'smallness' on the one hand, and its 'Grotian exceptionalism' on the other, retains a somewhat mysterious character. Building on research in Dutch, Swiss, Scandinavian government archives, as well as those of the LoN, she convincingly explains how both extremes played into the positions taken in the PCIJ negotiations. A longitudinal view indicates nonetheless the glaring discontinuities that cropped up in this positioning. What is more, the chapter highlights how the Dutch belief in international adjudication and conceptualisations of the broader discipline not only sprung from the missionary zeal found among prominent public international lawyers, but also by a the 'merchant' or maritime tradition originating from private international lawyers. She hereby rightly foregrounds Dr Bernard Loder, erstwhile judge of the Dutch Supreme Court, and his major impact on a great variety of ACJ decisions – a theme we will be reverting to further below.

The torch is taken over in the next chapter, focusing on the underexposed thinking of three distinguished Brazilians. Its author, Lucas Lima, not so much wishes to pay tribute to their separate activities, but rather grasp how their collective effort could be framed as a national legal position, in turn expressing a version of Latin-American regionalism. Lima deftly elaborates what were the central coordinates of the works of these scholars, Rui Barbosa, Clóvis Beviláqua and Raul Fernandes, which informed their views on the road towards the establishment of the PCIJ. Importantly, his study zeroes in on Fernandes' demeanour in the ACJ, who emerges as the true *auctor intellectualis* of the aforementioned optional clause. Moreover, going against an *idée reçue*, Lima contends that the regionalism that was espoused by the studied scholars constituted a philosophy that advocated the insertion of Brazil as such into the international scene, rather than an attempt to fit out the nascent judicial institution with elements of Latin American legal culture as a whole.

Another specific regional actor, the 'Empire of the Rising Sun', and the Japanese interventions in the run-up to the founding of the Court, are gauged by Itai Apter. His contribution paints a longitudinal picture by first charting the country's political shift from staunch isolation to radical internationalism at the dawn of the 20th century, inter alia through its partaking in the First and Second Hague Conferences. The chapter moves on to consider Japan's influence on the construction of the LoN and the PCA, the ill-fated 'racial equality' proposal, its national preferences as shared within the ACJ, as well as the dealings of its delegate Mineichirō Adachi. Instructive here is inter alia how much importance the Japanese attached to the election of PCIJ judges by governments, instead of resorting to other possible procedures. It turns out too that Adachi's resistance to endowing the Court with jurisdiction over international crimes hardened the opposition that ultimately put an end to that initiative. Furthermore, in the refusal to broaden the standing at the PCIJ beyond states, it turns out that Japan's opposition was equally instrumental. As it happens, several of the basic principles of its operation, like the appointment of judges and the need for jurisdiction based on consent, originated almost exclusively from the submissions of Japan.

Opening the second part of the book, devoted to the Permanent Court in Action, Antoine Ollivier addresses a number of other questions about its setup and functioning that have hitherto remained unanswered. His chapter starts with a review of the embryonic plans for the organisation of the Court, and the miscellaneous considerations on its 'permanence', before turning to the design of its eventual procedures. As known, in its preparatory work, the ACJ to a considerable degree drew from provisions which had been set out in the Hague Conventions for the Pacific Settlement of International Disputes of 1899 and 1907. Simultaneously however, it was well understood that the workings of the PCIJ raised novel challenges that called for limited adjustments. As Ollivier handsomely exemplifies, much room was left for the further development in practice, relating to mundane matters touching on the administration of proceedings, as well as to horizontal issues of a more fundamental relevance for the exercise of the international judicial function. Most of these came to be codified in successive revisions of its Rules of Procedure, surviving up to the present day to govern the modus operandi of the ICJ. Ollivier hereafter turns to the procedure for internal deliberations and the drafting of decisions, showing how these were intensely discussed by the judges, with an initial approach involving a special *chambre du conseil* being progressively complemented by the distribution of written notes, as consolidated later on in official resolutions. He finally reflects on some other features of the proceedings, including their length and the structure of the hearings. The chapter overall makes clear how much flexibility the PCIJ managed to afford itself, by avoiding to detail every aspect of its working methods, maintaining a principal freedom to deviate.

A related issue is how the PCIJ operationalised international law as a concept, and to which extent it thereby relied on existing scholarship. Purporting to deliver a tentative answer to that question, the chapter by Sean Morris zooms in on the Court's Advisory Opinions from the 1922–1930 period. His essay reveals that many of these did not bother to reference the notion or seek to build on the available scholarly sources. He moreover demonstrates how invocations of the notion often occurred to the background of the broader international legal environment, especially the aforementioned general principles. In some ways, the few visible conceptual exchanges resemble an effort to align the paradigm with the law of nations, and later on, with the 'new' international law of the 20th century. One of the distinctive characteristics of the era, or so Morris posits, is the framing of the law of nations as a 'jurisprudential mode', which incrementally may have been giving way to an alternative adjudicatory approach that was premised on 'mutual transactions'.

A specific procedural query, addressed in the chapter by Momchil Milanov, concerns how the Court choose to deal with preliminary objections directed against its subject-matter jurisdiction. Returning to the origins of the PCIJ, analysing the relevant conversations in the ACJ as well as the subsequent debates in the Assembly and the Council, it appears possible to uncover the main factors determining the treatment of such objections – yet Milanov argues convincingly that this story begins already in the 19th century, necessitating a review of international court projects from that epoch. A closer look at the PCIJ's case law signals there exists a tension between two competing approaches, a 'sovereign friendly' versus an 'expansive jurisdiction' one, which continues to hold sway. It emerges that one of the tests employed mirrors that in *Oil Platforms*, but predates it by more than 70 years.[6] Milanov also shows how the absence of rules on preliminary objections between 1922 and 1926 and the brevity of the first provision on the matter were a conscious choice, with the Court gradually realising how these have the power the course of the proceedings. On the aside, he illustrates how familiar *topoi* like consent and the dichotomy between arbitration and adjudication do not have an immutable meaning, but evolved considerably. He similarly points out how various ideas we have meanwhile taken for granted, like the *domaine réservé* or the rejection of non-justiciable disputes, result from a truly spectacular evolution.

The no less pioneering piece by Michel Erpelding showcases how the creation of the Permanent Court right after the First World War did not represent the only major innovation in international adjudication. Multiple Mixed Arbitral Tribunals (MATs) had been established even before the booting-up phase of the PCIJ was complete, which would go on to become the busiest judicial bodies of the whole interwar period. Whereas the Court refrained from any deep engagement, it is unsurprisingly that its own output made at least some mention of their practices. More importantly, Erpelding avers how these two phenomena mutually impacted one another

6 *Case concerning Oil Platforms (Islamic Republic of Iran v. United States of America)*, Judgment of 6 November 2003, ICJ Reports (2003), 161.

in ways that underlined their fundamentally different status. Hereby, he inter alia muses on ACJ deliberations as regards the relevance of the MATs precedent for determining the PCIJ's jurisdiction, as well as on the delicate inter-personal connections that existed between the respective members. In conclusion, his chapter touches on the 'paper legacy' of the MATs, reminding us that the unequal character of the relations between the two would succeed to outlive the institutions themselves.

In his epilogue, taking his cue from several previous chapters, Christian Tams chooses to ponder on three notable *fils rouges* that signify the added value of the current volume. He first engages with the familiar debates on the Euro-centredness of the PCIJ, opining that in the existing sources, the contributions of non-European participants continue to be underappreciated. If nothing else, the contributions collected here should succeed in convincing a wider audience that the World Court, as created in 1922, was at least partly shaped by their powerful interventions. Second, Tams suggests the *communis opinio* that the Court was too deferential of its sovereign clients is in dire need of being countered. Proceeding from our novel evidence, it might be argued instead that at times, it actually appeared quite interventionist, exhibiting the qualities of a 'savvy case manager'. In spite of this, Tams does admit that it remains correct to believe that 'muddling through' was a common *modus operandi*, then and now. The epilogist leaves us with a few captivating thoughts on the PCIJ's situational context, the possible influence it may have had on the conduct within the institution, as well as on how international justice was ultimately delivered.

C. The Hague Seat – Against All Odds?

Beyond the gaps the contributors to the present volume mean to fill, there is one other facet of PCIJ history that, to the mind of the editors, has not received the scholarly attention it is due. Today, one might still verily wonder: why did the Permanent Court end up in The Hague? However logical this may seem with the benefit of hindsight, at the time, the odds were actually stacked heavily against this location. The celebrated sentence in Article 14 of the League Covenant left open the choice of seat:

> The Council shall formulate and submit to the Members of the League for adoption plans for the establishment of a Permanent Court of International Justice.

While the underlying course of events is generally known, no author has fully plumbed its depths so far. In this volume, the chapter by van Leeuwen provides unparalleled insight into how the Dutch generally positioned themselves in the run-up to the PCIJ's establishment, yet does not go further than marking the decision of the ACJ that sealed the deal. For a completer picture, it is essential to retrace the steps that led to the outcome, drawing on a small score of primary sources that for foreign readers have been unhelpfully inaccessible.

In the aftermath of the First World War, the Netherlands had painted itself into a rather dire corner indeed. In the years before, it refrained from choosing sides and preferred to sit on the fence, a posture inciting suspicion and distrust from the neighbouring belligerents. European media commonly referred to it as 'the profiteer country par excellence'.[7] In November 1918, placing further strain on its official neutrality, the Dutch government allowed the German army to retreat more rapidly, granting an immediate passage from Belgium by crossing through the Limburg province. In addition, US President Woodrow Wilson harboured especially strong reservations towards the Netherlands because of its monarchical system of government, even regardless of the cosy relations the royal family dared to entertain with the imperial *Hohenzollern* cousins.[8] Worst of all, the Dutch elected to give shelter to the former *Kaiser* Wilhelm II, and repeatedly refused to accede to Allied extradition requests. In reaction, the British threatened to sever all diplomatic ties, and deny the country League membership.[9]

Initially, the Netherlands government attempted to persuade the Great Powers that The Hague would be a suitable venue nonetheless.[10] Foreign Minister Herman van Karnebeek exerted himself to tempt the League orga-

7 Johannes Houwink ten Cate, 'Deutschland und die neutralen Kleinstaaten in Nord- und Nordwesteuropa in der Zwischenkriegszeit' in Harm Schröder and Clemens Wurm (eds), *Politik, Wirtschaft und internationale Beziehungen. Studien zu ihrem Verhältnis in der Zeit zwischen den Weltkriegen* (von Zabern Verlag, Mainz 1991), 4.

8 Theodore Green, *Woodrow Wilson and the Paris Peace Conference* (Heath & Co., Lexington 1972), 31.

9 Rohan Butler, J.P.T. Bury and Margaret Lambert (eds), *Documents on British Foreign Policy 1919-1939, First Series – German Affairs* (HMSO, London 1960), nos. 577 and 579.

10 *Rijks Geschiedkundige Publicatiën* 117, nr. 924, 'Letter from Minister van Karnebeek to Former Minister Loudon', 12 February 1919; *Rijks Geschiedkundige Publicatiën* 117, nr. 948, 'Letter from Minister van Karnebeek to the Representative of France Mr Bourgeois', 19 February 1919.

nisation as a whole to establish itself there, finding himself rebuffed in the face of stiff competition – for multiple other countries had been vying for the seat just as much.[11] When it became clear this was a lost cause, with Switzerland winning the day, he enjoined that an energetic lobby be set up in order to lure the Permanent Court instead.[12] Correspondingly, van Karnebeek's predecessor John Loudon, who had become Dutch envoy in Paris, wrote to the US President:

> (…) [A]s You are aware the Covenant for the League of Nations does not mention the seat of the Permanent court of international justice. Some time ago I ventured to suggest to You in the interest of the League itself the advisability of separating the seat of the judicial from that of the executive and legislative branches. I was glad to notice that You concurred in this suggestion and intended to earnestly consider it. My government, to whom I reported our conversation, is now anxious to have the attention of the Conference drawn to this question and The Hague formally offered as the eventual seat of the new court of international justice.[13]

Wilson replied on 24 April that "the matter of the establishment of a permanent court under the League of Nations must necessarily wait some time until the organs of the League can give it full consideration", but that he would keep in mind "what you have urged about the seat of the court as distinguished from the League".[14] On the instruction of van Karnebeek, Loudon upped the ante in a letter to the US Secretary of State:

> My government earnestly hopes the Peace Palace which, as you know, is particularly suitable as a court of Justice, might then be accepted by the League of Nations as the abode of the newly established Court. Not only would the League of Nations at once have a palatial building at the disposal of its judicial branch, but to Holland, the country that has done so much for the cause of international law and justice it would give a genuine satisfaction. In that event my government is prepared

11 *Rijks Geschiedkundige Publicatiën* 117, nr. 936, 'Letter from the Paris Envoy Mr Loudon to Minister van Karnebeek', 17 February 1919.

12 *Rijks Geschiedkundige Publicatiën* 156, nr. 114A, 'Letter from Minister van Karnebeek to the Paris Envoy Mr de Stuers', 30 April 2019.

13 *Rijks Geschiedkundige Publicatiën* 117, nr. 1030, 'Exchange of Letters between Former Minister Loudon to US President Wilson', 22 and 24 April 1919.

14 Ibid.

> to grant the new Court of Justice the capitalized amount of the yearly contributions of all the powers that signed the agreement regarding the Court of Arbitration.[15]

Though prima facie, it appears striking that these manoeuvres were taking place even before the Covenant had entered into force (on 10 January 1920), it should be noted out that Mr Eric Drummond was appointed Secretary-General of the League as early as 5 May 1919.[16] As this official would probably stick to a neutral stance, Minister van Karnebeek was advised by the head of the League's legal section, the Dutchman Joost van Hamel, to officially forward him the Hague offer, but that it made little sense to try to win him over.[17] The Great Powers had anyway opted to pass the hot potato to the special Committee entrusted with the drafting of a Statute.[18]

Of crucial importance in the long run proved the recommendation to Drummond by the aforementioned van Hamel to invite his uncle, Bernard Loder, as member of the ACJ. Remarkably, Minister van Karnebeek was informed of this gambit after the deed was done, in a muffled writing asking for an official governmental endorsement of the candidature.[19] Van Hamel contrived that with Loder on the Committee, the Hague still stood a chance to win the seat, provided he would not claim its presidency, but rather leave that to the avid British representative Lord Phillimore. He equally suggested to couch in moral terms any forthcoming decision not to extradite the German Emperor, and to phrase it in a non-absolute fashion.[20] The advice was duly heeded, with the government's response declaring that Dutch legal system, "based on universally recognised principles of law", nor the country's reputation of being "a land of refuge for those vanquished in international conflicts" allowed it to accede to the extradition – since "right and national honour, the respect of which is a sacred duty, oppose

15 *Rijks Geschiedkundige Publicatiën* 156, nr. 32A, 'Letter from the Paris Envoy Mr Loudon to US Secretary of State Lansing', 9 July 1919.

16 Clasina Cluyver, *Documents on the League of Nations* (Sijthoff, Leiden 1920), 256.

17 'Letter from Mr van Hamel to Minister van Karnebeek', 31 March 1920, reprinted in Ernst van Raalte, *Den Haag, Zetel van het Internationale Gerechtshof* (W.E.J. Tjeenk Willink, Zwolle 1974), 20.

18 League of Nations, *Official Journal*, Vol. I, March 1920, p. 37.

19 *Rijks Geschiedkundige Publicatiën* 156, nr. 117, 'Letter from League Functionary Mr van Hamel to Minister van Karnebeek', 6 October 1919.

20 Ibid.

such action".[21] The elegantly framed memorandum obviated a key reason for Allied resentment – sparing them the ordeal of actually having to go through with a trial for which the appetite had waned considerably.[22]

At the end of 1919, van Hamel had been under the impression that the ACJ was to meet in London or Paris, but believed that at that point nothing was fixed in this respect. He insisted that Loder, not van Karnebeek, was best placed to take it up with Drummond, after consulting with Phillimore, who was apparently predisposed towards The Hague.[23] As recounted by van Leeuwen, shortly thereafter, Loder and Phillimore indeed met up privately in London, reaching an agreement on both the Committee's chairmanship and the location for its meetings, exactly along the lines of van Hamel's preferences.[24] No less cordial *tête-à-têtes* took place with Loder's future peers Mineichirō Adachi (who would become judge as well) and Dionisio Anzilotti (destined to serve as Committee secretary).[25] Loder also twice staged an encounter with Léon Bourgeois, then President of the League Council, who personally regarded The Hague to constitute the most logical option. The Belgian member of the ACJ, Édouard Descamps, had floated Brussels as an alternative, and two other colleagues favoured gathering in Paris. Pressed for time however, Drummond apparently presented the Committee only with the Dutch invitation, which (partly owing to Loder's interventions) was gladly accepted by a majority of the would-be participants.[26] The Secretariat-General then planned the first official ACJ meeting for 16 June 1920, which was preceded by a secret session wherein

21 *Rijks Geschiedkundige Publicatiën* 156, nr. 215, 'Note verbale from Minister van Karnebeek to the President of the Peace Conference Clemenceau', 21 January 1920; *Rijks Geschiedkundige Publicatiën* 156, nr. 279A, 'Letter from the British Prime Minister and Leader of the Supreme Council Lloyd George to Foreign Minister van Karnebeek', 20 February 1920.

22 William Schabas, *The Trial of the Kaiser* (Oxford University Press, Oxford 2018), 269 and 294-295.

23 *Rijks Geschiedkundige Publicatiën* 156, nr. 117, 'Letter from League Functionary Mr van Hamel to Minister van Karnebeek', 6 October 1919.

24 'Letter from Mr Loder to Minister van Karnebeek', 15 April 1920, reprinted in Ernst van Raalte, *Den Haag, Zetel van het Internationale Gerechtshof* (W.E.J. Tjeenk Willink, Zwolle 1974), 22-23.

25 *Rijks Geschiedkundige Publicatiën* 156, nr. 325, 'Letter from Mr Loder to Minister van Karnebeek', 22 April 1920. On Adachi, see also the chapter by Apter in the current volume.

26 Karin van Leeuwen and Morten Rasmussen, 'A Political and Legal History of the Advisory Committee of Jurists and the foundation of the Permanent Court of International Justice' in P. Sean Morris (ed), *Transforming the Politics of International Law*

Descamps (and not Phillimore) found himself elected President and Loder Vice-President.[27]

Among his colleagues, Loder was one of the few who had acquired extensive experience in legal practice, both as an attorney and a judge. On top of that, he partook in high-level international affairs, inter alia as co-founder of the *Comité Maritime International*, head of a committee for the *Organisation centrale pour une paix durable*, and chair of the group of neutral countries that aimed to align their positions on the text of the League Covenant. In January 1919, he had been of counsel to the Dutch government on the matter of the *Kaiser*'s extradition. His subsequent influence on multiple decisions of the ACJ is unsurprising, and masterfully depicted in the chapter by van Leeuwen. The Committee itself was convened in the picturesque Peace Palace, where the attractive surroundings, but also Loder's presence and gravitas, should have helped to obtain a most benevolent view of The Hague.

At its 9th meeting on 25 June 1920, which was designated 'private yet 'fully recorded, President Descamps opened at 9.30h, wishing to table an item that in his eyes could be settled without a long debate: the definitive choice of the Court's seat. He proposed to choose The Hague, but not merely as an act of courtesy towards the host country, grounding his proposal on two other arguments:

> [F]irst, the Hague is already the seat of the Permanent Court of Arbitration; and second, the President thought there was reason to separate the political functions of the League of Nations from its judicial functions by assigning different seats to the two groups of institutions. If the proposal were adopted, exception of course should be made for cases in which it might be necessary to convene the Court away from its normal seat.[28]

The echo of the arguments that were advanced before by van Karnebeek and Loudon can obviously not be overlooked. Of those present, nobody except Adachi shared a piece of their mind. He explained that he had warmed to the idea, notwithstanding prior hesitations, expanding as follows:

– *the Advisory Committee of Jurists and the Formation of the World Court in the League of Nations* (Routledge, Oxon 2022), 85.

27 Advisory Committee of Jurists, *Procès-Verbaux of the Proceedings of the Committee: June 16th–July 24th 1920.*

28 Ibid, 202.

> If this idea is carried out, it is certain to be the interpretation of public opinion in the Asiatic nations. In Japan, when the Hague is mentioned, it means Peace and Justice. This has become a tradition among the people. Furthermore, it is necessary to separate the judicial from the political deliberations in order to permit the Court to examine and judge in tranquillity the cases submitted to it.[29]

Since everyone else present seemed to concur, Descamps dared to state there was a consensus within the Committee. Right hereafter, Albert De Lapradelle took the floor, asking that the reasons behind the decision not be recorded in light of possible reservations on his side.[30] For unknown reasons, his request was ignored. Loder then delivered a grateful statement:

> There is no need for me to tell you that the proposal made by our President and its adoption by all of you make me very happy, Gentlemen, especially in view of the reasons upon which the President was so good as to base the resolution. I think that I may say, in the name of my Government, as well as in the name of my country, that the resolution adopted by this Committee will be received with joy, and I think I can assure you that Holland, always faithful to its traditions, will do all in its power to accomplish the task given to it. I hope that the Council and Assembly will also adopt the decision taken here, and I give voice to the hope that the Court for whose coming we are preparing the way will be a source of happiness for the whole world.[31]

Wrapping up the discussion, Descamps had put on record that the decision was unanimous, and that the Dutch government was prepared to agree. The former inference is a tad confusing, as the minutes reveal that the Brazilian member Beviláqua (despite having resigned earlier, to the benefit of Fernandes) did not attend this session. Anyhow, neither the Council nor the Assembly sought to revisit the issue, with both institutions simply deferring to the bidding of the ACJ on this count.[32] Thus, the sly manoeuvring of the van Hamel–Loder tandem resulted in the manifold objections lodged against the candidature of the Netherlands being washed away in little under a year.

29 Ibid.
30 Ibid, 203.
31 Ibid.
32 League of Nations, *Records of the First Assembly – Plenary Meetings* (1920), 468.

D. Conclusion

Though officially disbanded in 1946, the Court was, as known, in fact merely rebooted in a slightly different form. Observed with the benefit of hindsight, in 1921, it may well have been a smart move to decouple its Statute from the Covenant of the League, so that it would not go down immediately if or when the latter organisation were to implode.

The Court's case law evidently connects with that of its successor, their constitutional texts are neigh identical, and it can hardly be called a coincidence that the first President of the ICJ had served as the last of the PCIJ. For sure, one century after the international judiciary got off the ground properly, the legacy of the First World Court is alive and kicking.[33]

Quite a bit of the early history of the PCIJ remains to be demystified nevertheless. The present volume seeks to rise to that challenge, whereby the current chapter contained a snapshot of what the reader may expect in the collected essays. The aim here was moreover to recount in novel detail the trajectory of how the Permanent Court landed, against all odds, in the city of The Hague, and why this came about. The outcome should strike those cognisant of the erstwhile context as remarkable, a feat accomplished through a series of clever shenanigans behind the scenes. Whereas credit is ordinarily given to Bernard Loder, an essential complementary actor was Joost van Hamel – a largely unsung hero who enabled his success.[34]

33 For a specific substantive illustration, see Ewa Sałkiewicz-Munnerlyn, *Jurisprudence of the PCIJ and of the ICJ on Interim Measures of Protection* (Springer, Berlin-Heidelberg 2021). On the exemplary status of the system of judicial governance, see Henri de Waele, 'Managing the Realisation of "The Hope of Ages": Governance of the Permanent Court of International Justice' in Sergey Vasiliev and Niels Blokker (eds), *The Governance of International Courts and Tribunals* (Oxford University Press, Oxford forthcoming).

34 Cf. Freya Baetens and Veronica Lavista, '"Where is Your Tribunal?" Bernard Loder (1849–1935) and the Quest for International Justice' in P. Sean Morris (ed), *The League of Nations and the Development of International Law – A New Intellectual History of the Advisory Committee of Jurists* (Routledge, London 2022), 207.

PART I
Establishing the Permanent Court

The Hope of Ages

Arthur Eyffinger

A. Introduction

The early 2020s are sobering times. A full century ago, at Versailles, the 'Alliance of the Peoples' felt confident it was at long last turning a bloody page of history. In a critical move, mankind was determined to replace the relentless conflicts of the nation states and the inveterate mistrust between the Great and the Small Powers with a New World Order of Solidarity. The League of Nations, the World Court, the collective security system were daring experiments. In this new dawn, there was no place for aloofness or neutrality. To top its hubris, mankind in 1928, in dewy-eyed reliance on the effectiveness of a paper interdiction of war, for a fleeting moment even daydreamed it had wiped out *Leviathan.*

A century later, a vacillating World Organization, kept hostage by its Member States, is left virtually toothless in its uphill fight to battle global warming, engraft sustainable development, implement social justice, or enforce a fair distribution of wealth. Worse, an energy crisis, short supplies of pharmaceutics, and the questionable production-lines of food and fabrics lead man to reconsider the wisdom of global interdependency and rekindle nationalism and protectionism.

But then, the other pole, the nation state does not fare much better. In an irreversible process, its once unassailable claim to sovereignty is increasingly being eroded. Multinationals claim more than their share of power. Modern technology has no regard for borderlines, local militias scoff at the Powers' claims to exclusivity of armed force. International governance experiences an impasse, giving cause for serious concern. In the early 1920s, millions of homeless migrants and refugees were crisscrossing Europe in desperate search of a restart in life. The repetition of moves we observe in our days does not just find political structures as disjoint as ever, more alarming yet is the lack of any palpable moral growth. In our darker moments, we feel lost in a twilight zone of crumbling authority wherein former parameters no longer apply.

Mankind has stood at these crossroads before, and the birthday of Modernity was a particular moment in point. At that historic juncture, two powers with competing universal claims, the one sovereign in the political domain, the other in the spiritual realm, by forceful inroads in each other's provinces and prerogatives, raised a storm they proved unable to ride. At these crossroads of despair, the discipline of international law was born. At that moment of deep moral and intellectual crisis, man conceived what we call the 'Hope of Ages'.

In the irony of history, our current crisis coincides with the celebration of some of the dearest moments in the track-record of our discipline. With war raging nearby, we stand on the eve of the fourth centenary of the publication, back in 1625, of the first comprehensive set of traffic rules for the international arena. Pioneering Hugo Grotius laid down general principles and pitched commandments against prohibitions to mark the zones of black and white in public and private relations. Out of sheer concern, he even ventured into that fleeting grey zone in-between, where but few lawyers dare: that slippery domain, which eludes formal indictment and where no duty applies. The precarious intersection, where the law, justice, and equity each claim a say, and man's conscience must guide him in sub- or supererogation.

These years teem with jubilees. December 2020 saw the centenary of the adoption of the Statute of the World Court. February 2022 recalled the installation of its first bench. The year 2023 carried our thoughts back to that memorable year 1873, when in the wake of a stunning war and a pivotal arbitral award, Belgium hosted the founding of two research bodies, the *Institut* and the ILA. In their unrelenting codifying efforts and parallel roadmaps, the two bodies bespoke the distinguished outlooks on the law from the perspective of the Civil Law and the Common Law. Our discipline would stand much the poorer for the lack of either of these bodies and traditions in their eminently complementary and balancing roles. The year 2023, *quatorze juillet* to be precise also marked the centenary of a third formidable organ of research and education. It came about under the auspices of the previous two bodies. But then, it was very intentionally brought within the framework of *L'Oeuvre de La Haye*. The Hague Academy of International Law was conceived as the touchstone of theory, as watchdog of the practical accomplishments of diplomacy as laid down in the conventions of conferences and the awards and judgments of courts.

Commemorations are fitting moments for a *siste viator*. At congresses and in publications, the abovementioned bodies wisely take a break for intro- and retrospection. The academic workshop that eventually gave birth to the present volume sought to reach even wider and cut deeper. It harked back to the cradle, and probed the rationale of concepts that have intrigued and yet teasingly baffled mankind for centuries. The project carries us well beyond the precincts of the law proper. It appraises the role of our discipline as ancillary to man's elusive yearning for self-fulfilling.

B. *The Riddle of the Quest*[1]

The quest for a World Court bespeaks what perhaps presents mankind's highest pursuit of all, stubbornly upheld amidst the gore of centuries, to improve on the fate of man, attain sustainable peace and establish the Rule of Law in this world. The title of the workshop held at Nijmegen in 2022 appropriately states both the unrelenting ambition and the recalcitrance of its implementation. One may suggest that the quandary comes only naturally and, in the last resort is retraceable to the ambivalent nature of man himself, and his inner conflict to rhyme self-assertion with altruism. Next to his innate social bent and solidarity to his fellow-man, and equally ineradicable ranks his incorrigible pursuit of self-interest.[2]

Man's quest for harmony was perhaps first suggested by analogy, by his observation of the euphony of the universe in what he coined the 'music of the spheres'. Plato reputedly probed its rationale, which Pythagoras famously sought to catch in numbers.[3] Mindful of his status as part and parcel of the universe man craved to arrogate this ideal. He extrapolated the concept in the image of the concentric circles[4] that encompassed all provinces of human endeavour, from the private domain of the *pater famil-*

1 This paper presents a synopsis of the author's findings from his research laid down in the volumes I and II of an intended trilogy on the history of the 'World Court'. Volume I addresses the Constitution of the Court (1870-1920), Volume II the PCIJ (1921-1946). Hereinafter, the volumes are referred to as '*World Court* I' and '*World Court* II' respectively.

2 As e.g. designated by Hugo Grotius, *De jure belli ac pacis* (1625), prolegomena, paras. 6-10.

3 The origins and rationale of the *musica universalis* were discussed by Plato in his *Timaeus* (c. 360 BC). For Pythagoras of Samos (570-500 BC), his concept of the harmony of the spheres and his doctrine of numbers see Diogenes Laertius, *Life of Philosophers*, 8.1-50. For the reception of the idea in early modern times see e.g. Johannes Keppler, *Harmonices Mundi* (1619).

4 As e.g. presented in Nicolaus Copernicus, *Systema Universi Totius* (1543).

ias, along the civil entourage of the shepherd of men to the political sphere of the *perfectissima societas,* the State entity.[5] He envisioned the perfect ruler as a great legislator[6] or philosopher-king[7] and presented the ideal Head of State as the "Living Law".[8]

No sobering experience of history has ever uprooted this longing, which proved so common to all human pursuits. Poets and painters portrayed the *Ideallandschaft;*[9] architects sketched the *città ideale.*[10] All Roman poets of Augustus' times longed for the Golden Age.[11] Virgil's call for the 'Saturnia Regna' is reflected in the stained-glass windows of the Great Hall of Justice of the Peace Palace.[12] St. Augustine imagined a 'better Rome', the City of God.[13] One misunderstanding should definitely be cleared up. The unfeasibility of the ideal never affected the comfort it offered man in dealing with harsh reality. Erasmus' pun 'Utopia' eminently brings the quest to the point. The ideal world (*eu-topos*) is nowhere to be found (*ou-topos*), but the search is one man cannot do without.[14]

Perhaps a second misconception calls for reassessment. The two worlds are commonly presented as outer poles bound never to meet. As it is, the lofty ideal is often discredited as 'unworldly' and 'unreal'. But then, history rather suggests a closer link, such as the one expressed in the metaphor of

---

5 For the implementation of the concept in politics see Cicero, *Somnium Scipionis* (= *De Republica*), 6.9-29.

6 As in Francesco Patrizzi's *Città Felice* (1551) or in Robert Burton's *Anatomy of Melancholy* (1621).

7 As represented in the *Fürstenspiegel* of humanists like in Erasmus' *Institutio Principis* (1516).

8 This is the way Hugo Grotius portrays Joseph, Vice-Roy of Egypt in his *Sophompaneas* (1635).

9 As represented by Nicolas Poussin in his pastoral *Et in Arcadia Ego* (1638) in the plastic arts, or by Hugo Grotius in his portrayal of Paradise in his drama *Adamus Exul* (1601).

10 As in the famous presentation of Urbino as the ideal township (c. 1490, by an unknown artist) or in the depiction of Siena in Lorenzetti's *Allegory of the Good and Bad Government* (1338).

11 The idea is met in Catull, Ovid, Properce, Tibull and Virgil alike.

12 Virg. *Ecl.* 4.6: 'Redeunt Saturnia Regna'. The line recalled the address by Sir Edward Fry in the Plenary of the Second Hague Peace Conference (1907). The window panels were the gift of the British Government (1912) and were produced by Douglas Strachan (1875-1950).

13 Augustine, *De Civitate Dei* (426).

14 Erasmus handed his dear friend Thomas More the title for his political satire (originally entitled *Nusquama*). The tract marked the birth of a genre and found endless expression up to H.G. Wells, *A New Utopia* (Chapman and Hall, London 1905).

the communicating vessels. The meandering of international law is a case in point. Nothing has as consistently and dramatically prompted the Rule of Law, if probably from repent rather than from wisdom as precisely the failure of the realm of power. The rivalry for the Spice Isles pitched Grotius against John Selden.[15] The atrocities perpetrated in the Indies triggered the humanitarian debate at Valladolid (1550)[16]. The shambles of the Wars of Religion set the law free from its straight-jacket of moral theology.[17] The Napoleonic Wars (1793-1814) sparked the Peace Movement on both sides of the Atlantic.[18] Henry Dunant's eye-witnessing the slaughterhouse of war brought about the Red Cross codes.[19] The Crimean War (1853-1856) kindled a Czar's initiative to curb privateering.[20] The American Civil War (1861-1864) brought about *Lieber's Code.*[21] The first conflict of the Industrial Age, the Franco-Prussian War (1870-1871) triggered the *Institut* and the *International Law Association,*[22] the *Brussels Declaration* on the Laws and Customs of War (1874),[23] and the *Oxford Manual* on humanitarian

15 Selden pitched his *Mare Clausum* (1635) against Grotius' *Mare Liberum* (1609). For the English-Dutch rivalry see the reports of the two 'Colonial' Conferences in London (1613) and at The Hague (1615), in which Grotius served as the main advocate and spokesman of Holland and the V.O.C.

16 The polemic between the Dominican Bartolomé De Las Casas (1484-1566) and Juan Ginés de Sepúlveda (1490-1573) on the treatment of the native peoples of Latin America opened the discourse on human rights.

17 It is an interesting whim of history, as Tobias Asser once acutely observed, that the first politician to propound the separation of State and Church was French Cardinal Richelieu (1585-1642).

18 Both the British and the American *Peace Societies* were founded in the days of the Congress of Vienna (1815).

19 Dunant's *Souvenir de Solférino* (1862) recalled a crucial battle in the Second Italian War of Independence (1859). It inspired the International Red Cross Movement (1863) and Convention (1864).

20 At the Congress of Paris (1856), Czar Alexander II (1855-1881) instigated the *Paris Declaration Respecting Maritime Law.*

21 The reference is to the political scientist Francis Lieber (1800-1872) and his *Instructions for the US Army in the Field* (April 1863, General Order No. 100).

22 The two research institutes were both founded in 1873, in Ghent and Brussels respectively, in the wake of the Franco-Prussian War (1870-1871) and inspired by the *Alabama Arbitration* (1872) in Geneva. The two bodies represented the Continental and Anglo-Saxon approach to the codification and development of international law.

23 The 'Project of an International Declaration concerning the Laws and Customs of War' (Brussels, 27 August 1874). This Declaration never entered into force, but served as roadmap in 1899.

law (1880).[24] The blatant abuse of the law in the Russo-Japanese War (1904-1905) made the Powers regulate that last domain of perfect licence, naval war in the Laws of The Hague (1907).[25] As if to put down the seal of history the first military conflict on a global scale, in proportional response one may say facilitated the implementation, at long last, of a World Organization and the substitution of the gratuitous procedure of arbitration with a standing global judiciary.[26]

Man, clearly, learns from failure and draws inspiration from repent. But then, the medal has its flipside. Man's dual nature works both ways. Even in his highest aspirations, he never betrays his ambiguity. The quest that was under consideration in the Nymegen workshop is a case in point. None of the allegedly 'unworldly' chimeras of a World Federation (and of a World Court as its steady corollary) which history has produced passes the scrutiny for bias and hidden agendas. The first documented instance, Pierre Dubois' scheme from 1306 already featured most ingredients of Wilson's League.[27] It even proscribed war in terms recalling the *Briand-Kellogg Pact* of 1928.[28] But its ultimate goal was the common stand against the infidel with a view to recapturing the Holy Land. Again, as a King's Counsellor, Dubois never lost sight of the interests of France as against the Hapsburg Emperor. It was much the same with comparable schemes developed by Marsilius of Padua or Honoré Bovet.[29]

Bohemian King George Poděbrady, to make his project for a Permanent Council and Federal Tribunal at all feasible had it put under the high patronage of Louis XI.[30] Cardinal Wolsey's subtle scheme for a European

24 The *Manuel des lois de la guerre sur terre*, adopted by the *Institut* at its 6th Session in Oxford in September 1880, served as basis for the Hague Convention of 1899.

25 Laid down in the Hague Conventions VI-XIII (1907).

26 The ambition joined two separate aspirations that both boasted a long heritage, the one for a World Organization, the other for a World Court of Law. For a survey of the numerous projects up to 1919 that inspired the Covenant of the League see *World Court* I, chapter 6.

27 Pierre Dubois (1255-1321), *De Recuperatione Terrae Sanctae* (1306). For a historical survey of projects for a World Organization, see *World Court* I, chapter 1.5.

28 The *Briand-Kellogg Pact* was initiated by the Foreign Ministers of France (Aristide Briand) and the USA (Frank B. Kellogg). It was signed in Paris on 27 August 1928 and intended to eliminate war as an instrument of national policy. For the text see LONTS 94, No. 2137 (57ff.).

29 Marsilius of Padova (1280-1342), *Defensor Pacis* (1324); Honoré Bovet (1340-1410), *Arbre de batailles* (c. 1430).

30 Georg of Podiebrad (1420-1471), King of Bohemia (1458-1471), the reputed author of a *Tractatus pacis toti Christianiti fiendae* (1463).

Union thwarted the Papacy.[31] The prerequisite for Eméric de Crucé's Permanent Assembly in Venice was the prior satisfaction of France's territorial claims.[32] The highly praised 'egalitarian' *Grand Dessein* of the Duke of Sully was above all an ingenious device to stamp out Hapsburg primacy.[33] De Béthune neatly obliged all territorial claims of the European Powers by the dodgery to have the Turks dispelled from the Continent.

The famous project for perpetual peace of the Abbé de St. Pierre, in its system of the rotation of membership for the Small Powers keenly anticipated the conundrum that baffled the delegates at The Hague in 1907 and the Advisory Committee of Jurists (ACJ) in 1920.[34] Its reliance on arbitration and sanctions to help execute awards sounds all too modern.[35] But the 'peace eternal' of the Abbé was based on perpetuating the *status quo*, thus warranting the primacy of France. William Penn's enlightened *Diet* in its economic postulates quite intentionally complied with the Anglo-Saxon outlook.[36] In short, peace was proclaimed from self-interest long before in 1898 Nicholas II's *Rescript* secured a moratorium to *reculer pour mieux sauter*.[37]

C. The Parameters for the Court

True to his nature, man learns the best the hard way. Real progress is invariably wrung from crisis, and the two junctures of most comprehensive crisis in European history stand witness to this sobering truth. The second

31 British Cardinal Thomas Wolsey (1473-1530) conceived a non-aggression pact among the European Powers, the *Treaty of London* (1518).

32 Emeric de Crucé (1590-1648), *Le Nouveau Cynée* (Au Palais sur le perron royal, Paris 1623).

33 Maximilien de Béthune, Prince de Sully (1560-1641), *Grand Dessein d'Henri IV* (c. 1600).

34 Charles Irénée Castel, Abbé de Saint-Pierre (1658-1743), *Projet pour rendre la paix perpétuelle en Europe* (1712). The riddle of the legal equality of States (as contrasted with their political inequality) baffled both the Second Hague Hague Conference and the ACJ; *World Court* I, chapter 5.2-4; chapter 12.1.

35 Cf. Dutch Cornelis van Vollenhoven (1874-1933) and his advocacy of sanctions in his *Drie Treden van Het Volkenrecht* (Martinus Nijhoff, 's-Gravenhage 1918) under specific reference to Hugo Grotius.

36 Quaker William Penn (1644-1718) developed the idea for a *Diet* or Council of Europe (1693).

37 The Czar's *Rescript* of 24 August 1898 was mistrusted from the day of its proclamation. Modern research has emphatically confirmed these reserves.

instance, the cataclysm of the First World War, facilitated the implementation of a World Organization at Versailles. The first social upheaval, four centuries earlier addressed at Westphalia,[38] was as deep as the second in unsettling moral normativity, political idiom and the socio-economic fabric. But then, that moment of crisis was perhaps no less pivotal to our subject-matter, in that precisely this cataclysm laid down the parameters for the League and the Court as we know it today.

The reference is to the birth of the nation state, and the lukewarm bid at Westphalia for what was called a State system. Up to Dante,[39] the parameter of the monolith Roman Empire, many centuries from its effective downfall (c. 476 A.D.) had remained axiomatic, if conversed into the doctrine of the *Two Swords* to appease the keen rivalry of the spiritual and secular realms.[40] With the Crusades, this medieval commonwealth imploded. The rise of commerce and banking, of a citizenry and a merchant class outwitted the feudal hierarchy. Modern science challenged spiritual authority. To bespeak the urgency of new parameters a mere three years, 1515-1517, saw Luther nail his theses in Wittenberg and the publication of Macchiavelli's *Prince*, Erasmus' *Institutio Principis* and Thomas More's *Utopia*.[41]

Neither Pope nor Emperor found the proper answer how best to ride the storm. In Augsburg (1555), fragmentation was consolidated in the *cuius regio*-principle.[42] A century later at Westphalia, solidified power-blocks stood horn-locked.[43] Well-advised by Cardinal Richelieu (of all people) to separate the realms of Church and State, rulers in an arduous process

38 A range of bilateral peace negotiations were opened as early as 1636 and took place at Munster and Osnabruck. Direct negotiations were complicated by personal incompatibilities and matters of *préséance*. Talks ensued in a range of separate and bilateral treaties, just like in Paris in 1919-1920.

39 As illustrated in Dante Alighieri (1265-1321), *De Monarchia* (1313).

40 Pope Gelasius († 496) in his doctrine of the 'Two Swords' (under reference to *Luk.* 22:38) propounded the dichotomy of the spiritual and temporal powers; it was a paramount concept throughout the Middle Ages.

41 Luther proclaimed his 95 theses in April 1517. The tracts by Erasmus (1516), Macchiavelli (1513-1515), and Thomas More (1516) represented three consistent mainstreams of political theory: constructionalism, realism, and idealism.

42 The Religious Peace agreed at the Council of Augsburg in September 1555 formulated the principle of *cuius regio, eius religio*, which put public authorities in control of religion in their lands.

43 By 1635, the initial demarcation of Powers in the Thirty Years' War (1618-1648) according to their religious denomination had by and large been substituted by that of political interests in the keen rivalry of the hegemonic Hapsburg Empire and the rising Nation-States. A major ideological watershed was the alliance concluded by

of centuries sought how to rhyme unimpeachable State sovereignty with peaceful inter-State relations. The conundrum triggered a wealth of discourse on the theory of State. A first line of thought reasoned from the keen observation of sobering practice. It ran from Macchiavelli along Hobbes to Morgenthau.[44] In a second bid Erasmus' *Institutio* articulated the circumspect humanist tradition of State counsellors, which Grotius endorsed a century later in his *De Studio Politico*.[45] This line of thought insisted on legal principles and moral normativity.

Perhaps most intriguing, while often misunderstood, was a third proposition on the basis of 'idealistic' speculation. Plato had adumbrated the concept of the ideal State in his *Timaeus* and his parables of the grotto and mythical Atlantis.[46] Columbus' and Vespucci's reports from the New World, if blatantly at odds in their appraisal rekindled the ancient fables of the Isles of the Blessed.[47] Coined by Thomas More, the utopian genre became an instant vogue, never to lose its impact. Eluding censure from grim authorities by its literary veil it saw noteworthy highlights of political satire at the able hands of Rabelais, Bacon, Harrington, de Bergerac and Swift.[48]

Remote, abstract, timeless and static as these ideal societies may appear, the substance matter they tackled was anything but unworldly or non-committal, indeed epitomized the acute moral and intellectual predicaments posed by nascent Absolutism. It found a telling parallel in another genre of high classical pedigree, political drama, as when Buchanan censured

---

Roman Catholic France and Lutheran Sweden. Hugo Grotius pointedly served as Special Envoy of the Swedish Crown at the Court in Paris (1635-1645).

44 Thomas Hobbes (1588-1676) authored *De Cive* (1642) and *Leviathan* (1651); Hans Morgenthau (1904-1980) in 1948 published his *Politics Among Nations.*

45 The tracts represented the concept of the 'Prince's Mirror' or *Fürstenspiegel.* Macchiavelli's *Il Principe* was dedicated to Lorenzo II de Medici (1492-1519); Erasmus' *Institutio Principis* was addressed to young Charles V; Grotius' *De Studio Politico* of 1626 originated as a tract written in 1615 for the education of the son of a befriended French diplomat, Benjmin Aubéry du Maurier (1566-1636).

46 For Plato's ideal State headed by the philosopher-king, see his *Republic* 5.473ff.; for the Allegory of the Grotto, *Republic* 7. 514A-520A; for the mythical Atlantis, *Kritias* 113A-121C and *Timaeus* 24E-25B.

47 Cf. Columbus, *Diario* (1492) and Vespucci, *Mundus Novus* (1503). References to the 'Isles of the Blessed' are found in classical authors from Pindar (*Olymp. Od.* 2.57) and Plutarch (*Vit. Sertor.* 8) to Loukianos (*True Hist.* Bk. 2).

48 François Rabelais, *Abbaye de Thélème* (1534); Francis Bacon, *Nova Atlantis* (1627); James Harrington, *Oceana* (1656); Cyrano de Bergerac *Empires de la lune, Empires du soleil* (1657, 1662); Jonathan Swift *Gulliver's Travels* (1726).

More's beheading in his play on John the Baptist,[49] or when Grotius keenly addressed predestination in his *Adam in Exile* (1601), or typified the ideal ruler as the 'living law' in his play on Joseph as Vice-Roy of Egypt (1635).[50] One does well to pierce the veil of this allegedly 'unwordly' idealism. As in Augustine's *Civitas Dei*, speculation on a better world came in natural response to grim reality.

The nation state asserted itself in ruthless battle with rivalling secular and spiritual powers. At its inception, authority had to be absolute, if only to withstand centrifugal headwinds as evidenced by the *St. Bartholomew's Day* massacre in France (1572), the Remonstrant Troubles in the Low Countries (1610-1619), or the trampling of the German lands in the Thirty Years' War (1618-1648). In a rather impressive process of centuries, this early 'conflict model' attained a natural balance in Montesquieu's *trias politica*[51] and in the juxtaposition of interlocking and inter-monitory legislative, executive and judicial powers. Still, as before, its rock-bed was its untrammelled sovereignty. Precisely this paramount asset kept paralyzing international relations in perfect deadlock. Never (neither at Nymegen, Utrecht, Vienna or Berlin)[52] did the so-called 'State System' – whether seen as a monolith Concert or the counterbalancing of the Great and the Small[53] – live up to its self-imposed claims to preserve sustainable peace and harmony in Europe.

Was Westphalia the best bid, or was it the last straw for lack of a reasonable alternative? In 1625, a humanist suggested a different roadmap. On the tripartite basis of natural law, the positive law of treaties, and the

49 George Buchanan (1506-1582), *Jephthes sive Votum* (1554); *Baptistes sive Calumnia* (1577).

50 For a review of Grotius' political drama, see Arthur Eyffinger, 'Literary Writings' in Randall Lesaffer and Janne E. Nijman (eds), *The Cambridge Companion to Hugo Grotius* (Cambridge University Press, Cambridge 2021), 293.

51 Montesquieu (1689-1755), *De l'esprit des lois* (1748).

52 The Treaties of Nijmegen (1678-1679) put an end to the Franco-Dutch War (1672-1678); the Treaty of Utrecht (1713-1715) ended the War of the Spanish Succession (1701-1715); the Pact of Vienna (1815) ended the Napoleonic Wars (1793-1814); the Congress of Berlin (1878) came in the wake of the Russo-Turkish War (1877-1878). The treaties were mere stepping-stones along the thorny path of the Powers to durable peace.

53 The Concert of Europe (1814-1914) was the bid of the Great Powers to uphold a sustainable Balance of Power in Europe without the interference of the Small Powers. The claims of the small and neutral sovereign nations to legal equality marred political consensus at the Hague Peace Conferences. In 1920 the dilemma was transplanted into the keen rivalry of the Council and Assembly of the League.

accumulated wisdom of the philosophers and poets, those unacknowledged legislators of mankind,[54] Hugo Grotius, in a majestic comprehensive proposition, suggested reconciling religious schism, political rivalry, and social tension under the banner of the law.[55] There is little coincidence that the signing of the Pact at Versailles was hailed as 'the Hour of Grotius'. In 1925 the members of the *Institut* paid homage in Delft to this visionary alternative concept that had so sadly been ignored.[56]

D. The Constitutional Phase (1870-1920)

The course set at Westphalia was an all-decisive watershed. In the bid for a supra-national order and world organization, the claims to sovereignty of the nation states grew into the burden of history and a major obstacle to change. As its corollary came a second historical drawback. This concerned the overall outlook on the settlement of international disputes other than by dint of arms. It proved consequential to the intellectual discourse on the parameters for a World Court. Classical antiquity, medieval and early modern society had jointly handed over rather sophisticated and fairly subtle formulas of mediation, conciliation and, to crown these efforts, devices of arbitration. In all fairness, practice had been ambivalent and success intermittent. Whereas ancient Greece and the medieval commonwealths had seen a heyday of the instrument, Imperial Rome never accepted arbitral intervention by third parties, in line – one might say – with the 'leonine' pacts it granted. The modern sovereign State entertained much similar reservations. The role of arbitrator was long considered the prerogative and reserved domain of Heads of State or the Papacy. [57]

---

54 The phrase stems from Shelley (1792-1822), *A Defence of Poetry* (1821).

55 Grotius' *De jure belli ac pacis* (1625) was an instant classic.

56 On the occasion the former President of the *Institut* and of the *Advisory Committee of Jurists* (1920), Baron Edouard Descamps (1847-1933) addressed Grotius' legacy and put a wreath on his tomb. The gesture recalled the initiative of the US Delegation to the First Hague Peace Conference. On 4 July 1899 Andrew Dickson White (1832-1918) invited all Delegations to a pilgrimage to Delft in honour of "one of the Founding Fathers of the American Revolution".

57 For a concise survey of the history of the instrument of Arbitration see *World Court* I, chapter 2 and the Documentation Section.

A historic breakthrough was achieved in the *Treaty of Washington* (1871).[58] In the ensuing *Alabama Arbitration* (1872),[59] an expert panel of jurists peacefully settled the thorny legacy of British-American conflict from the American Civil War. It opened new vistas to the law, and the discipline jumped at the opening. Arbitration was hailed as a veritable panacea.[60] In 1873, the world of the law launched two research bodies, the *Institut* and ILA, which in subsequent years projected a whole range of schemes for arbitral procedure. Soon, the world teemed with bilateral arbitral treaties, in anticipation of the universal or general arbitration treaty.[61]

Over the past century and a half, and to the present day, both research bodies have eminently served the field of studies. Still, and as observed in our lines of introduction, from the first they championed a different philosophy, which effectively epitomized a major dilemma of the discipline. The *Institut* posed as the exclusive, prestigious think-tank of international lawyers, who were recruited by co-optation. It kept politics aloof as a matter of principle. The ILA, by contradistinction, and bespeaking its eminently pragmatic Anglo-Saxon perspective, welcomed the interaction of lawyers, economists, parliamentarians and captains of industry. From its ranks grew the *Comité maritime international* (CMI, founded in 1897).[62] The ILA thrived in its national affiliations[63] and in exchange with the *Inter-Parliamentary Union* (IPU, founded in 1889) and the *International Peace Bureau*

58 On 8 May 1871 the USA and the UK concluded the Treaty of Washington that in Art. I-XLIII settled lingering disputes. Art. VI contained 'Three Rules on the Rights and Duties of Neutral Powers'.

59 RIAA XXIX, 125-134.

60 *World Court* I, chapter 2.3-6. For schemes drawn up by IDI, ILA, IPU (f. 1889) and Peace Societies, and a survey of arbitration treaties (1791-1914), *Ibid*, Document Section. To exemplify, in 1895, at its 17th session in Brussels the ILA chaired by Sieveking produced *Rules of Procedure for International Arbitration.*

61 For the diverging outlook and keen rivalry of the two research bodies see Arthur Eyffinger, *T.M.C. Asser (1838-1913),* 2 volumes (Brill, Leiden/Boston 2019) Vol. I, chapter 18 (IDI) and chapter 19 (ILA).

62 Ibid, Vol. I, chapter 35.

63 For a review of its national affiliations, including its oldest branch – the Dutch *Nederlandse Vereniging voor Internationaal Recht* (KNVIR, f. 1875) – see the commemorative volume of ILA: *Au service du droit international: les 150 ans de l'Association de droit international = To the benefit of international law: 150 Years of the International Law Association* (Panthéon-Assas, Paris 1923).

(IPB, founded in 1891).[64] To the *Institut*, we owe the deepening and expansion of international law, to the ILA and IPU the gradual acceptance of the legal component in the high circles of diplomacy.

The harvest of twenty-five years of legal research, in both schools so to speak, was reaped at the Hague Peace Conference in 1899, when the Czar's counsellor, Fyodor Martens (1845-1909), ingeniously embedded the justly mistrusted disarmament proposition of his sovereign in the *Institut's* in-depth research projects on the codes of war and the peaceful settlement of disputes.[65] Still, in the end, it was public opinion that facilitated whatever progress was made at The Hague. The Powers, on their part, made it perfectly clear what strict terms they imposed on progress. The essence of arbitration was freedom. In accepting the substitution of political and military means to settle conflict with peaceful devices of dispute settlement, they did not give in an inch on their sovereignty. Obligation, in whatever form, was anathema. And so was a standing court beyond their control.[66]

The outcome in 1899 was a stalemate. The trump of the Conference, the Permanent Court of Arbitration (PCA, founded in 1900) embodied whatever few concessions could be wrung from the Powers. Still, and to its high credit, the Hague Peace Conference defined the conundrum and drew up the agenda for the next two decades. Its sequel in 1907, in seeking to truly grapple with the paramount issue of compulsion embarrassingly produced the *dénouement* of all ambitions. A discourse of twice the length of 1899, and among twice as many Powers, brutally revealed the quintessential gap between a judicature within the domestic domain and its envisioned counterpart in the international arena. The stalemate evidenced the misconception of the widely shared idea of a functional parallel of spheres.[67]

A few words on the debate of 1907 are in order, if only on account of its eminent pertinence to the subsequent discourse. On the strength of the reports tabled by the panels in the mere handful of cases the PCA

---

64 The cross-fertilization of these bodies and bureaus was impressive. Prominent pioneers were Auguste Couvreur, William Randal Cremer, Elie Ducommun, Albert Gobat, and Frédéric Passy.

65 Martens was a veteran of the *Institut* (*membre* from 1874) and jointly with his intimate Tobias Asser organized the Hague Peace Conference, which *inter alia* adopted the so-called *Martens Clause*. Outcome of the Conference were the three Hague Conventions of 1899, notably the so-called 'Arbitration Convention', which created the Permanent Court of Arbitration (PCA) at The Hague.

66 *World Court* I, chapter 3 and the Document Section.

67 Ibid, chapter 4 and 5 and the Document Sections.

had handled between 1902-1907,[68] delegates decided on an overhaul of that first international Court with a view to repairing its major deficits: its lack of permanency and ready availability; the lack of consistency of its awards; its cumbersome procedure. They realized that it had been a misconception to entrust all disputes, regardless of their political or legal nature, to a body of diplomats without specific legal training. The discourse instilled on the Conference the overarching understanding that precisely the nature of the dispute was conditional to the qualification of the Court and the reach of its jurisdiction. The predicament made delegates incur the dilemma of either upgrading the PCA to a proper court of law, or rather to complement, alternatively supplant it with a permanent judiciary to tackle strictly legal disputes and questions. Pursuant to a full three months of bewildering debate, and suggestive of both the clashing ideologies of the Powers and the impasse of thought among lawyers, delegates unfortunately found themselves trapped in the compromise of an intrinsically contradictory concept of a 'Permanent Court of Arbitral Justice' (PCAJ). The idea was a misconception: the freedom of diplomacy and the compulsory role of the law were incompatible concepts: arbitration and adjudication were poor bed-fellows. The Conference miscarried.

Public censure was severe, and the Conference has forever taken the blame for its failure to reach palpable results. In all fairness, and as the history of international adjudication over the past century has amply pointed out, this outcome was inevitable. The pertinence of the Conference was precisely in its very intentional bid to frontally tackle the nucleus of the problem in an effort to cross the threshold that was the premise to progress. The Conference was by far the most enlightening exchange of views of the pre-war period in defining the core challenge ahead. Its disconcerting legacy was the brute awareness of two formidable challenges: the pertinent claim of the (small) nations to legal equality in the face of harsh political realities, next to the quandary as to how make the proud Powers accept the curbing of their sovereign rights by a proper court of law.

The paramount aspiration of the Conference to arrange for a composition of the bench that would do justice to all Powers was addressed in parallel bids for the PCAJ and an International Prize Court (IPC). The latter Court reflected what in the last resort was the core issue of the

68 Ibid, chapter 3.3; all panels laid down their findings and recommendations in Reports.

Conference of 1907 – which came in the wake of the Russo-Japanese War (1904-1905) – to finally curb licence in that most elusive of domains, naval warfare. In both trajectories, the Small Powers clearly demonstrated their lack of vision, wisdom, and sense of realities. They preferred to risk the whims of war rather than to bend their necks to the Great Powers in the composition of the bench. The riddle of representation was never solved. Three years later, when an expert Committee of Four, in a clever bid to kill two birds by one stone, agreed on a compromise which cemented both projects, the off-hand rejection of the *London Declaration* on the Prize Law sadly wrecked both propositions.[69]

The failure defined the agenda for the post-war debate within the ACJ, the Council and the Assembly of the League of Nations in 1920. That formidable exchange of views of a full six months emphatically confirmed the recalcitrance of the problem. It availed itself of endless propositions made by public, academic, and private parties prior, during, and after *La Grande Guerre*.[70] Satisfied with the momentous task awaiting them, from 1912 onwards National PrepComs for the intended Third Hague Peace Conference – projected for 1915 – had elaborated on the Court project, then to find their endeavours dramatically cut short by the Guns of August. At first, war served to intensify the debate along former patterns. Only when, in time, the enormity of the watershed in all social domains dawned upon them, jurists and diplomats in a distinct reorientation of thought dismissed the logic of the past and the Hague Formula.

The sheer wealth of projects launched and the range of thoughts developed in the four years of war mirrored the depth of the crisis. Suggestive of normative change, the clarion-call was first raised by the female gender. In a massive conference at the Hague Zoo chaired by Nobel Peace Prize laureates, women assembled from all over the world in 1915 formulated a range of pivotal ideas and demands.[71] Spread by a subsequent world tour, these ideas substantially inspired Woodrow Wilson's *Fourteen Points Decla-*

69 Both with respect to the intended Permanent Court of Arbitral Justice (PCAJ) and the International Prize Court (IPC). For the aftermath of the Peace Conference and including the Naval Conference in London (1908-1909) *World Court* I, chapter 5.2-4 and chapter 6.1-5.

70 For a survey and ample documentation of projects *World Court* I, chapter 6.

71 On the role of women *World Court* I, chapter 6.8.

ration (1918).[72] Again, in the prelude to Versailles private parties – featuring politicians, philosophers and lawyers alike –, research institutes from all over the globe, national PrepComs and governmental bodies, whether from among the Allied and Associated Powers, the Central Powers or, notably, the Thirteen Neutral Powers, volunteered projects by the dozen. They readily agreed on the urgency to deepen and expand on the incidental pre-war Conference system into a permanent World Organization. For the greater part, they also insisted on a World Court. However, the institutional link between the two institutions was never taken for granted, indeed became a major bone of contention in Paris.

The aims at Versailles were twofold: to draw up Peace Treaties and to create a League of Nations. In the end it was the entwining of the two goals, mainly from strategic considerations, that wrecked the lofty aims. In envisioning a reformed Europe, the missionary US President championed the self-determination of the Peoples, and voiced high ideals of a network of self-sufficient nation states. As against this, the European Powers headed by France rather sought to exploit the spoils of war in the enforcement of harsh terms of peace. The concepts of global solidarity and national rivalry clashed to the point of debilitating the intended League of Nations, and imperilling peace.[73] At Versailles, to the embitterment of the world at large, not just the conquered Central Powers, but even the Thirteen Neutral Powers were left beyond the pale and out of the equation. The intensely politicized League had become a far cry from the "Hope of Ages'. Its policy emphatically belied the *incipit* of its Covenant: "We, the Peoples".[74]

The Court project was likewise left disoriented. Wilson envisioned a political organization without a judicial branch. London insisted on a judiciary.[75] In Washington, the adherents of the *Monroe Doctrine* of splendid isolation (as ever) clashed with the disciples of Roosevelt's call for a 'Policeman of the World'.[76] In order to outwit opposition at home, Wilson

72 On 8 January 1918, in an Address to Congress, Woodrow Wilson (1856-1924, President of the USA 1913-1921) famously sketched the norms for post-war world society in his *Fourteen Points Statement.*

73 *World Court* I, chapter 7.1-2, 4.

74 The PrepCom of the League was controlled by the Great Powers and sought to preserve the Concert system. Among its initiatives was the concept of advisory opinions. For the composition and role of the Committee, see *World Court* I, chapter 7.3.

75 *World Court* I, chapter 7.1-4.

76 In 1823, US President James Monroe (1758-1831, incumbent 1817-1825) formulated a doctrine to oppose European Colonial expansion in the Western Hemisphere.

had the Covenant integrated into the Treaty of Versailles. Ignoring Elihu Root's warnings not to haul the Court within the League, that body, too, was incorporated. So much so indeed that the PCIJ was vested with an assignment alien to a proper court of law, and which many felt was utterly inappropriate, *viz.*, to render legal advice to the political bodies of the League. The concept boomeranged in one signal respect. Precisely this feature made the US Senate obstinately withhold its signature from the Protocol of Signature of the Statute, and this in spite of a full decade of stubborn negotiations.[77]

It has often been argued that the two-tied system of the League, its two 'houses' consisting of the Council and the Assembly, facilitated the breaking of the deadlock of 1907 regarding the fair assignment of seats on the Court. If formally correct, the construction never solved the underlying problem of the inherent antagonism between the Great Powers and the small nations. Distrust was merely diverted towards the two political organs. A prominent issue that kept the minds divided early in 1919 was precisely which of these two Houses was to take the lead in the Constitution of the Court. A critical role in this process was reserved for the Preparatory Commission of the League. Arguing against majority opinion, its members entrusted this role to the Council.[78]

The Prepcom made more questionable decisions of lasting consequence. Thus, it categorically refused to entertain the enlightened propositions two lawyers of great repute, German Walther Schücking (1875-1935) and Austrian Heinrich Lammasch (1853-1920) submitted on behalf of their defamed nations.[79] To bespeak the fundamental switch of mentality in Berlin and Vienna, these projects intriguingly propounded the Sovereignty of the

---

Theodore Roosevelt (1858-1919; incumbent 1901-1909) modified this policy in his New Diplomacy of 'The World's Constable', and as mediator between Latin America and Europe.

77 The absence of the US pursuant to a so-called 'Round Robin' Resolution, launched by senators Knox and Lodge in the hearings of the US Senate of 3 March 1918, was one of the major setbacks in the early days of the League. The move was widely anticipated as being provisional. Up to 1929, strenuous efforts were made to haul in the USA, lastly by the Advisory Committee that revised the Statute of the PCIJ at Geneva that year. A major role in these efforts was reserved for Elihu Root (1845-1937), the Court's greatest advocate in the USA. Whereas the USA never entered the League nor subscribed to the Statute of the Court, American judges served on the Bench throughout the period of the PCIJ; see *World Court* II, chapter 13.

78 On the Preparatory Committee of the League *World Court* I, chapter 7.3.

79 For a portrait of Walther Schücking see Ole Spiermann, 'Professor Walther Schücking at the Permanent Court of International Justice' (2011) 22 *European Journal of Inter-*

Peoples, and entrusted the Court with competence in the private and public domains of the law indiscriminately. Even if the Council pledged itself to later on weigh the two propositions, no palpable evidence of any such course of action is on record, either with the ACJ or at Geneva.

Neither did the Preparatory Commission at first consider the very pertinent schemes the Thirteen Neutral Powers had by then tabled. In the end, its members gave in to pressure, invited a delegation to Geneva, then summarily dismissed all its propositions. Unabashed, five Neutral Powers early in 1920 met at The Hague and submitted a joint draft, the so-called *Five Powers Plan*, which became a major beacon for the ACJ in June-July.[80] In one other respect, the Preparatory Commission clearly showed its colours. It adamantly turned down all propositions to include the PCA in its deliberations on the Constitution of the League. This policy, too, would incur repercussions.[81]

E. The Drafting of the Statute: An Overall Appraisal[82]

The drafting of the Statute of the PCIJ came about in a prolonged process that featured five successive stages. It covered a full sixth months of intense discourse, from mid-June to mid-December 1920. A central role in this endeavour has commonly been reserved for the opening stage, the debate of the Advisory Committee of ten jurists that convened in the Peace Palace in June-July.[83] Accordingly, the burden of whatever blame the bid has incurred – and censure has indeed been severe – has mostly landed on

---

national Law, 783; For a portrait of Heinrich Lammasch see Markus P. Beham, 'A Forgotten Lighthouse of International Law: Heinrich Lammasch and the League of Nations' (2019) 62 *German Yearbook of International Law*, 245.

80 The *Five Powers Plan* was elaborated by the Scandinavian Powers, the Netherlands and Spain at a Conference held in the Peace Palace from 16-27 February 1920 under the chairmanship of Dutch Bernard Loder.

81 Notably so in the policy of the ACJ in 1920; see *World Court* I, chapter 13.1.

82 For a history of the Statute see Berthold Schenk Graf von Stauffenberg, *Statut et Règlement de la CPJI: Eléments d'interprétation* (Carl Heymanns Verlag, Berlin 1934); Andreas Zimmermann et al. (eds), *The Statute of the International Court of Jusice; A Commentary* (3rd edn, Oxford University Press, Oxford 2019), and notably the 'Historical Introduction' by Ole Spiermann, 39.

83 For the minutes of its thirty-five meetings, see Advisory Committee of Jurists, *Procès-Verbaux of the Proceedings of the Committee: June 16th–July 24th 1920.*

its shoulders.[84] To be sure, there is ample ground to question the wisdom of the Committee's policy, and we will address this aspect in a moment. Still, the reach and impact of the Committee's labours was fairly limited, and this arrangement was very intentional. The legal experts operated in a strictly advisory role to the sovereign Council of the League.[85]

Paradoxically, precisely this well-understood constraint of its assignment may have misguided the Committee in overstepping the mark of political feasibilities in the draft text it submitted. But then, regardless of the Committee's misconceptions or waywardness, the ultimate decisions were from the first well understood to be made by the two political bodies of the League, and beyond the Committee's immediate control. It was the Council that, on grounds of political opportunism – if under the veil of the imperative terms of the Covenant – uprooted the core concept of the Committee's draft, which erroneously took the acceptance of the Court's compulsory jurisdiction for a foregone conclusion.[86] In a single strike, the Council fatally struck the entire proposition out of balance. To its lasting discredit, the ACJ never anticipated the eventual rejection of this core element of its draft or cared to plot an alternative itinerary. This lack of foresight is the less understandable in light of the timely warnings the Committee had received even from amongst its midst. From first to last, two of its ten members, Japanese Mineichirō Adachi and Italian Arturo Ricci-Busatti despaired at the political feasibility of the concept of compulsory jurisdiction. Time and again, the Italian jurist suggested having that part of their draft embedded in a separate document. His calls fell on deaf ears.[87]

---

84 For a highly instructive review, see Ole Spiermann, '"Who Attempts Too Much Does Nothing Well": The 1920 Advisory Committee of Jurists and the Statute of the Permanent Court of International Justice' (2002) 73 *British Yearbook of International Law*, 187.

85 For the constitution of the ACJ, see *World Court* I, chapter 8.

86 The Committee's misconception was based on the alleged 'acceptance on principle' of the concept at the Second Hague Peace Conference (1907). For the successive stages of the debate, see *World Court* I, chapter 15.4; 21 II; chapter 22.4-5; chapter 23.4; chapter 24.5; chapter 26.3.

87 Adachi spoke up against compulsory jurisdiction as politically unfeasible; Ricci-Busatti, from fear of the Council's dismissal of the idea wished to distinguish matters of the Court's Organization and Competence in two separate propositions to the Council. For Adachi's position, see *World Court* I, chapter 12.1.1; chapter 13.2.4; chapter 20.1.2. For Ricci-Busatti's alternative views, ibid chapter 12.1.6; chapter 13.3.5; chapter 17.3.2; chapter 20.1.2.

But then, the Committee's draft of mid-July was by no means the last word. In August-October, the Council reviewed its political implications, with disastrous results for the overall concept as we have seen.[88] The legal analysis of this revised draft Statute was reserved for the First Assembly of the League in November-December.[89] That political body wisely entrusted the expert task to its (Third) Legal Committee, made up of expert lawyers representing thirty-six Powers. This Committee, in turn, appointed a Subcommittee of Ten to venture on a complete overhaul of the text. The draft Statute of the ACJ, in other words, went back and forth through three stages and at three distinct levels of concerted research in the First Assembly for its final assessment.[90] Half of the body of the Subcommittee was very intentionally made up of former members of the ACJ. The other half featured jurists who, with a single exception, later on served as judges of the World Court.[91] In short, the final outcome of the Statute was never impaired for the lack of commitment of the discipline or of juridical analysis. If from the midst of this Subcommittee due protest was raised against the Council's stern verdict, it never steered a course of square confrontation, and it never handled the crowbar.[92] The major outcome of the intense legal debate was the (rather controversial) lightning rod of the *Optional Clause*.[93]

As it is, a last truly brave and desperate stand in favour of 'the real thing' – untrammelled compulsory jurisdiction – was made, of all places, in the Plenary of the Assembly, in electrifying speeches by the First Delegates of the neutral Powers and the Latin American nations.[94] Some of these diplomats even turned down the optional clause as blocking the way to real progress. All eloquence was smothered in the sobering 'reason of State' of the Great Powers, and their plea for patience as well as growing confidence

88 The Council's dismissal of the Court's compulsory jurisdiction (in July-October 1920) seriously unbalanced the scheme; ibid, chapter 22.5.1.

89 The First Assembly addressed the matter in November-December 1920; see *World Court* I, Chapter 23.1.

90 For the successive stages ibid, chapter 23.1 and chapter 26 (Assembly); chapter 23.2-5; chapter 25 (Third Committee); chapter 24 (Subcommittee).

91 Ibid, chapter 24.1.

92 For the review of the aspect of Compulsory Jurisdiction in the respective bodies ibid, chapter 23.4; chapter 25.1.9 (Third Committee); chapter 24.5 (Subcommittee); chapter 26.2-7 (Assembly).

93 The concept of the Optional Clause, which harked back to an idea first developed by Max Huber in 1907 was launched by Raul Fernandes, the Brazilian (substitute-) member of the ACJ, in the discourse of the Third Committee; ibid, chapter 25.1.9.

94 For the seventeen impressive speeches ibid, chapter 26.3.

in the Court's credibility.[95] Whatever the shortcomings of the successive bodies, the outcome of affairs was never in the balance. It was also a fair appraisal, in being the true reflection of the effective state of the arts. As a full century has told us, the final terms of the Statute were hardly a matter of coincidence. The quintessential issue of the reach of the Court's jurisdiction has formally remained *sub judice* to the present day, but has never seriously been challenged. If, therefore, the verdict of time alone calls for constraint in our censure of the ACJ, we may in many ways benefit from a second glance and closer look at its proceedings.

95 For the position of the UK (Lord Balfour) ibid, chapter 26.3.15; for the position of Léon Bourgeois (France) chapter 26.6.

F. The Advisory Committee of Jurists[96]

I. The Socio-Political Backdrop

The constitution of the ACJ, Léon Bourgeois' brainchild,[97] proved a nettlesome affair. The criteria for the selection of expert jurists were never clarified. Half of the twelve original nominees turned down the invitation on various grounds. In the end, the Committee was reduced to ten members equally divided between the Great and the Small Powers, and this was begging the question whether these jurists attended its meetings on a personal title or rather as the representatives of their nations.[98] True to

96 The formal source of the discourse of the ACJ are Advisory Committee of Jurists, *Procès-Verbaux of the Proceedings of the Committee: June 16th–July 24th 1920*. Additional information is gained in the reports of the members of its Secretariat, Dionisio Anzilotti and Åke Hammarskjöld to the Permanent Secretariat of the League at Geneva, and in later publications of members of the Committee, most pertinent perhaps its informal attendant, James Brown Scott. For recent critical reviews, see the two volumes edited in 2022 by P. Sean Morris, *Transforming the Politics of International Law: The Advisory Committee of Jurists and the Formation of the World Court in the League of Nations* (Routledge, London 2021); P. Sean Morris, *The League of Nations and the Development of International Law: A New Intellectual History of the Advisory Committee of Jurists* (Routledge, Oxon 2022). In the first-mentioned volume, a range of scholars focus on the intellectual ambiance of the undertaking, whereas in the last-mentioned collection of essays emphasis is on the biographies and tenets of the members of the ACJ. General overviews of the political and legal context of the discourse may be found in Karin Van Leeuwen and Morten Rasmussen's contribution 'A political and legal history of the Advisory Committee of Jurists and the foundation of the Permanent Court of International Justice' in P. Sean Morris (ed), *Transforming the Politics of International Law The Advisory Committee of Jurists and the Formation of the World Court in the League of Nations* (Routledge, London 2021), 69, and Jakob Zollmann, 'Civilization(s) and 'Civilized Nations' – of History, Anthropology And International Law' in P. Sean Morris (ed), *Transforming the Politics of International Law The Advisory Committee of Jurists and the Formation of the World Court in the League of Nations* (Routledge, London 2021), 11. For an extensive bibliography and biographies of all members of the discourse throughout June-December 1920, see also *World Court I*.

97 Léon Bourgeois (1851-1925) was a central figure throughout the constitutional process of the League and the Court (1899-1922). For a biographical sketch, see *World Court* I, *Biographies*; Alexandre Niess and Nathalie Altinok 'Léon Bourgeois' in P. Sean Morris (ed) *Transforming the Politics of International Law: The Advisory Committee of Jurists and the Formation of the World Court in the League of Nations* (Routledge, London 2021), 213.

98 For the laborious selection process of the ACJ, see *World Court* I, chapter 8; for its installation, ibid, chapter 10.

diplomatic tradition, this issue was comfortably left hanging in the air. Even the members of the Committee clearly felt differently in the matter, and most of them felt less than secure. So much for certain, Italian Arturo Ricci-Busatti in his very particular proposition for a Court, exactly copied the submission of his Government at an earlier stage in Versailles and later on in the First Assembly[99] Again, Japanese Mineichirō Adachi and British Lord Phillimore likewise had their specific legal traditions, their nation's interests, and public opinion at home foremost in their minds throughout the exercise.[100]

The choice of venue for the ACJ turned into a major bone of contention between Berne, Brussels and The Hague. It was the upbeat to their keen rivalry in securing for themselves, first, the seat of the League, then of the Court.[101] The tense relations between The Hague and Brussels were still something else. Belgium (and France) severely censured the rather profitable neutrality policy of the Dutch during the war years and its Government's barely veiled German sympathies. Two specific incidents burdened the relations. In November 1918, The Hague granted permission to whole contingents of German military – loaded with loot in a hurried retreat to the *Heimat* – to take the shortcut through Dutch Limburg. A few days later, the Netherlands readily gave shelter to the alleged war criminal,

---

99 Ibid, chapter 7.3.2; chapter 22.3.1 (proposition Italy); chapter 12.1.6; chapter 13.3.5 (Ricci-Busatti). For a sketch of Arturo Ricci-Busatti see Elisabetta Fiocchi Malaspina, 'The Italian Jurist and Diplomat at the Advisory Committee of Jurists: Arturo Ricci Busatti (1868 – 1923)' in P. Sean Morris (ed.), *The League of Nations and the Development of International Law: a New Intellectual History of the Advisory Committee of Jurists* (Routledge, Oxon 2022), 218.

100 For Adachi's sociological approach and insistence on the representation of non-Western legal traditions and civilizations see chapter 12.1.1; 12.1.9; chapter 13.2.4; chapter 18.1.11; 21.4. For the wider context, see Jakob Zollmann, 'Civilization(s) and 'civilized nations' – of history, anthropology and international law' in P. Sean Morris (ed), *Transforming the Politics of International Law The Advisory Committee of Jurists and the Formation of the World Court in the League of Nations* (Routledge, London 2021), 11; for Adachi's views, see Tetsuya Toyoda, 'A Civilizational Pluralist and Inegalitarian: Mineichiro Adachi (1869–1934)' in P. Sean Morris (ed), *The League of Nations and the Development of International Law: A New Intellectual History of the Advisory Committee of Jurists* (Routledge, Oxon 2022), 74. For Lord Phillimore's insistence on public opinion in Britain, see *World Court* I chapter 12.1.3; chapter 13.2.1; for a personal sketch, see P. Sean Morris, 'The Judicial Churchman for Peace: Walter George Frank Phillimore (1855-1933)' in P. Sean Morris (ed), *The League of Nations and the Development of International Law: a New Intellectual History of the Advisory Committee of Jurists* (Routledge, Oxon 2022),180.

101 On the keen ambitions of the Netherlands, see *World Court* I, chapter 9.

Emperor Wilhelm II. Belgium insisted that the Netherlands should be provisionally banned from the League.[102]

There is no way around it, Queen Wilhelmina *schwärmed* with the German military and *Junkertum*. Foreign Minister Van Karnebeek on his part likewise never hid his German sympathies.[103] The latter's *tour de force* to turn affairs his way and earn himself the Presidency of the Second Plenary of the Assembly (1921) in the bargain is a rare feat of consummate diplomacy in Dutch history.[104] On another tack, in defiance of urgent requests from the Allied Powers, and stone deaf to public opinion, The Hague pertinently refused to put on trial or extradite *der Kaiser*. The man who articulated his Government's legal plea to appease the issue with an appeal to the principle of *nulla poena sine lege* was Bernard Loder, the Dutch Member of the ACJ and bound to become the first President of the PCIJ.[105] In the end, Brussels and the Hague agreed on a *quid pro quo* which, very likely, included Belgian Baron Descamps' Presidency of the ACJ.[106]

II. The Burden of History

Verdict on the operating of the ACJ and its draft proposition has been stern, and indeed on solid grounds. Still, in all fairness, the Committee's

---

102 On these incidents ibid, chapter 9.2-3.

103 The resentment against Great Britain on account of the Second Boer War (1899-1902) was still lingering in the Netherlands by 1914.

104 Herman van Karnebeek (1874-1942) was a highly gifted diplomat; for his policy, see *World Court* I, chapter 9.4-7. for a portrait see ibid, Biographies.

105 For Loder's pertinent role in the constitution of the World Court, see *World Court* I, chapter 7.3.5; chapter 9.6-7. For his legal tract on extradition, ibid, chapter 9, Document Section. On the ACJ, Loder professed to very pertinent views as regards a number of core issues: advisory opinions, unilateral applications, the access of private persons and bodies, national judges, chambers; the representation of non-Western cultures; ibid, chapter 13.1.7; 13.3.1; 13.3.6; chapter 14.2-3; chapter 15.2.1; 15.4.1-3; chapter 17.4.1. Loder also attended the meetings of the Third Committee and rendered a sounding address in the Assembly (ibid, chapter 26.3.1); in *World Court* II, Loder's role as (the not uncontroversial) First President of the PCIJ is evaluated; *World Court* II, chapter 15.1-4; Chapter 16.17. For a recent biographical appraisal, see Freya Baetens and Veronica Lavista, '"Where is Your Tribunal?" Bernard Loder (1849–1935) and the Quest for International Justice' in P. Sean Morris (ed), *The League of Nations and the Development of International Law: a New Intellectual History of the Advisory Committee of Jurists* (Routledge, Oxon 2022), 195.

106 On these issues, see *World Court* I, chapter 8.7; chapter 9.8-9; chapter11.1.1.

handicaps were at least as momentous as were its shortcomings. The drawbacks ranged from the unrelenting impact of politics[107] to the clash of legal traditions.[108] What did not help either were some blatant *incompatibilités d'humeur* of its members.[109] Still, in the last resort, the discourse was heavily impaired by the entirely different professional expertise of its members and their divergent outlook on the law.[110] This, too, proved anything but incidental. As we will see, the same conundrum emphatically resurfaced on the bench of the PCIJ.[111] It bespoke an embarrassing truth. In spite of a full half century of intense discourse in the circles of the *Institut* and ILA, the discipline, by 1920, had failed to reach an appreciable agreement on even the most elementary aspects of doctrine. Also, and notwithstanding pertinent claims as to the essential unity of international law the cleft between the Civil Law and Common Law traditions, which back in 1873 had driven Continental and Anglo-Saxon lawyers apart in two competing research bodies,[112] had not nearly been bridged.[113]

Yet another argument on principle burdened the discourse of the ACJ and this element, too, had a major impact on the way the World Court was to be implemented. This controversy touched the legacy of the Peace Conferences, the PCA, and *l'Oeuvre de La Haye* as such. At Versailles, and at Woodrow Wilson's instigation, the overall feeling had prevailed that wisdom told them to simply cut short the 'gratuitous' Hague tradition of arbitration that had failed to forestall war, and to discontinue the PCA. This understanding was emphatically transferred to Geneva and the officialdom of the League.[114] A role for the PCA in the World Organization was never

107 For the overall political ambiance and the unrelenting discourse on the legal equality of the sovereign nations ibid, chapter 11.1.2; chapter 12.1; chapter 13.3.2; chapter 14.1; chapter 21.2.1.

108 Notably so the incompatible outlooks of the Civil Law and Common Law traditions, and the pertinence of Non-Western law traditions; ibid, chapter 12.1.9; chapter 13.3.4; chapter 17.4.4; chapter 18.1.1; chapter 21.4.

109 On these distressing matters, see ibid, chapter 11.1.4-6; 12.1.10.

110 These diverging outlooks became apparent on every level and were reflected in the widely different propositions for the constitution of the Bench; ibid, chapter 12, 13, 17.

111 *World Court* II, chapter 15.

112 On the quarrels during 1873-1875, see Arthur Eyffinger, *T.M.C. Asser (1838-1913) vol. I*, chapter 18.3; chapter 19.2.

113 For the critical comments by Presidents Huber and Anzilotti, see *World Court* II, chapter 15.2-4.

114 Critical comments on the PCA had been raised on the eve of the Hague Peace Conference of 1907; see *World Court* I, chapter 4.5; chapter 5.1; chapter 6.5. These

considered. As late as mid-December 1920, Argentina in the First Assembly raised the claim to forthwith suppress the PCA.[115]

Still, the proposition was heavily contested, indeed to the point of provoking strong reaction.[116] Truth be told, precisely to this disputation we owe the curious anomaly that the election of the judges of the PCIJ, the judicial branch of the League of Nations, came to be based on the nomination by the National Groups of an institution, the PCA, that never formed part of the World Organization. On the rebound, the formula may actually have saved the PCA from oblivion, and carried the institution through its long decades of withering (1920s-1990s).[117]

III. Rudderless Off Track

The above controversy unbalanced the ACJ from the first. Possibly at the instigation of Léon Bourgeois – by far the most ardent champion of the aforementioned Hague tradition – the President of the ACJ, Baron Edouard Descamps, himself another outspoken protagonist of the PCA, in the opening days of the discourse took his colleagues by surprise in catapulting upon them a tripartite project for what he called a "General Office of International Justice".[118] Whatever its other aims, the proposition was at heart aimed at securing an institutional link between the PCA

feelings were emphatically shared at Versailles and by the Preparatory Committee of the League; ibid, chapter 7.2.2.

115 Ibid, chapter 24.6.

116 Legendary became Léon Bourgeois' appeals with Wilson and Clemenceau to uphold the Hague tradition.

117 From the day the PCIJ became operational, interest with the PCA withered. The last case submitted was the famous *Island of Palmas Case (USA–Netherlands)* handled by Max Huber, the former judge and President of the PCIJ, as sole arbitrator. The next inter-State arbitration before the PCA occurred only in 1996 *(Eritrea-Yemen, Sovereignty and Maritime delimitation in the Red Sea).*

118 *World Court* I, chapter 13.1. For an appraisal of Descamps' views, see Saskia Millmann, 'Making the Case for Arbitration – Edouard Descamps's Long Advocacy for Peaceful Dispute Resolution' in P. Sean Morris (ed), *Transforming the Politics of International Law: The Advisory Committee of Jurists and the Formation of the World Court in the League of Nations* (Routledge, London 2021), 134 and Frederik Dhondt, 'Edouard Descamps (1847-1933): From Negative Neutrality to Positive Pacigerate' in P. Sean Morris (ed.), *The League of Nations and the Development of International Law: a New Intellectual History of the Advisory Committee of Jurists* (Routledge, Oxon 2022), 156-179.

and the PCIJ. In his original concept, which included a reformed PCA, a PCIJ along much similar lines and, to top it all, a court that *inter alia* was to operate as an International Criminal Court.[119] Descamps initially even entrusted not just the nomination but the effective election of the World Court to the National Groups of the Powers that adhered to the Hague Conventions of 1907.[120] It was a rather daring bid, and was justly countered as reaching well beyond the Committee's assignment, as well as a rather artificial proposition. It also created practical problems in that the Contracting Powers to the Hague Conventions did not by any length overlap the Member States of the League.

Regardless of the intrinsic qualities and deficits of Descamps' project, his surprise attack brutally undermined personal relations. Norwegian Francis Hagerup, for one, was adamantly opposed to the concept of a Criminal Court, and all but called it a day.[121] Again, his preconceived project made Descamps summarily dismiss the elaborate agenda the Legal Secretariat of the League had drawn up for the Committee.[122] His strategy made the Committee lose all sense of compass for a full two weeks. Its eminently capable Secretaries, Dionisio Anzilotti and Åke Hammarskjöld, reported back to the Secretary-General and the Permanent Legal Secretariat at Geneva in the blackest terms.[123] By early July, various members of the Committee

119 In the face of strong opposition Descamps upheld his claim, which in the end was transferred into a (personal) Recommendation for an International Criminal Court. The idea was turned down by the Council and the Assembly alike; for the discourse, see *World Court* I, chapter 13.1.3; chapter 16.2.1; chapter 19.2; chapter 22.6.2; chapter 25.2.2; chapter 26.8.

120 Ibid, chapter 13.1.5.

121 Hagerup was adamantly opposed to the idea of an ICC in the absence of a proper penal law. On Hagerup's policies, see Dag Michalsen, 'Francis Hagerup (1853-1921): A Norwegian Legal Internationalist' in P. Sean Morris (ed), *The League of Nations and the Development of International Law: A New Intellectual History of the Advisory Committee of Jurists* (Routledge, Oxon 2022), 91 and cf. Haakon A. Ikonomou and Morten Rasmussen, 'Scandinavian Legal Internationalism and the Creation of the Permanent Court of International Justice' in Morris (ed.), P. Sean Morris (ed), *Transforming the Politics of International Law: The Advisory Committee of Jurists and the Formation of the World Court in the League of Nations* (Routledge, London 2021), 236.

122 *World Court* I, chapter 11.1.3.

123 For an analysis of Dionisio Anzilotti's views, see Giorgio Gaja, 'Positivism and Dualism in Dionisio Anzilotti' (1992) 3 *European Journal of International Law*,123; Georg Nolte, 'From Dionisio Anzilotti to Roberto Ago: The Classical International Law of State Responsibility and the Traditional Primacy of a Bilateral Conception of Inter-state Relations' (2002) 13 *European Journal of International Law*, 1084-1098

were close to taking their leave.[124] Descamps, if an expert diplomat, proved thick-skulled. Midway the discourse, he launched another high-handed proposition of his own, which unilaterally imposed a dictate in terms of sources of law to be applied by the Court – and including their strictest hierarchy.[125] These self-willed actions fatally eroded his authority with Lord Phillimore and American Elihu Root.[126] Two years later, Descamps paid dearly for his lack of diplomacy. The Assembly to his embarrassment stubbornly rejected his election, first as judge, then even as deputy-judge of the Court.[127]

---

and Francesco Salerno, 'State Practice, the First World Court and Dionisio Anzilotti' in P. Sean Morris (ed), *Transforming the Politics of International Law: The Advisory Committee of Jurists and the Formation of the World Court in the League of Nations* (Routledge, London 2021), 171. For Åke Hammarskjöld, see Haakon A. Ikonomou and Morten Rasmussen, 'Scandinavian Legal Internationalism and the Creation of the Permanent Court of International Justice' in P. Sean Morris (ed), *Transforming the Politics of International Law: The Advisory Committee of Jurists and the Formation of the World Court in the League of Nations* (Routledge, London 2021), 236; Ole Spiermann, 'Fighting for Justice: Åke Hammarskjöld at the Permanent Court of Justice' in Ola Engdahl and Pål Wrange (eds), *Law at War: The Law as it Was and the Law as it Should Be: Liber Amicorum Ove Bring* (Brill Nijhoff, Leiden 2008), 257.

124 *World Court* I, chapter 11.1.6. Root and Phillimore stood horn-locked with Descamps throughout the exercise, both on account of the Belgian's authoritarian style of chairmanship and of the substance of his propositions. For a portrait of Elihu Root, see William G. Ross, 'Elihu Root (1845–1937): Architect and Advocate of the Permanent Court of International Justice' in P. Sean Morris (ed), *The League of Nations and the Development of International Law: a New Intellectual History of the Advisory Committee of Jurists* (Routledge, Oxon 2022), 112.

125 Ibid, chapter 15.5, and cf. P. Sean Morris, 'The Advisory Committee of Jurists and the Historical Origins of Scholarly Writings as a Source of International Law' in P. Sean Morris (ed), *Transforming the Politics of International Law: The Advisory Committee of Jurists and the Formation of the World Court in the League of Nations* (Routledge, London 2021), 107.

126 The assessment of James Brown Scott, who attended the meetings in the capacity of personal secretary to Elihu Root, were mordant: see *World Court* I, chapter 11.1.7, and numerous quotations in successive Document Sections. For a portrait, see Paolo Amorosa, '"Leg over Leg, The Dog went to Dover" – James Brown Scott's Long Road to the Advisory Committee of Jurists' in P. Sean Morris (ed), *Transforming the Politics of International Law: The Advisory Committee of Jurists and the Formation of the World Court in the League of Nations* (Routledge, London 2021), 153.

127 The outcome went to the detriment of Belgium. A major player in the discourse over the preceding decades, in 1921 it ended with no judge on the Bench; see *World Court* II, chapter 1.7.

As a consequence, and for lack of a proper helmsman the Committee was never quite on top of affairs. From the first, it went all over the place in chaotic discourse. As time went by, the imminent meeting of the Council added an element of pressure. Double sessions, evening sessions and private meetings were inserted to meet deadlines.[128] Impromptu resolutions were passed in a rush and without proper deliberation. Among the many lacunae of its draft, the ACJ never considered addressing the way the Statute should best be passed, by simple Resolution of the Assembly or by the Powers' formal ratification of a multilateral Convention.[129] The same held true for its failure to contemplate the eventuality of revision of its Statute. The disease appeared endemic. In 1929, a second ACJ, which in Geneva addressed the revision of the Statute, laboured from the same handicap of haste in frantic anticipation of the forthcoming second General Elections.[130] It is perfectly astounding to which lengths the reputedly meticulous discipline time and again allowed itself to be wrongfooted and cornered by the world of politics.

IV. The Intangible Law

Still, the above, and external influence were only part of the tale. More perplexing indeed was the lack of consensus these ten legal luminaries faced at virtually every item they touched, and these included the so-called basic principles and axioms of the discipline. Most Committee-members were seasoned veterans of the research institutes and the Hague Conferences. Still, apparently, nothing had prepared them for the intellectual clash that awaited them. It attests to their firm determination to reach safe harbour at all costs that at long last they overcame their pride and prejudice in the common interest. But then, the riddle was never solved. In a perplexing

128 *World Court* I, chapter 20. Three meetings were held on 19 July, two on 20 July, 23 July, and 24 July. The stringent time-schedule accounts for the lack of proper research on many issues, as the Subcommittee of the Third Committee felt fit to observe later on.

129 It prompted an intriguing debate and Special Reports by Anzilotti and the Dutch Head of the Legal Secretariat at Geneva, Joost van Hamel; see *World Court* I, chapter 23.5. For a portrait of Van Hamel, see Biographies.

130 On the role and record of this Second Advisory Committee, see *World Court* II, chapter 12 and 13.

repetition of moves, the first bench of the PCIJ emphatically faced the same quandaries.[131]

To exemplify the predicament, a telling tale touched the ramification of views on the qualifications of aspirant-judges. As against the insistence of the Anglo-Saxon members of the ACJ on the expertise of the national magistrate, Continental jurists pressed for the prerequisite of academic training in international law. Deliberations got stuck in endless debate on the comparative assets of the municipal and international domains, of judicial training and academic learning, only to reach qualified agreement on the need for the judge's high *moral* qualifications.[132] The deadlock was symptomatic of the bifurcation of the two great law traditions that asserted itself at all stages. Lord Phillimore, Elihu Root and James Brown Scott were stunned at the nature and length of the Report to the Council their French *rapporteur*, De Lapradelle had drafted.[133] It was hardly a matter of coincidence: the cultural cleft emphatically resurfaced on the first bench of the Court. It incapacitated its Drafting Committees, and struck perfect outsiders in the way agents and counsel presented their pleas in the Court Room.

The ideological cleft permeated the discourse of the ACJ for a full six weeks. It crystallized in the drafts its members tabled with respect to the procedure for the nomination and election of judges, the item that the Committee soon identified as critical for its quest. The issue hinged on the respective roles of the Council and Assembly, and on the way the National Groups of the PCA might facilitate the process as lightning-rod to neutralize the inherent conflicting interests of these two political bodies. [134]

The arduous quest for harmony on the basis of the comparative analysis of clashing views and drafts called for rather stormy sessions.[135] In the end, a pragmatic scheme developed by Elihu Root and Lord Phillimore

131 *World Court* II, chapter 15.

132 For a review of the discourse, *World Court* I, chapter 12.1.4 and chapter 18.2.

133 Lord Phillimore, for one, openly ridiculed the 'literary' approach of his French colleague. For a summary of De Lapradelle's *Report* (which amounted to some 60 pp.), see *World Court* I, chapter 21. For a portrait of De Lapradelle, see Toni Selkälä, 'Forgetting Albert Geouffre De Lapradelle (1871-1955) and Ignorance as Remembering' in P. Sean Morris (ed), *The League of Nations and the Development of International Law: a New Intellectual History of the Advisory Committee of Jurists* (Routledge, Oxon 2022), 135.

134 For the successive stages of the discourse, see *World Court* I, chapter 18.1; chapter 21.2.1; 21.5; 22.5.7; chapter 24.3.1; chapter 25.1.1; chapter 26.2.1-2.

135 On several occasions Descamps exploded.

prevailed, if not for lack of protest from the part of the President, who had elaborated an otherwise ingenious draft of his own.[136] By that time, however, the personal authority and superior statesmanship of the expert American former Secretary of State - nicely seconded by the legal acumen of his personal secretary, James Brown Scott - had long been established.[137] In the eyes of many observers, Elihu Root was the true chairman of the Committee. Root's re-election for the position in 1929 in spite of his fairly advanced age was hardly coincidental. On that occasion, it came with an additional bonus. Throughout the 1920s, Root had stood out as the Court's greatest advocate in the USA, and had frequently made interventions in the Senate on its account. A major goal of League authorities and the Revision Committee was precisely to haul in the USA.[138]

V. Musical chairs

The discourse within the ACJ predictably invited repetition of the keen competition from 1907 between the Great Powers and the Small regarding the distribution of seats and the claim to legal equality of all Powers. As Lord Phillimore laconically observed, without teeth the Court was doomed.[139] The support of the Great Powers was indispensable for the execution and compliance with judgments. A permanent seat seemed the reasonable *quid pro quo.* It was begging the question for the highest number of judges the bench might reasonably allow for not to thwart its effective functioning - on which issue the members again differed to the extreme.[140]

136 The so-called 'Root-Phillimore Plan' was at the heart of the article-by-article discourse. It was adjusted with the help of emendations suggested by the other members; *World Court* I, chapter 13 for the various propositions; Chapter 17 for the appraisal of the competing projects; Chapter 18 for the analysis of the Root-Phillimore Plan.

137 For the antecedents of Elihu Root and James Brown Scott, see *World Court* I, Biographies. Root's authority was undisputed; he returned in 1929 on the Revision Committee for the Statute. In Washington, Root and Scott headed the *Carnegie Endowment for International Peace* (f. 1910). On the ACJ, Root and Scott successfully recommended the speedy implementation of the Hague Academy of International Law (f. 1914), Asser's project that had been all but abandoned after WW I. The Assembly ignored their Recommendation, but the Academy was effectively inaugurated on 14 July 1923, and up to 1940 generously sponsored by the *Endowment.*

138 *World Court* II, chapter 13.

139 *World Court* I, chapter 12; for Lord Phillimore's tenets, see ibid, chapter 12.1.3.

140 Ibid, chapter 12.1.9; 13.2.4.

To complicate matters, Adachi and Spanish Rafael Altamira laid down claims for the fair representation of the Asian and Latin American cultural and legal traditions.[141] These claims were unceremoniously countered by Loder under reference to the essential unity of international law, which he argued, did not allow for regional ramifications.

Truth be told, in nearly all matters of Organization of the Court, the ACJ found itself overtaxed. Whereas a fair majority insisted on the Court's exclusive performing *in pleno* and summarily dismissed Chambers,[142] Ricci-Busatti championed a Court split up in three Sections, each with a specific competence and featuring a President of its own.[143] The complexity of the subject-matter posed riddles to no end. The term of office of judges was a case in point. Most members rejected life-terms, in favour of terms of six up to fifteen years, with or without re-election.[144] The need to secure the most-qualified jurists raised the issue of adequate salaries and pensions, and here Anglo-Saxon and Continental traditions once again differed substantially. The matter was only settled in the concluding meeting of the First Assembly on 16 December 1920.[145]

The personal interests of the candidates (and the willingness of the nations to yield their most competent lawyers) also touched matters of incompatibilities. Could judges hold on to semi-political positions, as at the *Quai*

---

141 Ibid, chapter 13.2,2 and 4. For a portrait of Rafael Altamira y Crevea see Yolanda Gamarra, 'The Legal Conscience of a Universal Man: Rafael Altamira y Crevea (1866 – 1951)' in P. Sean Morris (ed), *The League of Nations and the Development of International Law: a New Intellectual History of the Advisory Committee of Jurists* (Routledge, Oxon 2022), 8. For the Latin American perspective on the law, cf. also Jakob Zollmann, 'Civilization(s) and 'civilized nations' – of History, Anthropology and International Law' in P. Sean Morris (ed), *Transforming the Politics of International Law: The Advisory Committee of Jurists and the Formation of the World Court in the League of Nations* (Routledge, London 2021), 11 and Arthur Roberto Capella Giannattasio, 'Crouching Scholars, Hidden Civilizations' in P. Sean Morris (ed), *Transforming the Politics of International Law: The Advisory Committee of Jurists and the Formation of the World Court in the League of Nations* (Routledge, London 2021), 39.

142 The discourse on the Chambers of Summary Procedure and the Special Chambers for Labour issues and matters of Transit and Communications preoccupied protagonists up to December 1920; see *World Court* I, chapter 14.3; chapter 24.3.10-11; chapter 25.1.5; 25.1.8.

143 On Ricci-Busatti's particular views and his reservations to the Draft Statutes, see ibid, chapter 12.1.6; chapter chapter 13.3.5; chapter 17.3.2; chapter 20.1.2. On Italy's amendments in the Council Ibid, chapter 22.3.1; chapter 26.3.12.

144 Ibid, chapter 14.4-6; chapter 18.2.2; chapter 21.5.1; chapter 24.3.5.

145 Ibid, chapter 18.2.13; chapter 22.5.6; chapter 25.2.1; chapter 26.9.

d'Orsay in France or in the House of Lords in London, and upkeep their law firms, or lucrative positions as barristers? Some members of the ACJ discredited all side-activities and secondary functions *tout court*, whereas others merely rejected political connections. Others again maintained that all judges should be deemed qualified to serve who were accepted as such by the Parties. The overall feeling prevailed that first-rate jurists should rather not be lost at home to merely serve an idling bench at The Hague.[146]

All of the above was not for the lack of debate on substance. A first baffling issue presented itself in the Committee's choice of policy with regard to the legacy of the Hague Conferences, and the wealth of projects for a World Court subsequently tabled. The ACJ felt ill at ease to ignore this 'pride of the nations' so dearly treasured by public opinion.[147] In embracing these propositions, the ACJ incurred the perhaps not quite fair blame of later commentators to have looked backwards rather than ahead.[148] At all events, there was no way around two perplexing left-overs of the Peace Conference of 1907 – and the ACJ bravely resolved on frontally tackling both. The first concerned the composition of the Court, and the adamant claim of the Small Powers to perfect equality before the law in challenge of the Great Powers' insistence on permanent representation. Lord Phillimore's demand was stern. British public opinion would never accept the authority of a Court without being represented.[149]

VI. The Reach of the Court

The jurisdiction of the Court likewise invited keen debate, and this touched its competence *ratione personae* and *ratione materiae* alike. Various schemes over the years 1917-1920 advocated the Court's jurisdiction over private and public parties indiscriminately, a line of thought that was never extinct.[150] However, in obedience to the terms of the Covenant, the

146 Ibid, chapter 14.5; chapter 18.2.6; chapter 21.5.2; chapter 24.3.6; chapter 26.2.3.

147 Ibid, chapter 11.2.3; chapter 13.1.1.

148 See Ole Spiermann, '"Who Attempts Too Much Does Nothing Well": The 1920 Advisory Committee of Jurists and the Statute of the Permanent Court of International Justice' (2002) 73 *British Yearbook of International Law*, 187.

149 In blatant dismissal of the time-honoured principle of *nemo judex in causa sua*. On the legacy of the abortive debate in 1907, see *World Court* I, chapter 5.3.3; chapter 12.1; chapter 13.1.2; 13.3.2; chapter 17.4.5; chapter 18.1.2; chapter 21.2.1.

150 See e.g. the German and Austrian propositions; ibid, chapter 7.3.7-8.

members of the ACJ strongly held that an *inter-national* court should, on principle, operate exclusively in the relations between *nations*. With one exception, that is: Bernard Loder. A maritime law expert and prominent in Asser's *Hague Conferences on Private International Law*,[151] the Dutch Supreme Court judge insisted that the competence of the PCIJ should cover the full canvas and include the two additional layers of private parties and supra-national organizations.[152] Loder's proposition was based on a rather idiosyncratic interpretation of the multi-interpretable Article 14 of the Covenant.[153] Still, in the last resort Loder's stance was inspired by his philosophy of a World Organization of Peoples. His discretionary interpretation of the terms of the Covenant made him also insist – in another solitary stand – on the Court's rightful title to entertain unilateral summons from Parties.[154]

Loder's viewpoint with regard to the private domain is not without interest in light of the impressive case-load of the PCIJ in matters of nationality questions, minority issues, complaints of discrimination, and disputes over private concessions.[155] The idea to vest the Court with competence in matters of minority issues was readily backed by commentators at the time, if only from sheer pragmatic considerations in that it might help the Court through its anticipated early years of 'drought'. This apprehension of idleness and its impact on public opinion and the Court's credibility was likewise at the roots of the call to have the PCIJ address labour disputes. The anxieties, clearly the outcome of experience with the PCA were belied from day one – and the ILO played a prominent part in the matter.[156]

Still, even in matters of the Court's competence with respect to the public domain issues were never clear-cut. Many observers wrecked the stringent conditions the Council imposed on the access to the Court by non-Member States of the League as singularly counterproductive to the institution's paramount objective to monitor global justice and peace.[157]

151 Loder chaired the 5th and 6th Sessions in 1925 and 1928; Arthur Eyffinger, *T.M.C. Asser (1838-1913) vol. II*, chapter 26.7.

152 *World Court* I, chapter 15.2; chapter 21.4.1; chapter 24.5.1.

153 For the readings of the cryptic Art. 14 of the Covenant, see ibid, chapter 13.3.6; chapter 15.4.1.

154 For the discourse of the ACJ on Unilateral Summons, see ibid, chapter 15.4.

155 *World Court* II, Part IV, Section III, chapter 26-31.

156 The first three advisory opinions handled by the PCIJ concerned labour issues at the request of the ILO; ibid, chapter 22.

157 *World Court* I, chapter 15.3; chapter 18.2.19; chapter 21.II.2.

Here again, the experience of the PCIJ, notably so with regard to the role reserved for Germany in Court proceedings was to belie all expectations. It was much the same with the debate of the Committee regarding the Court's jurisdiction *ratione materiae*. Time and again the ACJ, to its discomfort, felt compelled to accept harsh realities. To start with, the Court was in no position to summon Parties. It was merely the recipient body and could only be activated by voluntary applications. To highlight another complicating element, any authority the Court might lay claim to was to be subtracted from the sovereignty and prestige of the nations, and this inevitably came at a price. The Powers made sure to curb the jurisdiction and clip the wings of the Court. Under no condition should the institute be vested with anything remotely akin to a legislative role.[158] Again, and to remain on the safe side, the effect of its judgments should not reach beyond the Parties directly involved and, then again, only with regard to the specific dispute at issue.[159]

VII. The Size of the Bench

Last but not least, in fair reward of their willingness to substitute might for right, and throw their interests in with a bench of judges, the Powers insisted on keeping some say in the matter. This claim was translated into the institution of the national judge *ad hoc*, in clear infringement of the *nemo judex* principle in the municipal domain.[160] In all fairness, one could hardly deny these Powers the right to defend their claims *via-à-vis* a bench that, more likely than not was not at all familiar with their national legislation and its regional social backdrop. What counted most in the end, they advanced, was the fair and equal representation of parties. With two parties, just a single party, or neither party represented on the regular bench, the options were legion. Assessors, deputy-judges, or national judges might be called in or, alternatively, regular judges be invited to step down. It all boiled down to a matter of addition or precisely distraction. The members of the ACJ found it a hard nut to crack.

158 Lord Phillimore dismissed any legislative ambitions of the Court; see ibid, chapter 15.5.1.

159 Not to invite any unwelcome 'ulterior conclusions' as the UK insisted; see ibid, chapter 22.3.4; 22.4.1

160 It was a hot issue throughout the discourse and views differed to the extreme; see ibid, chapter 14.2; chapter 17.4.1; chapter 18.2.18; chapter 21.1; chapter 22.5.4.

The flipside of the medal was the concern for the size of the bench.[161] The claim to compactness and efficiency did not tally with the principle of fair representation of all the world's legal systems and cultural traditions. This left the Small Powers rather slim chances of representation. It was this dilemma that called the institute of the deputy-judge into being.[162] The formula was rather controversial. Still, against all expectations and for reasons never anticipated a great future was in store for the concept, as we will see in our review of the role and record of the PCIJ.

VIII. An Unseemly Proposition

A last blind spot of the ACJ should be highlighted. The Covenant of the League foresaw in two basic formulas of dispute settlement: the conciliatory intervention by the Council in disputes of a predominantly political nature, next to the binding adjudication of strictly legal issues by the PCIJ. With a view to linking the two concepts – and in the last resort the Council and Court – a forever controversial idea was developed in Paris to authorize the Court to render advice to the Council and Assembly in any legal problems these political bodies might face. Most jurists considered the role alien to a court of law, and understandably so. Still, the ACJ never even addressed the issue. In its draft Statute, the advisory role of the Court remained wholly implicit.[163] It was left to the first bench of the Court in its preliminary session early in 1920 to sort out the issue in the Rules of Court.[164] The formula remained a matter of controversy from first to last. Still, the way the device developed in the interbellum Period makes for one of the most intriguing aspects of the Court's role and record.[165]

161 Ibid, chapter 14.
162 On the institution of deputy-judges, see ibid, chapter 18.1.7; chapter 21.1.3; chapter 24.3.2; chapter 25.1.3.
163 The origin of the idea of advisory opinions harked back to the discourse at Versailles. The formula was definitely adopted by the Preparatory Committee of the League; cf. Chapter 7.3. Reference to the formula was made in the Report of the ACJ (see ibid, chapter 21). The idea was at length discussed by the Subcommittee of the Third Committee; see ibid, chapter 24.5.4.
164 In the Preliminary Session of the PCIJ in February 1922; see *World Court* II, chapter 2.3.
165 Ibid, chapter 3; 7.1.2; chapter 10; chapter 12.

IX. A Draft and a Report

The draft Statute the ACJ submitted to the Council on 24 July 1920 was consolidated by a full report.[166] It also included three recommendations.[167] Six months later, these three propositions had all been unceremoniously suppressed. Even so, their reach in the long run was impressive enough. The first concerned the call for institutionalized codification conferences as a follow-up to the Hague Peace Conferences. That call was first complied with at The Hague in 1930.[168] The second touched the relics of Baron Descamp's 'Tripartite Project' and suggested the launch of an International Criminal Court. It was the all too hesitant upbeat to the Nuremberg and Tokyo Tribunals (1945-1948), the Statute of Rome (1998), and the installation of the ICC at The Hague (2002). The third Recommendation called for the implementation of the Hague Academy of International Law, the project from 1907 that had virtually eclipsed after 1913. Not by incident, the Recommendation was instigated by Elihu Root and James Brown Scott, the two administrators at the head of the *Carnegie Endowment*, which asserted itself as the foremost benefactor of the Academy throughout the Inter-Bellum Period.[169] The proposition was turned down by the Council as beyond the competence of the League. Even so, the cursory hint worked wonders. On *quatorze juillet* 1923, the wish of the Committee was fulfilled in solemn ceremony. In this way, the first, strictly advisory phase of the discourse on the Statute was concluded. It was now left to the two political bodies in control to evaluate the findings of the ACJ.

G. The Discourse in the Council: August–October 1920

In August 1920 at San Sebastian, the Council, chaired with poise by Léon Bourgeois, observed admirable constraint.[170] It assessed the draft of the ACJ

166 The Report was put up in French and for pragmatic reasons drafted by the French member of the ACJ, De Lapradelle; see *World Court* I, chapter 21.

167 These Recommendations or Resolutions were at length discussed at all stages and levels; see ibid, chapter 16.2; chapter 19; chapter 22.6.2; chapter 25.2.2; chapter 26.8.

168 In the Hague Codification Conference that convened in Jan./Feb. 1930 in the Peace Palace.

169 On the history of the call for an Academy see Eyffinger in (2023) RdC 433, 9-97.

170 In its 8th Session at San Sebastian (30 July-5 August 1920). *World Court* I, chapter 22. The Council was chaired by Léon Bourgeois and composed of two representatives

exclusively from the political perspective and in light of the terms of the Covenant. Bourgeois praised the elegant solution the ACJ had arrived at in matters of nominations and elections. Still, the final conclusion the Council had drawn was devastating. It considered the proposed compulsory jurisdiction of the Court in infringement of Article 14 of the Covenant.[171] This conclusion was reached in the presence of three members of the Secretariat who had from the first been involved with the process (Anzilotti, Hammarskjöld and Van Hamel), of two members of the ACJ (Lord Phillimore and De Lapradelle) and of two prominent jurists, Henri Fromageot and Carlo Fadda, who had been among the original appointees for the ACJ.[172] It was the crucial moment in the entire discourse. If assailed from many quarters throughout the next four months the decision was never recanted. It has governed the functioning of the World Court to the present day.

In subsequent months, the Member States of the League submitted amendments to the Draft Statute.[173] Most severe was Italy in suppressing full two dozen articles. These touched the essence: compulsory jurisdiction; advisory opinions; deputy-judges; the publication of dissenting opinions. The UK likewise turned down compulsory jurisdiction and advisory opinions, and insisted on a clear hierarchy of the sources of law. It refurbished the concept of dissenting opinions, and constrained the binding force of the judgment to parties, and for that single case exclusively from fear that 'ulterior conclusions' of a legislative nature might be drawn from a judgment. Bourgeois drew up a final report[174] which, along with comments on behalf of the ILO, was on 15 November 1920 presented to the First Plenary of the Assembly in its opening session in the *Salle de la Réformation* at Geneva[175]

of the Permanent Members (British Empire, France, Italy, Japan), a single representative of four Non-Permanent Members (Belgium, Brazil, Greece, Spain), and was attended by the SG of the League, and Members of its Secretariat.

171 *World Court* I, chapter 22.1.4.

172 For their involvement and biographies, see ibid, chapter 8.4.

173 Ibid, chapter 22.3.1-4.

174 Ibid, chapter 22.5.

175 Ibid, chapter 23-26.

H. The Discourse in the Assembly: November–December 1920

I. The Third Committee

Without much ado the Assembly delegated the issue to its (Third) Legal Committee, in which all thirty-six Member States were represented.[176] This Committee was chaired by Bourgeois, seconded by Dionisio Anzilotti as secretary, and Francis Hagerup as reporter. The composition of the Committee was most impressive. It counted five former members of the ACJ (Adachi, Fernandes,[177] Hagerup, Loder, Ricci-Busatti), three future Presidents of the World Court (that is, on top of Loder, Anzilotti and Adachi), *viz.* Max Huber, Sir Cecil Hurst, and Bodislan Winiarski; three future judges (Fromageot, Negulesco and Urrutia) and yet another formidable lawyer, Greek Nicolas Politis. Joined by diplomats of the stature of Arthur Balfour and Lord Cecil, the Committee, in short, represented pre- and post-war expertise from all quarters of the globe.

Bourgeois entrusted five alleged hot-cockles to the Committee: compulsory jurisdiction; the appointment of judges; national judges; the right of intervention; salaries. Suggestive of the Assembly's absolute priorities the last three issues were never even tabled.[178] The core matter at hand was the reach of the Court's jurisdiction.[179] The Committee's reporter, Francis Hagerup, a standard-bearer of the Court's compulsory jurisdiction, in no uncertain terms distanced himself from the Council's verdict. Adachi predictably countered this move arguing that progress came only step by step. The Latin American delegations fervently pleaded the emendation of Article 14 of the Covenant, so as to facilitate the compulsory role for the Court and spare the public at large a major disillusion. Brazilian Fernandes tabled a compromise. He suggested constraining compulsory jurisdiction to a means of last resort only to be applied should agreement through Council and PCA have failed. Fernandes called the Council's fear for the Court's

176 Ibid, chapter 23.2-5.

177 For a portrait of Raul Fernandes (and his tutor Clóvis Beviláqua) see Arthur Roberto Capella Giannattasio, 'National Political Ideologies and International Legal Practices: Raul Fernandes (1877–1968)' in P. Sean Morris (ed), *The League of Nations and the Development of International Law: A New Intellectual History of the Advisory Committee of Jurists* (Routledge, Oxon 2022), 39.

178 Negulesco questioned the formula of nominations through the PCA (*The World Court* I, Chapter 23.1.7), but priorities were never in doubt.

179 Ibid, chapter 22.4.

interference with its exclusive sphere of competence wholly unfounded. As he argued, the conciliation of political disputes and the judicial appraisal of legal disputes were worlds apart.[180] Lord Cecil countered it all. Inasmuch as the Court's judgments were enforceable, the vital interests of the Powers had to remain within the competence of the Council, at least momentarily and awaiting the organic growth of the judicial formula and the enhanced repute of the Court. Frustrated Belgian Henri La Fontaine retorted that, as before, the idols of sovereignty and unanimity were blocking progress.

With Loder protesting that one should not put everything at peril and rather abide one's time, Portuguese Affonso da Costa and Colombian Francisco Urrutia made a final appeal to Bourgeois to try and have the Council recant and implement the rule of law in order to ban war. The vicious circle should be broken, the fetishes of vital interests and honour that impregnated the Covenant should be dropped, and justice made sovereign. It was rather illogical, as Urrutia argued, to settle minor disputes through a compulsory formula and the PCA (as provided for in Article 12), then in Article 14 to exclude from this arrangement major disputes that might end up in war. In a stormy meeting Sir Cecil Hurst - otherwise a protagonist of the Court from the first and a later judge (1929-1945) and President (1934-1936) of the PCIJ - countered all progress. As he stated, the draftsmen of the Covenant had never had the Court's compulsory jurisdiction in mind in the first place; bilateral agreements were the way ahead.[181] In response, Henri La Fontaine, the editor of the authoritative *Pasicrisie* drew attention to Article 13 of the Covenant, which he felt clearly foresaw compulsory jurisdiction. As he countered, well over 200 bilateral treaties between 1907-1919 had prompted the call for a General Treaty of the kind presented in the Statute of the Court.[182]

180 Ibid, chapter 22.4.1.
181 Ibid, chapter 23.4.9.
182 Ibid, chapter 23.4.8.

At that stage, Nicolas Politis[183] and Max Huber[184] rather embarrassingly introduced an item that in a remarkable oversight had never been considered by the ACJ. This concerned the way the Statute should be adopted, by Assembly resolution or by ratified international convention.[185] Two expert lawyers of the Secretariat, Anzilotti and Van Hamel, drew up draft propositions. Both preferred the formula of the convention, as they anticipated political deadlock in the Assembly. Their proposals met with stormy protest from the Third Committee, whose majority considered the matter the exclusive competence of the Assembly. To prove Anzilotti's point, and amid heated polemics, Adachi and Ricci-Busatti, Fernandes and Hagerup – all four of them former Members of the ACJ – stood horn-locked in their widely diverging tenets in the matter.

II. The Sub-Committee

In a bid to break the deadlock by in-depth research, the Third Committee, in the wake of a couple of stormy meetings, from its midst appointed an impressive legal Sub-Committee of Ten.[186] This body likewise included five former members of the ACJ *qualitate qua* (Adachi, Fernandes, Hagerup, Loder, Ricci-Busatti). These gentlemen were, so to speak, given another chance, albeit this time not in a private capacity, but formally as the representatives of their nations. Their numbers were added by five jurists handpicked by the Secretariat of the League: Huber, Fromageot, Sir Cecil Hurst, Politis and Canadian Charles Doherty.

The ensuing exchange of views was tantamount to a comprehensive overhaul of the findings of the ACJ. The Sub-Committee's article-by-article review of the draft Statute on the basis of the close to sixty amendments the Powers had tabled prompted emendations or refinements on a range of minor points. Still, if anything, the debate served to confirm that the

183 For a portrait of N. Politis see (2002) 23 *European Journal of International Law* (contributions by Kolb, Özsu, Papadaki, Tsagourias), and cf. Marilena Papadaki, 'Creating Traditions of International Justice – The Case of Nicolas Politis' in P. Sean Morris (ed), *Transforming the Politics of International Law: The Advisory Committee of Jurists and the Formation of the World Court in the League of Nations* (Routledge, London 2021), 199.

184 For a portrait of Max Huber, see Ole Spiermann, 'Twentieth Century Internationalism in Law' (2007) 18 *European Journal of International Law*, 115.

185 *World Court* I, chapter 23.5.

186 For a full report of the extensive discourse, see ibid, chapter 24.

dilemmas the ACJ had faced had hardly been a matter of chance. The exhausting polemics may have fatally affected the wavering health of the Chairman of the Sub-Committee, Francis Hagerup. He died within three months from the exercise.

The Subcommittee's research covered ten sessions.[187] It was intense and comprehensive, touching the Court's Organization, Procedure and Competence alike. It addressed the status of non-signatory Powers to the Hague Conventions in the process of Nominations (Hurst); the opposition to the institute of deputy-judges (Ricci-Busatti); the idea to split up the Court in three divisions with specific competence (Huber). It amply considered the number of judges, their terms of office and matters of incompatibilities. It reviewed the formula of the joint conference; the distribution of seats according to continents rather than Powers;[188] the need for continuity of jurisprudence next to the refreshment of the bench. The Subcommittee appreciated the reluctance of the ACJ to comply with the claims laid down by the ILO for additional technical expertise – whether through chambers, assessors, or judges *ad hoc* – and shared that Committee's compliance with the demand from fear of jeopardizing a higher asset, the unity of the international judiciary.

Turning from the Court's organization to its procedure, the ten experts dealt with stiff French opposition (voiced by Henri Fromageot) to the claim tabled by the Spanish-speaking world to have its language honoured as official language.[189] The Sub-Committee emphatically turned down an Argentinian amendment aiming at the definite suppression of the PCA. It called the matter beyond its competence, and argued that the move would take the bottom out of the process of nomination of judges. The Sub-Committee also addressed the British claim (Sir Cecil Hurst) to honour the livelier Common Law tradition with regard to the hearing of experts and witnesses. When Fernandes insisted on public hearings – a matter on which issue the two Hague Conferences had judged differently – as the prerequisite to the monitoring of judges, Hagerup protested that public influence impaired the course of justice. Ricci-Busatti and Politis countered that the concept of privacy was alien to judicial procedure. The publication

187 Between 24 November and 7 December 1920. The Subcommittee's research was at the heart of the Assembly's dealings with the Statute of the Court.

188 This idea was time and again suggested in 1920, and from various sources, but was consistently dismissed throughout the Inter-Bellum Period.

189 This claim, first raised by Altamira within the ACJ, was on this occasion repeated by Raul Fernandes.

of dissenting opinions likewise caused polemics, and the same held good for the concept of the revision of judgments, the major bone of contention between Barbosa, Choate and Martens back in 1907. The vehement debate within the Sub-Committee only confirmed the lack of agreement of the discipline.

The debate on the jurisdiction of the Court saw a repetition of the prolonged polemics regarding the access of private parties and non-member States of the League, before the core matter, the Court's compulsory jurisdiction was tabled.[190] To Ricci-Busatti's content, Politis warned against brushing the Great Powers the wrong way. Confidence in the Court had to be gained in a gradual process of growth. Huber fell in: the text of the Covenant did not justify compulsion. He advocated an alternative route, by means of the voluntary acceptance of bilateral agreements. In Fernandes' rephrased formula, this idea landed in the optional clause.[191] From the first, the formula of the clause was highly contested, both on grounds of substance (Adachi, Politis), and as being a matter beyond the competence of the Committee (Fromageot).

Two other controversial issues were settled, if only as the outcome of serious debate. It was concluded that under no condition should the Court lay claim to a legislative role. Secondly, advisory opinions should only touch abstract matters, no palpable disputes. Also, these opinions should have a strictly recommendatory status – and this held good both ways. They should never be binding on the Court either, meaning that the issue should not be considered *res judicata*.[192] As we will see, Court experience would be entirely different and feature a gradual process of assimilation of the advisory formula to the Court's judicial role.

In all, the Sub-Committee modified, refined or rephrased no less than two thirds of all Articles of the Statute. Still, the net harvest on substance was fairly moderate. On the whole, the Sub-Committee was rather hesitant to run against the Council. It only honoured a mere handful of the sixty amendments the Powers had tabled, notably so with regard to labour cases and issues of transit and communications.[193] The outcome must have come as a comfort to the five former members of the ACJ. Hagerup's *Report* of the findings of his Sub-Committee in the Third Committee rekindled

190 *World Court* I, chapter 24.5.2.
191 Statute Permanent Court of International Justice (1920), Art. 36.2-5.
192 *World Court* I, chapter 24.5.4.
193 Ibid, chapter 24.3.10-11.

discourse on the idea of Sections (Negulesco), on the regional distribution of seats (Urrutia) and on the number and balance of national and foreign nominees. Agreement was reached with Albert Thomas on Assessors in ILO cases. Meanwhile, Politis, Huber and Fernandes kept quarrelling over the proper way of implementation of the Statute. Argentina tabled an amendment that called for the exclusion from the League of any Power that refused to comply with a judgment of the Court. She wished to have sanctions imposed, should such conduct effectively endanger world peace. The idea was rejected as beyond the Committee's competence. Delicate matters of salaries were not solved by any length yet.[194]

The recommendations of the ACJ were likewise addressed.[195] The one with respect to the Hague Academy and Baron Descamps' personal advocacy of an international criminal court were courteously but summarily dismissed. The first was deemed beyond the Committee's competence, the second was considered premature and inopportune. The proposition for a prospective codification conference raised lengthier debate. Sir Cecil Hurst preferred relying on gradual growth. Henri La Fontaine insisted on the Committee's complying with the urgent demand of public opinion to finally see palpable results. Huber felt that any such initiative should be left to the Assembly. But then, Politis would rather entrust this role to the Council and Ricci-Busatti, in turn, to the Powers. To break deadlock, Politis suggested recruiting a Research Committee from the *Institut* and the ILA. The wide divergence of views underscored the provisional, tentative nature of much of the discourse, which in 1925 was rekindled by France and ensued in the Hague Codification Conference of 1930.

III. The Plenary

On 13 December, the First Assembly chaired by Paul Hymans heard Bourgeois, the inveterate optimist, call the outcome of their debate historic in having entwined durable peace and real justice.[196] Delegates attentively listened to Hagerup's report on the four weeks of discourse and to his urgent plea for agreement so as to uphold the credibility of the League. The Norwegian jurist extolled the merits of the exercise. The stalemate of 1907

194 For a full review, see ibid, chapter 25.
195 Ibid, chapter 25.2.2.
196 Ibid, chapter 26.1.

on the Court's composition had been broken, and political machinations effectively been excluded in the plebiscite of perfect equality of the National Groups and in the strict observance of incompatibilities. Technical labour disputes and issues of communications would receive flexible treatment through advisory assessors. Fernandes' *trouvaille* of the optional clause on the basis of reciprocity had met the conflicting views of ACJ and Council midway. The choice of implementation of the Statute, whether through resolution or convention, was left to the Assembly's discretion. The Protocol of Signature of the Statute was left open to facilitate later access by the USA and other Powers.[197]

In this way the stage was set for the last act, an impressive array of speeches by the representatives of seventeen Powers in the Plenary.[198] Moral conviction and legal acumen, sober *raison d'état* and diplomatic subterfuge were channelled into a wealth of passionate pleas of true eloquence and brilliant rhetoric. To bespeak the high stakes, the optional clause was hailed by some as a veritable breakthrough, and loathed by others as blocking the 'real thing'. In a desperate rally, the Latin American Republics and the Neutral Powers joined hands in an emotional final bid to turn tables and have the Great Powers drop their opposition to the compulsory role of the Court. Neither Loder's sharp censure, La Fontaine's compelling pleas or Fernandes' analytical coaxing softened inexorable Lord Cecil. Three judges-to-be, Urrutia, Negulesco and Wellington Koo (ICJ), had implored the Assembly to have the Council recant, when Nicolas Politis hammered down harsh reality: unanimity was beyond their grasp. Arthur Balfour personally settled the issue: *natura non facit saltus.* Time should be left to do its healing work. An embittered Loder countered that Great Britain's selfish blockage of progress was doomed: one could not hold back Spring. Regardless of the outcome, the two sessions of intense skirmishing on 13 December 1920 bear witness to the quintessential import of the debate and the sheer tenacity of its protagonists. It was, by all standards, a historic encounter.

With Hagerup severely ill and tired of battling Bourgeois still mustered optimism. The League and the Court, he claimed, were the living organisms of progress. The optional clause epitomized unstoppable moral growth. Between themselves, the Council and the Court were the guardians

197 Ibid, chapter 26.2.
198 Ibid, chapter 26.3.

of sustainable peace. Once established, the Court would soon overcome all current reserve. A star had risen on the firmament. The feeble light of an imperfect scheme would light their way: *ubi lux, ubi jus, ibi pax.*[199] On 15-16 December, in the Ninth and Tenth meetings of the Third Committee, the delicate issue of salaries was settled.[200] On 18 December 1920, the Assembly by unanimous acclaim adopted the Statute, Protocol, and optional clause.[201]

I. The First General Elections: September 1921

It still took some gentle reminders, but in July 1921, Sir Eric Drummond confidently projected the general elections for the first bench for September.[202] With hindsight, Max Huber heavily censured the intense political infighting between Council and Assembly on the occasion,[203] but on the whole, the first general elections went off smoothly, if not without surprising setbacks.[204] The frequently voiced reserve against the formula of nominations from fear of an unwieldy competition should all forty Powers nominate the maximum of four candidates, proved wholly unwarranted: only 89 candidates were proposed. Most Powers never bothered to nominate more than just two jurists.[205] But then, to general discomfort, the alleged universality of the law was definitely belied. More than half the nominees, forty-eight candidates to be precise, were exclusively nominated by their own National Group. Regional haggling in *quid pro quo* was thriving, notably so among the Latin American, the Baltic and the Balkan nations. Again, as against all expectations, in the elections for deputy-judges it effectively took a joint conference to break the distrust and stalemate between Council and Assembly.

199 Ibid chapter 26.6.
200 Ibid chapter 25.2.
201 Ibid chapter 26.7-9.
202 *Word Court* II, chapter 1.1.
203 Ibid, chapter 1.7. The First Elections took place on 14-15 September 1921. For Huber's Appraisal in *Denkwürdigkeiten* (1972), see ibid, chapter 15.4.
204 Such as the steadfast rejection by the Assembly of Edouard Descamps' candidature.
205 Great Britain had made just a single nomination (Lord Finlay, who was likewise nominated by Australia, Greece and Chile). Two other British candidates were nominated by foreign Powers. France had nominated two nationals and a single foreign scholar, but no less than seven other French scholars had been nominated by other countries; see ibid, chapter 1.6.

On 3 November 1921, Secretary-General Drummond invited fifteen jurists to assemble at The Hague by the end of January.[206] On 15 February 1922, in a Court Hall packed with dignitaries the judges took their solemn declaration to honourably, faithfully, impartially, and conscientiously exercise their powers and duties.[207] Centuries of speculation, fifty years of concerted research and six months of intense discourse and solid resolutions had carried the world onto the threshold of the fulfilment of the Hope of Ages.

J. The Permanent Court of International Justice (1922-1946)[208]

I. The Political Backdrop

The post-war generation sought to digest the shockwave it had endured in the hubris of its aspirations. In bids for a League, a World Court, and a collective security system, it sought to implant the rule of law in brave challenge of the untrammelled sovereignty of the Powers. A mere two decades later, the sad demise of this boundless idealism saw the world in a singularly traumatic experience roll back to the nadir of war. Still, unlike what the tragic outcome in 1939 might suggest, the League Era was no straightforward process of down-spiralling. In spite of unrelenting political tension, indeed belying scepticism all around, the Dawes Plan (1925) exemplified the feasibility of international co-operation. Cautious *détente* bore rich fruit in the Locarno Agreements (1925), the Briand-Kellogg Pact (1928), and the Hague Codification Conference (1930). At the time, these successes of diplomacy were widely interpreted as the beacons of veritable progress. The Wall Street crash in the Fall of 1929 came as a rude awakening. Baffling

206 Ibid, chapter 2.2.

207 Ibid, chapter 2.3. Due to the absence of regular judges, three deputy-judges had to be called in; these were ominous beginnings.

208 For an extensive, if by no means comprehensive Bibliography of the role and record of the PCIJ see *World Court* II. Major *stanze* in the history of commentaries on the PCIJ were Alexander Fachiri (1932), Manley O. Hudson (1943), Jan Verzijl (1965). For recent assessments, see Shabtai Rosenne, *Law and Practice 1920-1996, 4 vols.* (Nijhoff, Den Haag 1997); Ole Spiermann, *International Legal argument in the Permanent Court of International Justice; The Rise of the International Judiciary* (Cambridge University Press, Cambridge 2005); Christian J. Tams and Malgosia Fitzmaurice (eds) *Legacies of the Permant Court of International Justice* (Martinus Nijhoff, Leiden/Boston 2013).

the Young Plan (1929, adopted 1930) and US President's Hoover's Moratorium (June 1931), global depression cut short all optimism. Hence, an unstoppable process of conflicts – Manchuria (1932), Ethiopia (1935), the Rhineland claim (1936), the Spanish Civil War (1936-1939) and the Sudeten crisis (1938) – paved the way to Munich (1938), and the invasion of Poland (1939).

From wishful thinking, the world had all too readily condoned the manifest structural defects of geopolitics and the inherent shortcomings of the League. Rather than presenting the ambitioned brotherhood of man and the alliance of the peoples, the World Organization proved a helpless plaything at the whim of the powerplay of the nations. The legacy of the pre-war Concert era, the gap between the Small and the Great was never truly bridged. It was merely waylaid into the inveterate mistrust and paralyzing machinations of Council and Assembly. The League fatally laboured from the basic mismatch between high Wilsonian idealism and Clemenceau's stern objective to consolidate war by the victors' peace. With the Covenant embedded in the Peace Treaties, the PCIJ, for all its judicial autonomy was part and parcel of the severely flawed League system. It had serious repercussions for its functioning.

II. Growing Pains

However, in all fairness, the Court laboured as much from serious intrinsic drawbacks, and we will open our review from this angle. To put it bluntly, the institution of international adjudication was an experiment for which the world of law, despite fifty years of intense discourse, proved ill-prepared. The need for the steady revision of the Rules of Court, first drawn up in toilsome deliberation at the Preliminary Session in 1922, strikes as a telling symptom.[209] Practice soon pointed out the blatant lacunae and misconceptions of theory.

But the immediate problems for the Court were very basic. From the start, it was overwhelmed by events and wrongfooted in all departments of organization. Its heavy case-load took all concerned entirely by surprise. The response ran contrary to all expectations based on the experience with the PCA back in 1900 and to the assessment of the ACJ and academia in

209 For a survey, see *World Court* II, chapter 3.

1920.[210] It required a rapid expansion of staff.[211] It also created all kinds of logistical problems at the Peace Palace. These, in turn, led to tension with the administrating body, the Dutch Carnegie Foundation,[212] and triggered keen rivalry with the three other institutes on the premises, the PCA, the Peace Palace Library, and that other newcomer, the Hague Academy of International Law (1923).[213] Frictions were only solved by lengthy negotiations, endless refurbishing projects at high costs, finally the construction of an adjoining building in the grounds to lodge the Hague Academy as well as the stacks of the Peace Palace Library.

Personal repercussions were equally dramatic. In their schedule, the judges had anticipated a single Annual Session and a yearly sojourn at The Hague of two months on average.[214] Reality was far more demanding. Up to 1936, the Court had to insert no less than twenty Extraordinary Sessions[215] before, in a major revision of the Rules, one wisely concluded upon permanent Annual Sessions.[216] The non-Western judges never coped with the tight schedule. In the meetings of the Revision Committee (1929) at Geneva, Henri Fromageot justly complained that the Winter Sessions rarely saw any 'overseas' judges attending. Statistics are telling: judge De Bustamante missed out on 24 out of the 35 Sessions up to 1935; judge Pessõa attended 6 out of the 16 Sessions up to 1931; judge Moore attended 6 out of 14 Sessions, judge Kellogg a mere 3 out of 14.[217]

Very likely, what also assessed itself in these figures was the lack of direct commitment and personal interest of these non-European judges with the substance of the cases. Barring a single exception, these exclusively touched the dismal legacy of Versailles and the self-inflicted wounds of the European Powers. The institutional home-leaves these 'overseas judges'

---

210 Ibid, chapter 6.1

211 Ibid, chapter 4.3.

212 Ibid, chapter 5.

213 Ibid, chapter 5-3-4.

214 Ibid, chapter 2.4.

215 The total of Sessions over the period 1922-1935 amounted to thirty-five (fourteen Ordinary and twenty-one Extraordinary Sessions). With the implementation of its Revised Rules and Statute early in 1936, the Court adopted the system of Annual Sessions.

216 For the successive revisions of the Rules, see *World Court* II, chapter 3; for the revision of the Statute, *Ibid*, chapter 12.

217 For a survey, see ibid, chapter 6.2-3.

were entitled to only exacerbated the predicament.[218] As a consequence, the Presidents of the Court had a permanent struggle on their hands to reach a quorum. On various occasions, as in the *Serbian Loans* (1928) and the *Free Zones* (1930-1932) cases, hearings had to be postponed for lack of judges. In the latter case, President Anzilotti had to reconstitute the bench. At different stages of a case, parties faced a bench in a substantially changed composition. They raised sharp protest claiming they were entitled to a 'standing' Court and a 'consolidated' bench. To add insult to injury, overseas judges often took their leave in the (sometimes substantial) interval between hearings and the reading of the judgment or opinion. Judge Moore did as much in 1923 and 1927, judge Pessõa in 1927 (all the while delivering a dissenting opinion), judges Kellogg and De Bustamante in 1933. Pursuant to complaints by parties, this questionable *modus operandi* was suppressed in the revised Rules of 1936. Names of absent judges were stricken from the case, and their statements or opinions no longer accepted. [219]

The predicament had another major consequence never anticipated. This touched the upgrading of the role of deputy-judges. The concept as such had been reluctantly accepted by the Great Powers in 1920 to oblige the claims the Small Powers had tabled with a view to enhancing their chances of representation on the bench.[220] At the installation ceremony of the Court, on 15 February 1922, President Loder embarrassingly had to call in three deputy-judges to reach the quorum.[221] Hardly any case ever proceeded without the presence of one or more 'junior judges', as they were often called. Chinese deputy-judge Wang Chung-hui was summoned in seven of the nineteen sessions up to 1930 to help make the quorum.[222] The predicament raised the call in the elections of 1930 for the extension of the bench from eleven to fifteen regular judges.[223] Even so, and to remain on

218 In 1931, the predicament prompted the amendment of the Rules to ensure that no more than two judges simultaneously enjoyed a home-leave (Article 27).

219 On these issues, see *World Court* II, chapter 6.2-3.

220 For the discourse on the concept, see *World Court* I, chapter 18.7; chapter 24.3.2; chapter 25.1.3; for the Elections see *World Court* II, chapter 1.7.2.

221 *World Court* II, chapter 2.2. At the installation ceremony three deputy-judges joined nine regular judges. Still, judge Huber pertinently rejected the interference of deputy-judges with elections or with the drafting process of the Rules of Court.

222 Ibid, chapter 6.4.; on judge Wang, see Ole Spiermann, 'Judge Wang Chung-hui at the Permanent Court of International Justice in (2006) 5 *Chinese Journal of International Law*, 115.

223 Ibid, chapter 12.

the safe side, the institution of deputy-judges was provisionally retained for rainy days. No deputy-judge was ever 'activated' on the second bench.

III. Clashing Legal Cultures

So much for the predicaments of organization. A far more severe hindrance to Court proceedings, indeed a serious menace to its proper functioning, was the divergence of outlook of the judges. It could hardly have come as a surprise. In 1920 the ACJ, and in its wake the Third Committee of the Assembly, had been taken aback by the lack of consensus among international jurists on even the most elementary aspects of their assignment. On the first bench, the civil law magistrate and the international legal scholar stood horn-locked. Two more blood types bespoke the fundamental bifurcation of views between the representatives of the Common Law and the Civil Law traditions on the role of the judge and the status of the Court in the international arena. Keen personal frictions sadly revealed that the difference of perspective, which back in 1873 had driven the pioneers of the *Institut* and the ILA apart,[224] had still not been bridged.

As the record of the PCIJ showed the world, to identify and appreciate the conundrum was not to solve the dilemma. The judges became painfully aware of these inconveniences the moment they tackled the drafting of the Rules of Court in their Preliminary Session in 1922.[225] Their professional intercourse on a daily basis in subsequent years only exacerbated the predicament. Two authoritative judges and Presidents, Max Huber and Dionisio Anzilotti, both expert scholars and seasoned diplomats, in public addresses on the bench and in their private papers and memoirs, amply reflected on their serious concerns. They voiced despair at their colleagues' lack of openness for compromise, at their impotence to observe the principle of *audi et alteram partem*, in short, at the lack of 'esprit de corps' and solidarity on the bench. In their joint perception, these handicaps paralyzed deliberations and impaired the quality of judgments and opinions, and in the last resort the prestige of the Court.[226]

224 Arthur Eyffinger, *T.M.C. Asser (1838-1913) vol. I*, chapter 19.2.

225 See *World Court* II, Chapter 3, for the discourse on the Rules of Court in January-February 1920.

226 On Anzilotti's and Huber's fairly critical appraisal of the (mal)functioning of the First Bench in its opening years, see ibid, chapter 15. 2-4.

The incongruities of outlook and the recalcitrance to compromise became particularly embarrassing with respect to the position of parties. Both Huber and Anzilotti kept hammering down the quintessential difference of the national and the international courtroom. As they posited, the status, psychology and susceptibilities of sovereign States were worlds apart from the position of private parties in civil jurisdiction. Huber called it a fundamental error of judgment to treat sovereign Powers like suspects before the police judge. As he insisted, this was just a matter of common sense, which had nothing to do with the 'independence' of the judiciary. The agent of a Power simply was an actor not comparable to the barrister of a private party. The PCIJ had to meet the needs of the Powers to the extent that this rhymed with the basis of good justice, *viz.*, the fair and equal treatment of Parties.

But then, as Huber intimated in his private papers, fewer than half of the judges properly understood international law. Most of them were civil procedure experts who had no inkling of the different conditions on the international plane. To Huber, Bernard Loder was the prototype of the national magistrate who did not understand, or accept the proper status of the Powers. The Court's first President was an eminent civil jurist and a man of undisputed integrity, but entertained sanguine feelings and had a hot temperament. He never accepted the interference of politics in his courtroom.[227] In Huber's final assessment, the judges never managed to strike a deal. If a 'guilty party' should be designated at all, it was perhaps the discipline as such. It was left to the judges to solve the riddle. But then, as Huber and Anzilotti readily agreed, the key was collegiality, the willingness to open up to the legitimacy of alternative views. Legal expertise had little to do with it.

The above 'factions' within the Court are readily retraceable in the consistent tenor of dissenting opinions. The formula of dissent was, of course, itself a source of controversy from the days of the Hague Peace Conferences.[228] It was widely felt that dissent might affect the prestige of the Court and the authority of its judgments and opinions. As against this, it was argued that precisely these contrasting positions were invaluable tools for the interpretation of the Court's true mission. They exposed the full

227 The personal drama reached its pit on the day of Loder's 75th birthday, when Huber's last-minute candidature for the Presidency prevented Loder's re-election.

228 See *e.g. World Court* I, chapter 21.3.7; chapter 24.5.5.

canvas of the discourse, the balancing act of law schools, the equipoise of *lex lata* and *lex ferenda*, and the progressive harmony of the discipline.

Anzilotti and Huber, it must be said, were rather critical commentators of Court proceedings. Their censure on the process of deliberations is a case in point. Both readily acknowledged that the elaborate formula chosen had the merit of creating a welcome buffer against political infringement. But then, the debate among eleven jurists who represented different systems of law was tiresome, and extremely time-consuming under the best of circumstances. In their experience, the exchange of views was strikingly chaotic, and the discourse embarrassingly ineffective, the more so as only three judges commanded French or English as their mother tongue. Last but not least, a collective judgment called for a compromise that was hard to get at, and never boasted the lucid reasoning and clear-cut verdict of a solitary judge.

Huber drew attention to still another drawback. Haste was the common denominator of all these deliberations, notably so in the critical final stages of the drafting of a judgment. By then, most judges had long booked their tickets and were ready to call it a day. Last minute changes were the order of the day. Somehow, Registrar Åke Hammarskjöld managed to keep his cool and remain on top of affairs. If most opinions and judgments were acceptable at all, this was thanks to the Swedish scholar. Anzilotti once intimated to Huber that he thought it was sheer providence.[229] Huber's outspoken unburdening in his memoirs covered the whole process: from the machinations at the general elections in 1921, along the vanity of his colleagues in matters of robes, to the uncompromising factions as exemplified in the elections for the Presidency in 1924.[230] It opens our eyes to a captivating spectacle of trial and error, symptomatic of the experiment the Court essentially was.

IV. The Court, the League, and the Powers

The above quandaries of organization and legal cultures set apart, the role of the Court was never to be envied. Its position towards the League and the Powers must have felt like sticking cramped between a rock and a hard

229 *World Court* II, chapter 15.4.1.3.

230 Max Huber, *Denkwürdigkeiten* (Orell Füssli Verlag, Zürich 1972); *World Court* II, chapter 15.4.

place. There is no way around the quintessential difference of functioning of national High Courts and the international judicature. The World Court organically developed as the fairly passive receptacle of applications and requests for opinions under terms submitted by the Powers or the Council at their perfect discretion. The PCIJ was in no position to initiate cases or of its own accord tackle any juridical entanglements it perceived.[231] Again, anything remotely akin to a legislative role had been stamped out from the first in 1920.

The first bench (1922-1930), to its infinite credit, ingeniously entwined *obiter dicta* of general purport in its judgments to help advance the law and by precedent establish normative rules.[232] It earned itself the undivided acclaim of academia. The World Court, scholars posited, should never let parties dictate its agenda the way the Powers were wont to juggle arbitrators. The second bench (1931-1940), increasingly cornered by growing political tension, felt wise to observe greater restraint, so as not to undermine its own credibility. It incurred severe censure on this account.[233] A first censure came from among its own ranks. In his very first attendance as judge, in December 1930, Frank Billings Kellogg in a rather stern observation of dissent to the second Order in the *Free Zones Case* censured the way the Court had bent the knee to the whims of the Powers. A versed diplomat, who in 1928 had authored perhaps the most enlightened political agreement of his times, Kellogg gave his colleagues on the bench fair warning never to compromise their high ideals and judicial integrity by letting themselves lured into adjudicating politically or, as the case might be, economically loaded disputes.

Another critical observer was Jan Verzijl.[234] Time and again, the stern Dutch scholar complained of the impotence of the Court:

---

231 Ibid, chapter 7 and 17.

232 In 1924, in the *Eastern Carelia Case* (see *World Court* II, chapter 26), the First Bench had firmly held its own and withstood the pressure from the Council in its refusal to render an Opinion. In the opening stages of the *Free Zones* case, the judges had openly reprimanded the joint bid of Parties to force their hands and render a provisional, private Order (ibid, chapter 25.1.3).

233 Keen observers had felt that the Court had mishandled the request of the Council on Danzig and the ILO (*World Court* II, chapter 29.3), and commentators had positively been alarmed at the way the judges had allowed litigants to led them astray in the case of the *Congo Concessions* (ibid, chapter 32.8.2), or in the case of the *Lighthouses on Creta and Samos* (ibid, chapter 32.7.3)

234 Jan Verzijl (1888-1987). Verzijl's rather severe but invaluable observations were published in various papers and languages throughout the 1930s. In 1965 they were

> This is one of those innumerable cases in which the society of States resembles a tract of international political jungle rather than an international legal community [...] in which the howling of beasts of prey is almost continuous. How could one hope to lay out in this jungle the «Lenôtre Gardens» of a neatly arranged law of international procedure which at the same time satisfies our sense of justice?[235]

Verzijl readily acknowledged the inherent problem:

> ...the lofty principles of international law which, from their empyrean height, dominate human affairs and which are invoked so frequently by the litigant States, often seem to become transformed into pale phantoms as soon as one wishes to bring them down to the earth, where national passions rage. This is because the bright rays of divine and eternal justice are only imperfectly reflected through the prism of the human mind and because, whenever we try to seize it, our clutching hands merely grasp a void.[236]

V. Advisory Opinions

The interaction between the Court, the Council and the Powers can perhaps best be instanced under reference to the Court's acceptance of its position in matters of advisory opinions. If forever controversial, the Court's advisory capacity never malfunctioned.[237] In fact, it brought the PCIJ half its case-load.[238] Thanks to the ILO, the formula even secured the Court a flying start.[239] But then, from the first, political considerations governed and soon redirected the application of the formula to make the device drift far away from its original purport. Strictly reserved for the Council and Assembly – and jealously withheld from the Organization as such or its Secretary-General – the option was never honoured by the Assembly. All requests without exception reached the Court through the Council. But

---

collected and published in *The Jurisprudence of the World Court* (Vol. I; Vol. II addressed the first decades of the ICJ).

235 Jan Verzijl, *The Jurisprudence of the World Court I* (A.W. Sijthoff, Leiden 1965), 439.

236 Ibid, I, 197-198.

237 *World Court* II, chapter 7.2.

238 In all, 65 cases reached the Court; 10 were withdrawn. The Court rendered 27 advisory opinions and passed 32 judgments.

239 Three requests came the Court's way within a year; for the review; see *World Court* II, chapter 22.

then again, this, too, only held good formally speaking. Soon enough, the Powers realized the opportunities the device offered them – and seized control. Weighing the odds, they shrewdly calculated which particular variety, the adjudicative or the advisory procedure better served their interests.

Their next step was to secure the assimilation of the two formulas. The ACJ had intended the advisory formula to serve doctrine and solve the legal riddles that baffled the political bodies of the League. The Powers, instead, availed themselves of the Council to submit very concrete disputes. As early as 1924, they claimed and the following year effectively obtained judges *ad hoc* in these procedures.[240] By 1930, the Court, finding the substance and objectives of the adjudicative and advisory formulas inextricably blurred, bowed to realities and in its Publications dropped the formal distinction of its Series of Judgments (A) and Opinions (B).[241] In short, the substance of a dispute rather than the way it was submitted should guide us in the arrangement and interpretation of cases.

VI. Legal and Political Disputes

Another source of rivalry and tension should be highlighted. This touched the interaction of the two bodies of the League engaged with the settlement of disputes in their respective assignments. The Council's role was to settle political disputes by conciliation, that of the Court to settle legal disputes by adjudication. The distinction, the typical product of theory, was rather artificial. For one thing, political disputes might involve major legal conundrums. For another, and more to the point, no legal controversy between Powers in this world was ever devoid of (overbearing) political motives. This held true indiscriminately for contentious cases and requests for Opinions, for major and minor disputes submitted, and whether by the Great Powers or the Small. To exemplify, the cases with respect to the *Upper Savoy*, the *Greenland* cases, or the dispute with respect to the *Waters of the Meuse* showed beyond a shimmer of doubt that even the traditional Neutral Powers – Switzerland, Norway, Denmark, Belgium and the Netherlands – could as easily be aroused to bellicosity. In other words, one should not shut the eyes for realities. Whether for better or worse, the PCIJ was

240 For a historical analysis, see ibid, chapter 3 and chapter 10.

241 On the Series of Publications of the PCIJ (A-E), see ibid, chapter 4.5; Series A 1-24 (1923-1930); Series B 1-18 (1922-19300; Series A/B 41-80 (1931-1940).

part and parcel of a through-and-through politicized organization. The Covenant of the League and the Statute of the Court were less than perfect instruments. Their perplexing lack of legal lucidity, their enigmatic phraseology and baffling ambiguity were the very intentional tools of diplomacy to claim elbow-room at all times.

What, then, should be the Court's policy? Most commentators agreed with Kellogg's adamant verdict: neither the nature of the Court nor its Statute allowed it to touch politicized disputes. But then, Verzijl for one did not agree unconditionally. As he readily conceded, some cases combined "the slipperiness of the eel, the changeable colour of the chameleon, and the mimicry of some insects".[242] These cases the Court should never touch. But then, this did not categorically exclude all political disputes. In Verzijl's book, the Court might by all means address political disputes, always provided it kept itself within the strict boundaries of its task to speak up as a veritable Court of Law. That is to say, the Court should pronounce binding decisions, and this exclusively on the basis of law. What the Court should abstain from at all costs was to decide a case not on a strictly juridical basis, but pursuant to that disastrous loophole provided for in the Statute (Article 38.2), which allowed the bench at the request of parties to render a judgment *ex aequo et bono*, in short, along the lines of diplomacy. [243]

As Verzijl advanced in a nice paradox, the Court would effectively more compromise itself by thus 'mediating' legal disputes than by adjudicating 'political' disputes. And, as he added in a shrewd observation, come to speak of it, by excluding political disputes on principle the Court would generate an additional problem. General jurisdiction treaties between the Powers as a rule entrusted the PCIJ with the adjudication of all disputes regardless of their nature. Separating the category of political disputes was begging the question to what body these disputes should then be conferred.

VII. A Deceptive Case-Law

The better to appreciate the above, we will have a closer look at the case-load of the PCIJ. There is something peculiar about these cases. At first glance one is positively struck at the seeming triviality of the disputes

242 Cf. *World Court* II, *Epilogue* 6.

243 The device had been introduced by the Third Committee of the First Assembly. In his celebrated *Corsi* (3 vols., 1915-1928) Dionisio Anzilotti called the device "most infelicitous".

submitted: a solitary lighthouse; a closed-down railway track; a remote primary school; a crooked entrepreneur; phosphate concessions; a Greek-Orthodox convent; postal services in Danzig. The sheer insignificance of the cases would seem to scoff the dignity of a World Court and affront the assembled legal genius of its bench. First glances can be deceptive. Paradoxically, the very substance-matter of the sixty odd cases submitted to the Court, be this in the contentious or advisory capacity serves to illustrate the underlying, hidden motives of the Powers. Time and again, the Court found itself caught up in legal intricacies that constituted only a tiny part, and rarely the critical element of disputes with much wider moral, social or political implications. The legal skirmishes were, so to speak, the tip of the iceberg, mere symptoms of deeper trouble.

The Court, in short, never was the Ivory Tower many jurists and politicians – both categories for reasons of their own – had preferred it to be. Many cases were very intentional political soundings by parties. They bespoke immensely higher stakes: the rivalling interests or the challenged prestige of the Powers in question;[244] the ambiguous nationality of millions of emigrants;[245] the discrimination and suppression of huge minorities;[246] the credibility of the world's finance system,[247] the high political stakes of concessions.[248] By way of example, on the second day the German forces invaded Poland, in early September 1939, her military in a well-considered move had the Polish staff of the (extraterritorial) Danzig Post Office executed.[249] One may indeed argue that precisely the pettiness of the cases betrays the almost pathological sensitivities of these allegedly Sovereign Powers.

---

244 As in the disputes between Norway and Denmark on the *Legal Status of Eastern Greenland* (1932; see *World Court* II, chapter 24); or the dispute between Belgium and the Netherlands on the *Diversion of Water from the Meuse* (1937, ibid, chapter 23).

245 As in the disputes between Turkey and Greece; see *World Court* II, chapter 31 (three cases).

246 As in the case on the *Greco-Bulgarian Communities* (1930; see ibid, chapter 30) or on the *German Minority Schools in Upper Silesia* (1931; see ibid, chapter 28).

247 As in the two cases of the *Serbian Loans* and the *Brazilian Loans* (1929; see ibid, chapter 32).

248 Fifteen cases in all touched matters of claims for compensations and indemnities in this domain, the *Mavrommatis Case* (1924-1927) being a prominent incident in point; see ibid, chapter 32.

249 The reference is to the advisory opinion on *Polish Postal Services in Danzig* (1925; see ibid, chapter 29).

What the PCIJ dealt with were the wandering ways States groped and probed their way to power. Often enough, the Court merely skirted the edges of the underlying friction. Rarely did the Powers let the judges come anywhere nearer. To its infinite credit, the Court readily seized the one handle it could grasp. As a rule, it stood firm in keeping the Powers from dragging justice and the law along in their sordid stride.[250] By the same token, there is never room for misunderstanding. At the core of the Court's challenge stood the Powers. The judgments of the Court went to the heart of the power-play at Versailles at the close of World War I and touched the gist of the problematic that twenty years later crystallized in World War II.

VIII. Developments Never Foreseen

Still, unwittingly, these allegedly sovereign Powers had somehow trapped themselves. Precisely the privileged kind of world the Allied and Associated Powers had created for themselves at Versailles undermined their exclusive claims. On the occasion they had willfully excluded all other social strata and actors from access to the Court, be they private parties, or supra- or international organizations.[251] On top of this, they had imposed stern conditions on rivalling actors at their own plane, these being the Non-Member States of the League.[252] Foremost among these, of course, were the conquered Central Powers.[253]

To its distress, the League found its proud claim of representing a true World Organization soon eroded by events beyond its control. Two World Powers on the rise, the USA and the USSR – which both had been pivotal to the implementation of the *Oeuvre de La Haye* in pre-war years – abstained on political grounds. In the *Eastern Carelia* case (1923), the USSR

250 *Pace* some very critical remarks by Verzijl, himself counsel for Bulgaria in the case of the *Greco-Bulgarian Emigration Convention* (1930; see *World Court* II, chapter 30.3). Verzijl did however acknowledge the tightrope the Court walked on occasions. As he observed in his analysis of the case on the *ILO Convention on the Employment of Women at Night* (1932; see *World Court* II, chapter 22.5), the footholds the Court found here "lent little more support than those which mountaineers have often precariously to rely on." (Jan Verzijl, *The Jurisprudence of the World Court I* (A.W. Sijthoff, Leiden 1965), 313).

251 *World Court* II, chapter 7.

252 Ibid, chapter 7.4.

253 Germany, Austria, Bulgaria, Turkey, the Parties in the successive and separate 'Paris' Peace Treaties.

showed perfect disdain for the Court and the League alike.[254] Neither was the USA ever hauled in, notwithstanding concerted efforts to persuade the US Senate up to late in 1929. [255] Fortunately, and in spite of French opposition, American judges graced the bench throughout its span of activity, thus to enhance the balance of its verdicts in encompassing the voice of a great law tradition.[256]

However, nothing had prepared the Allied Powers for the dramatic role Germany was to play in the process.[257] Wilson's championship of Nation States and the Sovereignty of the Peoples was no doubt idealistic, and perhaps even visionary. Still, more to the point, it was irresponsibly light-hearted, very likely due to the President's lack of intimate understanding of the many scars by which history had long disfigured the Old Continent. The implementation of Wilson's unjustified optimism had dramatic consequences for the map and the social stratification of Europe. At the core of all trouble were the immeasurable consequences of the overnight eclipse of Empires that, for better or worse, had given guidance to the world for centuries on end: the Romanov, Hapsburg, and Hohenzollern dynasties, next to the Sultanate and the Chinese Empire. The substitution of the philosophy of the multi-national Empire with the concept of national sovereignty gave rise to a whole range of new, ambitious States in the huge and densely populated region – and patchwork of races and religions – that ran from the Baltic to the Balkans and had already been the crucible of unrest in pre-war years.[258]

To cut finesses, the implementation of Wilson's philosophy entailed the voluntary or compulsory migration of millions and millions of German and Polish, Hungarian, Romanian and Serbian, Greek, Bulgarian and Turkish civilians, as a rule at the cost of their nationality. It exposed huge minorities to the revengeful equalling of old scores and to discrimination and perpetration on racial, religious or linguistic grounds alike.[259] The dismal legacy of Versailles, its discrediting ambiguity in seeking to yoke

254 On the position of the USSR, see *World Court* II, chapter 7.5.2; on the *Eastern Carelia Case*, ibid, chapter 26.1

255 For the role of the USA, see ibid, chapter 7.5.3 and chapter 13.

256 For the role of the four American judges (Hudson, Hughes, Kellogg, and Moore) see their Biographies, ibid, chapter 16.

257 For the position of Germany at Versailles, see *World Court* I, chapter 7.3.8.

258 Finland, Bulgaria, Serbia and Turkey being cases in point.

259 For a survey from the perspective of the case-law of the Court, see *World Court* II, chapter 26-31 (Part IV, Section III: Minorities).

visionary concepts to sober *raison d'état* created the social unrest from appalling injustice that kept Europe durably unbalanced and made it two decades later plunge back into war.

IX. The Hand of the Court Forced

An integral part of the League, the PCIJ, in defiance of its fairly restricted mandate – which formally excluded access by private parties – landed smack in the middle of the onslaught. Throughout the span of the Court's operation its Registrar was overwhelmed with urgent requests for help from desperate civil applicants to suggest the perfect inadequacy of the League system.[260] Both the ACJ and the Third Committee of the Assembly had taken it for granted that the tried and trusted formula of diplomatic protection would smoothen out any inconveniences in this domain of law. To be sure, the device functioned to some degree in helping out major firms and concession-holders.[261] However, this left the small fish, read millions and millions of penniless, denationalized honest citizens out in the cold. Here its limited mandate left the Court perfectly helpless.

To exemplify the predicament, Versailles had rekindled a former major entity in Europe, the Polish-Lithuanian Commonwealth (1569-1795) that had first been dismembered, then altogether suppressed at the hands of three empires, Russia, Prussia, and Austria.[262] The new Polish State that emerged in 1919[263] filled most of the vacuum left by these three eclipsed thrones. Regained self-confidence and boisterous nationalism in Warsaw dictated expansionist policies at the expense of her former German masters.[264] As a net result Germany, perhaps the most controversial nation during the entire Inter-Bellum Period – kept at bay until 1927, then to quit on the double in 1933 – was the Power that most frequently appeared before the Court, be this in the role of Applicant or Defendant. Time and again, Berlin called in the help of the judges to redress the provocation of its authority and the discrimination of its nationals at the hand of Polish

260 Witness the *Annual Reports* of the Court; for a summary, see *World Court* II, chapter 7.1 and the Document Section.

261 For a review of the fifteen cases in this domain, see *World Court* II, chapter 32.

262 Due to the *Three Partitions* (1772-1795).

263 By the Polish Minorities Treaty or so-called 'Little Treaty of Versailles' (1919).

264 On German-Polish issues that ended up with the Court, see *World Court* II, chapter 27-29 (14 cases in all).

authorities, whether in Danzig,[265] or in (Polish) Upper Silesia.[266] From first to last, German minorities were at the core of the repercussions prompted by the territorial and humanitarian implications of the Peace Treaties.

A closer look at statistics may illustrate the implications of the above. It tells us that ten cases touched aspects of international governance. They ranged from the transition of sovereignty in former colonies loosely monitored by Mandate Commissions (as in Tunis and Morocco),[267] to issues concerning international waterways, as exemplified by the troubling *Wimbledon Case* (1923)[268] or the infrastructure of the ILO.[269] Another ten cases touched territorial and boundary issues,[270] matters of delimitation, or customs.[271] However, the bulk of cases, twenty-one to be precise, and among them some touching the most heated disputes, sought to appease minority issues ranging from the Baltic, along Poland and Germany, to Bulgaria, Greece and Turkey.[272] Cases included the dire consequences for civilians of their loss of nationality; the social upheaval caused by massive migration projects all too loosely monitored by short-term League Commissioners or Mixed Arbitral Tribunals; the creation of huge minority groups and their blatant discrimination and persecution on a range of scores. Forceful education and the brainwashing of youngsters constituted yet another dismal category.[273]

In a last, closely related category of its own came fifteen cases of diplomatic protection, in which Powers identified the (financial and economic) interests of their subjects as their own.[274] Most of these cases came as the consequence of State succession. At stake was the reassessment of pre-war

265 For the bilateral conflicts with regard to the Free City of Danzig (6 cases), see *World Court* II, chapter 29.

266 For the disputes with regard to Upper Silesia (5 cases), see ibid, chapter 28.

267 *Nationality Decrees in Tunis and Morocco* (1923; see ibid, chapter 21)

268 Four cases in all, ibid, chapter 21.

269 Five ILO-cases, most notable the one regarding the position of women, see ibid chapter 22.

270 Assembled ibid in chapter 24.

271 Two highly controversial cases concerning the issue of the *Free Zones of Upper Savoy* (1929-1931) and the intended *Customs Union of Austria and Germany* (1931); see ibid, chapter 25.

272 Ibid, chapter 26-31.

273 As e.g. the 'Language Tests' in the case of the *German Minority Schools* (1931; see ibid, chapter 28.4).

274 As in the *Oscar Chinn* (1934), *Losinger* (1936) and *Borchgrave* (1937) cases; see ibid, chapter 32.

concessions. At times this was meant to sort out legal ambiguities, but most cases were dictated by thinly veiled political motives. A typical instance was the way British authorities in the wake of the Balfour Declaration (1917) handled the (pre-war contracts for) electricity projects in Jerusalem, to which a sharp Greek business tycoon laid claim, a Mr. Mavrommatis. Foremost on the minds of officialdom in London was to favour the (post-war) claims of a no less shrewd competitor of the Greek tycoon, but he a Jewish-Russian immigrant, Mr. Rutenberg.[275]

The consequences of the above assortment of cases for the Court were dramatic. To start with, the orientation of the Court was by necessity essentially backwards, rather than forwards, in redressing the endless legal flaws, logical riddles or intentional ambiguities of the Peace Treaties. Secondly, the case-load covered the preoccupations of just a single Continent and never really touched (the wealth of) Asian or Latin American disputes.[276] One corollary, as we have seen, was the steadily growing disinterest of non-European judges in Court proceedings. Thirdly, the great majority of cases the Court faced touched the twilight zone of the public and private spheres and compelled the judges to make arrays into national as much as international legislation.[277] Symptomatic were their early complaints of the lack of relevant literature at the Peace Palace Library, perhaps the world's foremost international law library proper of the period. Persistent failure to solve the conundrum led to the anomaly of a second library in the grounds for the Court's exclusive use.[278]

X. A Prudent Appraisal

In critically appraising the sustainable impact of the Court on the basis of its case-law one, therefore, should above all observe restraint. To start

275 The case went through several stages that kept the Court preoccupied over 1924-1927; see ibid, chapter 32.1.

276 None of the numerous wars, insurrections, revolts or civil wars in Latin America or Asia ever made it to the Court at The Hague. For a survey of these conflicts, see *World Court* II., Part III, *Introductory Note* and Document Section.

277 The conundrum prompted a range of courses at the Hague Academy to sound the interaction of the private and public, the domestic and the international domains of law. The quandaries invited notorious polemics on monism and dualism between scholars like Triepel, Anzilotti, Kelsen, Scelle, and Ago. Cf. *World Court* II, chapter 5.4.

278 *Word Court* II, chapter 4.7 and chapter 9.8-9.

with, the Court was cut short in its stride. Two decades are no record to speak of in the international arena, even under the best of circumstances. And the circumstances the PCIJ met with were far from encouraging. In its early years, the Court faced widespread mistrust and reserve. The obsessive apprehension of the Powers lest the Court might take on a legislative role is a telling point. The Court's impotence itself to emendate its Statute and the strong reserves the Powers made to the Court's claim to be at least entitled to adjust its own Rules speak volumes. During its second decade, growing political polarisation undermined the reliance on the law as a feasible catalyser of conflict, much the way the ICJ was to experience during the Cold War era.

Secondly, on the basis of the wide variety and divergent nature of the morsels and chunks the Powers threw at it, the Court could never have been expected to construe anything akin to a comprehensive judicial system or a refined maze of legal concepts. In the last resort, the quintessential impact of the Court reached perhaps beyond its legal dealings with the disputes it addressed. The Court was watched argus-eyed with regard to the way it met with the preliminary challenge whether a standing court of law could at all operate to the benefit of the world in the cauldron of the international arena. San Francisco unequivocally settled that issue in confidently upgrading the formula to ambitiously address a truly global discourse.[279]

The above is not to belittle the impact of the case-law of the PCIJ. The Court played a prominent part in the less politicized domain of international governance. It substantially helped expand and deepen world organization as such, the League system and, more in particular the effectivity and credibility of the ILO. The latter endeavour cut at the roots of social progress. This in itself was no mean achievement in light of rising socialism and communism and the re-shifting of social strata – the changing role of womanhood being a prominent case in point.

In no technical domain of the law the Court's impact was as sustainable as in its dealings with the Law of Treaties. To that extent the Court never belied the high expectations of its founding fathers, who justly considered this domain the Court's core business. The countless ambiguities left by the Paris Peace Treaties and the manifold reappraisals in their wake served

279 See *World Court* II, chapter 14, for a summary review of the Allied Committees that successively dealt with the future of the World Court.

as *Fundgrube* for the interpretation and application of agreements, or the obligations they entailed for contracting Powers and Third Parties.[280] There is little coincidence that two decades of the PCIJ and an additional twenty years of case-law of the ICJ amply sufficed for jurists and diplomats in 1969 in Vienna to draw up one of the most impressive multilateral conventions of the early United Nations period.[281]

The record of the PCIJ was far from impeccable. But then, such high claims can never be applied to pioneering bodies. Still, at the time, the role the Court performed amply satisfied the world. The intellectual acumen and moral integrity of the judges convinced commentators of the feasibility of the institution. Operating as it had been under the darkening skies of clashing ideologies, amidst sharp social discord and paralyzing economic malaise, the Court had emphatically corroborated the pertinence of the legal component. Through its judgments and opinions, the Court had not just developed the law, but effectively enhanced the status of the law. At San Francisco, disillusion did not affect the appraisal of the PCIJ in similar harsh tenor as it had struck the PCA at Versailles. The World Court, it was realized, was not the institution to be held to account for the loss of the peace. There might be sound reasons to discontinue the particular formula of the interbellum, but the concept of the World Court as such was upheld by general acclaim, and its Statute adopted as proposition for its successor without amendments to speak of.

280 For the paramount role of treaties in the case-law of the Court, see the review in *World Court* II, chapter 20.2.

281 *The Vienna Convention on the Law of Treaties* of 23 May 1969 (UNTS 1155, 331).

'Land of Grotius', or Representing the Small Nations? The Role of the Netherlands in Establishing the 1922 World Court

Karin van Leeuwen[*]

A. Introduction

In October 1913, in the margins of a correspondence on the opening of the Hague Academy of International Law, the director of the Carnegie Endowment for International Peace's (CEIP) International Law Division, the American law professor James Brown Scott (1866-1943), put an idea before the new Dutch minister of Foreign Affairs John Loudon (1866-1955). What if the Netherlands took the initiative for convening a Great Power conference that could establish a World Court at the occasion of this festive opening in the summer of 1914? During the 1907 Second Peace Conference, the world already had been very close to the establishment of a such court. Moreover, in the aftermath of the 1908 London Conference on the establishment of a Prize Court, the Great Powers had in fact settled on taking the court question up immediately afterwards, so Scott reminded Loudon. Sadly, this promise had been wrecked when the British Lords had afterwards failed to accept the Prize Court. To Scott, the opening of the Hague Academy offered an excellent occasion to pick up on this promise. Scott hoped to find an ally in Loudon, the former Dutch ambassador in Washington, whom he knew was generally sympathetic to the cause he pleaded.[1]

* Research for this paper was undertaken as part of the collaborative project *Laying the Foundations. The League of Nations and International Law, 1919 to 1945* (University of Copenhagen) and gratefully builds on many exchanges regarding the establishment of the Permanent Court of International Justice with Morten Rasmussen, Haakon Ikonomou (University of Copenhagen) and Andrei Mamolea (Boston University), with other workshop participants and with the editors.

1 Loudon to Brown Scott 20 June 1913 and 27 June 1913, and Brown Scott to Loudon 23 June 1913, 21 October 1913, 9 December 1913 and 21 December 1913, all in box 561, vol. 257, Carnegie Endowment for International Peace, New York and Washington Office Records, Columbia University Rare Books and Manuscripts Library (CEIP records).

Clearly, the ideas of the director of one of the main philanthropic organisations of the USA had no official diplomatic status. Yet, Loudon was tempted. The Netherlands had consistently supported plans for international arbitration – and even more so after the Hague Peace Conferences of 1899 and 1907 and the establishment of a Permanent Court of Arbitration (PCA) in the Hague had inspired Dutch public opinion to increasingly identify with its reputation of 'Land of Grotius' and support the advancement of international law. Moreover, Scott's request played into Dutch ambitions to improve its rank in international politics. In 1908, the Dutch government had moved heaven and earth to be invited to a conference of great naval powers. Now, Scott addressed the Netherlands as a major player in the field. Eventually, Loudon rejected Scott's suggestion nevertheless. Following the advice of an expert committee of diplomats and lawyers, such as former foreign minister Willem Hendrik de Beaufort (1845-1918) and the prominent law professor and member of the *Institut de Droit International* (IDI) Jan de Louter (1847-1932), Loudon concluded that the price of establishing the much-desired World Court during a 'Great Power' conference would be too high for the Netherlands. More precisely, the committee worried that choosing to join and host the 'great powers' only would severely disappoint other small states.[2]

With hindsight, it may be hard to imagine how the Netherlands, and the Hague more in particular, could ever have not been the 'legal capital of the world', or, as city marketeers prefer, 'city of peace and justice'.[3] Yet, from a historical perspective, it was far from self-evident that a World Court would be established on Dutch soil, or that the Dutch government would commit itself to a such project. In light of recent historical interest in the political origins of the Permanent Court of International Justice (PCIJ), this chapter analyses how the Netherlands, as the future host country, contributed to the establishment of the court.[4] Starting from the early engagement of

2 Commissie ter Voorbereiding van de Derde Vredesconferentie (CVDV) to Loudon, 28 October 1914, inv. no. 10, archive CVDV (2.05.40), National Archives of the Netherlands (NL-NA), the Hague.

3 Peter J. van Krieken and David McKay, *The Hague: Legal Capital of the World* (T.M.C. Asser Press, Den Haag 2005); https://denhaag.com/en/the-city-of-peace-and-justice.

4 P. Sean Morris, *Transforming the Politics of International Law: The Advisory Committee of Jurists and the Formation of the World Court in the League of Nations* (Routledge, Oxon 2021); P. Sean Morris, *The League of Nations and the Development of International Law: A New Intellectual History of the Advisory Committee of Jurists* (Routledge, Oxon 2021).

Dutch diplomats and lawyers with a 'world court' in the late 19th century, it explores how the Dutch often manoeuvred between two extremes. On the one hand, lawyers and diplomats alike claimed a 'Grotian' exceptionalism on matters of international law, especially when 'The Hague' became almost a synonym to international peace and justice in the early 20th century.[5] On the other hand however, the Dutch oftentimes sought alignment with other small neutral European states – whereby 'smallness', considering the vast empire of the Netherlands, must merely be understood as a self-referential quality.[6] Building on new archival research in both Dutch, Swiss and Scandinavian government collections and the archives of the League of Nations, this chapter traces how both extremes played into the positions taken by the Netherlands in the negotiations over the court.[7]

By zooming in on some of the legal associations, advisory bodies and individual 'craftsmen' of international law that importantly contributed to the development of a Dutch position on the matter, this chapter moreover picks up on recent exchanges about a Dutch 'national tradition' in international law.[8] In line with previous studies of Dutch internationalism,

---

5 Pepijn Corduwener, 'Risee van de wereld of land van Grotius? De synthese tussen nationalisme en internationalisme in het Nederlandse fin de siècle' (2012) 2 *Tijdschrift voor Geschiedenis*, 202 (203); Maartje M. Abbenhuis, *The Hague Conferences and International Politics, 1898-1915* (Bloomsbury, London 2019), 169.

6 Samuël Kruizinga, 'Introduction' in Samuël Kruizinga (ed), *The Politics of Smallness in Modern Europe: Size, Identity and International Relations since 1800* (Bloomsbury, London 2022), 1 (7). For parallel work on other small states see eg Haakon A. Ikonomou and Morten Rasmussen, 'Scandinavian Legal Internationalism and the Creation of the Permanent Court of International Justice' in P. Sean Morris (ed), *Transforming the Politics of International Law: The Advisory Committee of Jurists and the Formation of the World Court in the League of Nations* (Routledge, Oxon 2021), 236; Andreas Graf and David Lanz, 'Conclusions: Switzerland as a Paradigmatic Case of Small-State Peace Policy?' (2013) 3 *Swiss Political Science Review*, 410.

7 For earlier accounts, see e.g. Michael Riemens, *De passie voor vrede. De evolutie van de internationale politieke cultuur in de jaren 1880-1940 en het recipiëren door Nederland* (De Bataafsche Leeuw, Amsterdam 2005); Remco van Diepen, *Voor Volkenbond en vrede. Nederland en het streven naar een nieuwe wereldorde, 1919-1946* (Bert Bakker, Amsterdam 1999).

8 Henri de Waele, 'A New League of Extraordinary Gentlemen? The Professionalization of International Law Scholarship in the Netherlands, 1919–1940' (2020) 3 *European Journal of International Law*, 1005; Janne E. Nijman, 'Marked Absences: Locating Gender and Race in International Legal History' (2020) 3 *European Journal of International Law*, 1025. On 'craftsmen', see Marcus M. Payk and Kim Christian Priemel, *Crafting the International Order: Practitioners and Practices of International Law since c.1800* (Oxford University Press, Oxford 2021).

it first of all establishes that the Dutch engagement with international adjudication was fed not only by the idealistic, 'missionary' zeal found among some prominent public international lawyers.[9] Instead, this chapter highlights that the interest in adjudication also built on more 'merchant' or maritime traditions in Dutch international law originating from private international lawyers such as the famous Tobias Asser (1838-1913) as well as for example Bernard Loder (1849-1935), the maritime lawyer and former Supreme Court judge who would become the most prominent Dutch voice in the PCIJ negotiations in 1919-1920.[10] By pointing out how Dutch conceptualisations of international adjudication were importantly tied to notions and interests typically encountered in private international law, this chapter thus addresses another 'marked absence' in recent studies of Dutch international law in this period – the somewhat anachronistic neglect of the contributions of private international lawyers.[11]

The chapter follows a largely chronological order. Section 2 explores the expectations of peace and justice associated with the 1899 and 1907 Hague Peace Conferences that importantly shaped the debates on the world court in 1919-1920 – even when the PCIJ was essentially a creation of the 1919 Paris Peace Treaties.[12] In particular, this section traces the emergence and various interpretations of the proclaimed Grotian tradition, which would return also in later discussions. Section 3 then analyses how the Netherlands came out of the First World War. With other 'small and neutral powers', it firmly supported the establishment of a permanent court as part of the new League framework, but on its own, it moreover fought to restore

9 E.g. Niek van Sas, 'De kracht van Nederland: Nationaliteit en buitenlands beleid' in N.C.F van Sas (ed), *De kracht van Nederland: Internationale positie en buitenlands beleid* (Becht, Haarlem 1991), 9.

10 On the merchant and the missionary in Dutch diplomatic and international law history, see J.J.C. Voorhoeve, *Peace, Profits and Principles. A Study of Dutch Foreign Policy* (Nijhoff, Leiden 1985); Nico J. Schrijver, 'A Missionary Burden or Enlightened Self-Interest? International Law in Dutch Foreign Policy' (2010) 2 *Netherlands International Law Review*, 209.

11 Janne E. Nijman, 'Marked Absences: Locating Gender and Race in International Legal History' (2020) 3 *European Journal of International Law*, 1025. Private lawyers do appear in C.J.H. Jansen, 'Nederlandse juristen en het streven naar wereldrecht en wereldvrede in de eerste helft van de twintigste eeuw' (2005) 2 *Pro Memorie*, 309.

12 Karin van Leeuwen and Morten Rasmussen, 'A Political and Legal History of the Advisory Committee of Jurists and the Foundation of the Permanent Court of International Justice' in P. Sean Morris (ed), *Transforming the Politics of International Law: The Advisory Committee of Jurists and the Formation of the World Court in the League of Nations* (Routledge, Oxon 2021), 69.

its 'Grotian' reputation and bring the new court to The Hague. A fourth section then zooms in on Loder and assesses the Dutch contributions to the Advisory Committee of Jurists and the final decision-making on the PCIJ in the League Assembly, before some concluding observations are made on (dis)continuities in Dutch positioning.

B. Before 1919: A 'Small' State with a Grotian Mission?

From the late 19th century onwards, Dutch legal and political debates on a World Court were importantly shaped by what has become known as the 'Grotian tradition': an invented tradition referring to the Dutch 'founding father of international law' Hugo Grotius.[13] In his 1913 appeal to the Dutch government, Scott for example explicitly addressed the Netherlands as the 'very birthplace of the law of nations'.[14] As historians have highlighted, such references to Grotius notably mirrored the popularity of the Dutch Golden Age more generally, and ignored the imperial imprint of Grotius' work.[15] Yet, the narrative did not miss its effect on the development of international law in the Netherlands, and on the debate on the World Court in particular. At the same time, the exceptionalism of the Netherlands should not be overstated, as this section illustrates by also considering the regular Dutch alignments with other small, neutral states.

As a sign of the continuing impact of the Grotian narrative, the Dutch contribution to the development of international law in the 19th century generally is considered as rather minimal. Historians often highlight how the Dutch commitment to international law in this period was limited, and mostly depended on one person: the 1911 Nobel Prize laureate Asser, who from the 1860s onwards had combined his Amsterdam law practice with a professorship in private international law, as well as legal counselling for the

13 Martine J. van Ittersum, 'Hugo Grotius' in Anne Orford and Florian Hoffmann (eds), *The Oxford Handbook of the Theory of International Law* (Oxford University Press, Oxford 2016), 82; Arthur Weststeijn, 'Provincializing Grotius: International Law and Empire in a Seventeenth-Century Malay Mirror' in Martti Koskenniemi, Walter Rech and Manuel Jimenez Fonseca (eds), *International Law and Empire: Historical Explorations* (Oxford University Press, Oxford 2017), 21.

14 'Memorandum proposing establishment of a Court of Arbitral Justice' [December 1913] p. 10, box 563, vol. 259, CEIP records.

15 Pepijn Corduwener, 'Risee van de wereld of land van Grotius? De synthese tussen nationalisme en internationalisme in het Nederlandse fin de siècle' (2012) 2 *Tijdschrift voor Geschiedenis*, 202 (215).

Ministry of Foreign Affairs.[16] However, this critical view on the backwards character of Dutch 19th century international law importantly builds on the work of early 20th century lawyers such as Cornelis van Vollenhoven (1874-1933) and Willem Jan Mari van Eysinga (1878-1961), who were at the forefront of 'reviving' the Grotian tradition.[17]

While this is not the place to extensively reassess Dutch legal internationalism in the late 19th century, it seems safe to suggest that the Dutch were less backward on matters of international law than sometimes suggested. Indeed, the engagement of Dutch lawyers and politicians with for example the question of arbitration had been rather minimal after a 1874 parliamentary resolution had recommended arbitration as 'the usual means to settle international disputes'.[18] For example, unlike some of their Belgian counterparts, Dutch lawyers did not prominently engage with the far-reaching schemes for arbitration developed by the Inter-Parliamentary Union and the Universal Peace Congress in the 1890s.[19] But at the same time, on the initiative of Asser, the Netherlands crucially hosted various conferences on the unification of private international law.[20] So, one might conclude that in the 19th century Netherlands, a 'Grotian spirit' may not have been absent altogether, but that it might have been more prominent within the Amsterdam merchant class in which lawyers such as Asser were rooted, than among the Hague political elites.

Backward or not, Dutch political leaders in 1899 cautiously welcomed the plans for a Permanent Court of Arbitration (PCA) to be established in the Hague. Initially, the Russian Czar's 1898 plans for a conference

---

16 Arthur Eyffinger, *T.M.C. Asser (1838-1913): in Quest of Liberty, Justice, and Peace* (Brill Nijhoff, Leiden 2019), 1133.

17 See e.g. Cornelis van Vollenhoven, *De drie treden van het volkenrecht* (Nijhoff, Den Haag 1923) and W.J.M. van Eysinga, *Huigh de Groot: een schets* (Tjeenk Willink, Haarlem 1945).

18 Proposal Bredius and Van Eck, *Handelingen der Tweede Kamer* 1874-1875 B 58 (1); Arthur Eyffinger, *T.M.C. Asser (1838-1913): in Quest of Liberty, Justice and Peace* (Brill Nijhoff, Leiden 2019), 894-895.

19 Vincent Genin, 'Un « Laboratoire belge » du droit international (1869-1940)? Réseaux internationaux, expériences et mémoires de guerre des juristes belges' (PhD thesis, University of Liège 2017), 128. But cf Michael Riemens, *Een vergeten hoofdstuk: de Nederlandsche Anti-Oorlog Raad en het Nederlands pacifisme tijdens de Eerste Wereldoorlog* (Wolters-Noordhoff, Groningen 1995); Frans van de Wijdeven, *Pacifisme in Nederland: Een transnationale geschiedenis (1889-1918)* (bachelor thesis, Utrecht University 2019).

20 Arthur Eyffinger, *T.M.C. Asser (1838-1913): in Quest of Liberty, Justice and Peace* (Brill Nijhoff, Leiden 2019), 735-806.

on disarmament had taken the Dutch government by surprise, while the press received these plans with similar high hopes as elsewhere.[21] The government was quicker to respond to a second circular issued in January 1899 that expanded the conference's programme to also include issues such as the laws of war and the application of alternative methods of conflict settlement such as 'good offices', arbitration and mediation. Upon receiving this second circular, the Dutch government immediately contacted Brussels, Stockholm, Copenhagen, Bern, Bucharest and Lisbon to align views among small states.[22] Only a day later, the Czar however surprised the Dutch government with his invitation to host the conference in The Hague. Henceforth, the Dutch minister of Foreign Affairs De Beaufort was too overburdened by organisational issues to further pursue a joint small state position.[23] Nevertheless, he gladly accepted the PCA as a token of the Dutch commitment to arbitration.[24]

The 1899 Hague Peace Conference, despite its limited success in terms of legal conventions, left a deep impression on international public opinion. 'The Hague' soon became a shorthand for the promise of international peace and justice.[25] Similarly, the conference had a deep impact on the self-perception of Dutch politicians and public alike.[26] In the years that followed, the Dutch government showed a growing commitment to the cause of international law in general, and arbitration in particular. Already during the summer of 1899, it explored the opportunity to establish a binding treaty between 'second rank powers'.[27] Although this treaty did not

21 Maartje Abbenhuis, *The Hague Conferences and International Politics* (Bloomsbury Academic, London 2019), 21.

22 De Beaufort to ambassadors in Brussels, Stockholm, Copenhagen, Bern, Bucharest and Lisbon, 24 January 1899, *Documenten betreffende de buitenlandse politiek van Nederland 1919-1945 3.1 (1899-1903) (GS 100)* (Nijhoff, Den Haag 1957), no. 2.

23 Maartje Abbenhuis, *The Hague Conferences and International Politics* (Bloomsbury Academic, London 2019), 58-60.

24 *Dagboeken en aantekeningen van Willem Hendrik de Beaufort 1874-1918 I* (Instituut voor Nederlandse Geschiedenis, Den Haag 1993), 61; De Beaufort to Van Karnebeek, 15 July 1899, *Documenten betreffende de buitenlandse politiek van Nederland 1919-1945 3.1 (1899-1903) (GS 100)* (Nijhoff, Den Haag 1957), no. 80.

25 Maartje Abbenhuis, *The Hague Conferences and International Politics* (Bloomsbury Academic, London 2019), 58-60.

26 Pepijn Corduwener, 'Risee van de wereld of land van Grotius? De synthese tussen nationalisme en internationalisme in het Nederlandse fin de siècle' (2012) 2 *Tijdschrift voor Geschiedenis*, 202.

27 The 'avant-projet' was to be concluded between Netherlands, Belgium, Denmark, Portugal, Sweden, Norway and Switzerland: De Beaufort to Van Heeckeren van

materialise, it eagerly participated in the arbitration frenzy by agreeing on arbitration agreements with France and the UK,[28] Denmark,[29] and Italy,[30] while also talking to Norway, Sweden, Belgium, Russia and the US.[31] For the broader public, the engagement with international law mostly focused on the PCA, and more particularly the plans to build a Peace Palace to host the court. The announcement that the American steel magnate Andrew Carnegie would endow one and a half million dollars to the Dutch government to build a 'palace of peace' in 1903 triggered a lot of attention for the court that so far had been housed in an unpretentious city mansion in the Hague. The controversies that marked the search for a location and the design competition for the Palace featured prominently on the front pages. Parallel plans for establishing a 'world city' surrounding the Palace reflected Dutch society's increasing engagement with its new, 'Grotian' identity.[32]

At the second Hague Peace Conference in 1907, the Dutch government took a remarkably restrained position on the question of a possible World Court. With the PCA on its soil, the Dutch government struggled to freely assess proposals for a new, more far-reaching court. Considering Belgium's passionate support for a such permanent court, former minister De Beaufort for example feared that this meant to wreck the PCA.[33] Thus, the overall position taken by the Dutch delegation in 1907 was one of restraint. This was not for a lack of views within the Dutch delegation. In response to the Russian draft programme issued in January 1906, featuring 'matters of court procedure' and 'obligatory arbitration', Asser had critically reviewed the PCA's lack of progress and had proposed to strengthen the court with

Kell, 18 August 1899, *Documenten betreffende de buitenlandse politiek van Nederland 1919-1945 3.1 (1899-1903) (GS 100)* (Nijhoff, Den Haag 1957), no. 85.

28 *Staatsblad* 1906 nrs. 249-250.

29 *Staatsblad* 1905, nr. 199.

30 *Staatsblad* 1910, nr. 213.

31 See the many sources published in *Documenten betreffende de buitenlandse politiek van Nederland 1919-1945 3.3 (1907-1914)* (GS 106) (Nijhoff, Den Haag 1958), such as the 'progress report' from Van Tets van Goudriaan to Queen Wilhelmina, 3 January 1908 (no. 132); and the discussions with US Secretary of State Root as reported by ambassador Royaards on 16 May 1908 (no. 251).

32 Maartje Abbenhuis, *The Hague Conferences and International Politics* (Bloomsbury Academic, London 2019), 171-176; Wouter van Acker and Geert Somsen, 'A Tale of Two World Capitals: The Internationalisms of Pieter Eijkman and Paul Otlet' (2012) 4 *Revue Belge de Philologie et d'Histoire*, 1389.

33 *Dagboeken en aantekeningen van Willem Hendrik de Beaufort 1874-1918 I* (Instituut voor Nederlandse Geschiedenis, Den Haag 1993), 398-99.

a more permanent element: a committee of three judges based in The Hague.[34] In addition, De Beaufort had favoured opening the discussion about obligatory arbitration, even though he felt its chances for success were limited.[35] Yet, the official instructions from minister of Foreign Affairs Dirk van Tets van Goudriaan (1844-1930) urged Asser and De Beaufort to sit on their hands.[36] Indeed, when Asser, as one of the most seasoned speakers around the table, intervened in the discussion to clarify some of the issues regarding obligatory arbitration, he was immediately reprimanded. No initiatives were to be expected from the Netherlands.[37] Similarly, on the issue of a permanent tribunal, Asser's plans for a permanent committee of three judges were not tabled as an official Dutch proposal.[38] Nevertheless, the Netherlands eventually supported the plans of the French representative Léon Bourgeois (1851-1925) for (limited) compulsory arbitration. These plans failed to reach agreement however over the question of equal representation of small and large states.[39]

How far the government's restrained policy had been out of tune with wider Dutch debate became clear when parliament critically discussed the matter shortly after the end of the conference. While the abundant programme of excursions, balls and other official and unofficial gatherings had done much to lift the Netherlands out of its reputation as the 'China of Europe', parliament observed that this had not been met by an equally progressive foreign policy.[40] MPs from various political backgrounds expressed their support for a more idealistic foreign policy. With Asser,

---

34 Asser to Van Tets van Goudriaan, 5 February 1906, *Documenten betreffende de buitenlandse politiek van Nederland 1919-1945 3.2 (1903-1907) (GS 106)* (Nijhoff, Den Haag 1958), no. 561.

35 De Beaufort to Van Tets van Goudriaan, 5 February 1906, *Documenten betreffende de buitenlandse politiek van Nederland 1919-1945 3.2 (1903-1907) (GS 106)* (Nijhoff, Den Haag 1958), no. 562.

36 'Nota nopens het standpunt, dat Nederland behoort in te nemen tegenover het Russische programma', 5 March 1907, *Documenten betreffende de buitenlandse politiek van Nederland 1919-1945 3.3 (1907-1914)* (GS 106) (Nijhoff, Den Haag 1958).

37 Van Tets van Goudriaan to De Beaufort, 19 July 1907, *Documenten 3.3 (1907-1914)*, no. 92; *Dagboeken De Beaufort I* (Instituut voor Nederlandse Geschiedenis, Den Haag 1993), 389.

38 Arthur Eyffinger, *T.M.C. Asser (1838-1913): in Quest of Liberty, Justice and Peace* (Brill Nijhoff, Leiden 2019), 1415-1420.

39 Christian J. Tams, 'Die Zweite Haager Konferenz und das Recht der friedlichen Streitbeilegung' (2007) 4 *Die Friedens-Warte*, 119.

40 *Handelingen der Tweede Kamer* 1907-1908, 483; Maartje Abbenhuis, *The Hague Conferences and International Politics* (Bloomsbury Academic, London 2019), 158-159.

they demanded that the government would instantly start preparing the next, 1913 conference by establishing a committee of experts to analyse which subjects of public international law would be ready for codification in treaties. Further, parliament demanded a more active policy with regard to arbitration treaties.[41]

Parliament's growing identification with the Dutch 'Grotian' reputation reflected a similar trend in Dutch scholarly and societal debates. International conferences as well as a boom in arbitration cases before the PCA between 1908 and 1914 intensified contacts with prominent international lawyers. For example, the French law professor Louis Renault (1843-1918) in 1910 extended his stay in The Hague as arbitrator for a guest lecture at the University of Groningen for the students of Van Eysinga, who in 1912 would accept the first chair in international law, at the University of Leiden.[42] Similarly, preparations for a Hague Academy of International Law laid the ground for further exchanges, as the above example of Scott's proposal illustrated.[43] The establishment of the *Nederlandse Vereniging voor Internationaal Recht* (NVIR, Netherlands Association for International Law) in 1910 provided an important new meeting space for lawyers and business leaders, as well as a local branch through which to organise representation in the transnational International Law Association (ILA).[44] The maturing of international law as an academic discipline also encouraged the debate on arbitration and on international courts in the Netherlands.[45] Broader public debate about the role of the Netherlands on the international stage was particularly stirred by the publication of the Leiden law professor Van Vollenhoven's pamphlet '*Roeping van Holland*'. Calling for the Netherlands to provide for a world police force serving to uphold rulings of interna-

41 *Handelingen der Tweede Kamer* 1907-1908, 488.

42 Van Vollenhoven to Van Eysinga, 16 May 1910, inv no 615, Van Eysinga family collection, Tresoar, Leeuwarden.

43 Van Leeuwen, 'Promoting a 'Common International Concept' of International Law: the Hague Academy and International Law Teaching, 1923-1940' (unpublished conference paper Copenhagen 2019, on file with the author).

44 'Verslag van de Oprichtingsvergadering' (1910) 1 *Mededeelingen NVIR*, 11.

45 E.g. Jan Kosters, 'Wat kan Nederland op dit oogenblik voor de zaak der internationale rechtspraak doen?' (1911) *Rechtsgeleerd Magazijn*, 454; Jan de Louter, 'L'avenir du droit international public' (1912) *Revue Generale de Droit International Public*, 281.

tional law, the pamphlet both strengthened and confirmed the Grotian narrative within and beyond the Dutch borders.[46]

The new minister of Foreign Affairs, Reneke de Marees van Swinderen (1850-1955) followed up on these demands by taking a more active stance towards the establishment of a World Court. In 1908, De Marees van Swinderen secured an invitation for the London Naval Conference to establish a Prize Court. This feat, for which the Netherlands used its status as maritime power and host of the PCA, was not much appreciated by its fellow 'small states' in Scandinavia.[47] The affair took a disappointing turn however when the proposals for an International Prize Court, that were further elaborated in talks between the four major naval powers, were rejected by the British House of Lords.[48] Meanwhile, De Marees van Swinderen also established a Committee for the Preparation of the Third Peace Conference (*Comité ter Voorbereiding van de Derde Vredesconferentie*, CVDV). Consisting of both seasoned diplomats and prominent legal scholars, the committee became an incubator for Dutch legal internationalism - and it considered matters of arbitration and a permanent court among the most urgent on its list.[49]

The proposals the CVDV developed for a future 'International Court of Justice' carefully balanced between Dutch exceptionalism and alignment with other small states. In response to the late 1913 request by Scott, the committee first of all advised minister Loudon to resist the temptation of convening a 'Great Power' conference that left out other small neutral states - a lesson learnt in 1908.[50] Moreover, the CVDV underlined the importance of equality in the nomination of judges as a key principle, even when one of its members suggested adding an alternative proposal granting more weight

46 Cornelis van Vollenhoven, 'Roeping van Holland' (1910) 74 *De Gids*, 185, for its preparations see the extensive correspondence with Van Eysinga in inv no 615, Van Eysinga family collection.

47 De Marees Van Swinderen to Gericke van Herwijnen, 10 March 1908, *Documenten betreffende de buitenlandse politiek van Nederland 1919-1945 3.3 (1907-1914)* (GS 106) (Nijhoff, Den Haag 1958), no. 185; Johan den Hertog, 'Klassieke diplomatie in een nieuw jasje. Reneke de Marees van Swinderen' in Dick Kuiper and Gerrit Schutte (eds), *Het kabinet-Heemskerk, 1908-1913* (Meinema, Zoetermeer 2010), 89 (96).

48 Francis Anthony Boyle, *Foundations of World Order: The Legalist Approach to International Relations (1898-1922)* (Duke University Press, Durham/London 1999), 60-63.

49 Minutes 22 February 1913, inv. no. 9, archive CVDV.

50 De Beaufort to Loudon, 28 March 1914, inv. no. 10, archive CVDV; also Minutes 6 March 1913 p.5, inv. no. 9, archive CVDV.

to the Great Powers.[51] Stepping away from the 1907 hesitations about a court that rivalled the PCA, the CVDV further clearly distinguished the new adjudicatory court – able to produce 'an international jurisprudence' – from the existing arbitration court. Pragmatically, the committee refrained from proposing obligatory jurisdiction, considering that this would lead to important objections, while treaties granting jurisdiction were emerging rapidly anyway.[52]

What made the Dutch ideas stand out internationally however – and again showed the influence of the 'Amsterdam' merchant roots of Dutch legal internationalism – was that the CVDV considered to not only grant jurisdiction for interstate conflicts, but also for disputes between states and (foreign) citizens. Reflecting commercial interests, such individual standing had been a key topic in Dutch debates already for some time, drawing inspiration from proposals raised during the Prize Court negotiations, as well as from a more recent campaign of the Berlin *Aeltesten der Kauffmannschaft*, the German chamber of commerce that had been dissatisfied with the lack of legal protection offered to the German tradesman Von Hellfeld when he came into conflict with the Russian government over the sale of a steamer during the Russo-Japanese war.[53] Building on these experiences, individual standing was meant to complement diplomatic protection of individuals and companies vis-à-vis other states, which Dutch lawyers found too dependent on state power and thus advantageous to the great powers versus the small states.[54] In its preparations for the Third Peace Conference, the CVDV thus drafted a separate protocol granting the new 'International Court of Justice' jurisdiction in conflicts between states and (foreign) citizens as well.[55]

51 'Voorstellen van C. van Vollenhoven', 1 March 1914, inv. no. 9, archive CVDV.

52 'Project d'une convention relative à l'établissement d'une Cour de Justice internationale', attached to De Beaufort to Loudon, 28 March 1914, inv. no. 10, archive CVDV.

53 This regarded proposals the *Aeltesten* sent to the Chancellor on 30 September 1910 and 20 May 1912. Inv. no. 197, Van Eysinga archive (2.21.060), NL-NA; for the original case see 'Von Hellfeld v. Russian Government (Anhalt Case)' (1911) 5 *American Journal of International Law*, 490–519.

54 Willem van Eysinga, 'Arbitrage obligatoire entre etats ou recours d'individus a une juridiction internationale?' (1911) *Zeitschrift für Völkerrecht und Bundesstaatsrecht*, 535.

55 Draft Van Eysinga and Van Vollenhoven and minutes 23 April 1914, inv. no. 10, archive CVDV.

Loudon's follow up of the CVDV's proposals was obviously interrupted by the outbreak of the First World War in summer 1914. Yet, the proposals built an important resource when in the final years of the war, plans for a post-war world order started to circulate.

C. 1919-1920: Repositioning 'The Hague'

At the end of the First World War, the Netherlands found itself in an intricate position. During the war, the government had been so cautious to preserve the country's neutrality that it even suppressed open domestic debates about the post-war order. Nevertheless, it was obvious that the formalist approach to international law that had guided Dutch neutrality policies – and the asylum granted to the former German Emperor in late 1918 – clashed with the ideas of 'international justice' for which the belligerent powers claimed to have fought the war.[56] Moreover, even though many Dutch lawyers and politicians considered the Dutch reputation as champion of international law to be untainted, and were eager to see 'the Hague' reestablished as the center of legal internationalism, Dutch aspirations were largely disregarded at the Paris Peace Conference, which negotiated a more political, Geneva-based League of Nations.[57] In order to restore the reputation of the Hague, while continuing its support for an 'International Court of Justice', the Dutch government more actively than before the war sought cooperation of other small and neutral states. At the same time, Dutch politicians and lawyers also revived the 'Grotian', exceptionalist narrative which already before the war had been narrowly intertwined with global conceptions of a 'Hague' order.

---

56 Maartje M. Abbenhuis, *The Art of Staying Neutral: The Netherlands in the First World War, 1914-1918* (Amsterdam University Press, Amsterdam 2006); Johan den Hertog, 'Dutch Neutrality and the Value of Legal Argumentation' in Johan den Hertog and Samuël Kruizinga (eds), *Caught in the Middle: Neutrals, Neutrality and the First World War* (Amsterdam University Press, Amsterdam 2011), 15; Isabel V. Hull, *A Scrap of Paper: Breaking and Making International Law during the Great War* (Cornell University Press, Ithaca 2014).

57 'Verslag der nationale zomerconferentie van de NVIR, 13 juli 1918' (1918) 10 *Mededeelingen NVIR*, 1; Karin van Leeuwen and Morten Rasmussen, 'A Political and Legal History of the Advisory Committee of Jurists' in P. Sean Morris (ed), *Transforming the Politics of International Law: The Advisory Committee of Jurists and the Formation of the World Court in the League of Nations* (Routledge, Oxon 2021), 69.

Even when the supporters of such a 'Hague' order of peace through law failed to dominate the negotiations, the Peace Conference brought together some prominent representatives of that vision.[58] One of them was Brown Scott, who in 1913 had tried to convince Loudon to take the initiative for a World Court conference. In May 1919, Brown Scott, who was in Paris to assist the U.S. government as a legal expert, again reached out to the Dutch government to seek its assistance in his campaign for a more fully developed World Court. Since the League of Nations Covenant only contained a very general clause about a court to be established by the League, Scott suggested that the Dutch government made its adherence to the League dependent on the establishment of the court. However, Brown Scott would again find the Dutch government unwilling to fully support his agenda.[59]

Already during the war, the Dutch government had been cautious in its positioning with regard to a future World Court. Again, it found itself balancing the country's unique reputation against its desire to align with other small states in order to protect neutrality. Prime minister Pieter Cort van der Linden (1846-1935) had explicitly declared his government's allegiance to a League of Nations in a parliamentary debate in November 1917, where he described this movement towards durable peace as 'in line with the Dutch national tradition' and 'of vital interest for a small state like we are.' [60] Meanwhile, in its detailed study of the plans for a such League circulated by the US-based League to Enforce Peace, the CVDV warned the government against the demands for mutual assistance these plans contained, which basically would bring an end to the neutral status of the Netherlands. Therefore, the CVDV recommended not only to make adherence conditional to the participation of all great powers – Allied and Central – but also to seek contact with other neutral states.[61] In late 1918, a resolution of the united Scandinavian parliament inspired the CVDV to in-

58 Stephen Wertheim, 'The League of Nations: A Retreat from International Law?' (2012) 2 *Journal of Global History*, 210.

59 Van Karnebeek to Patijn, 23 May 1919, *Documenten betreffende de buitenlandse politiek van Nederland 1919-1945 3.5.2 (1917-1919)* (GS 117) (Nijhoff, Den Haag, 1964), no. 1055; Patijn to Van Karnebeek 26 May 1919, , *Documenten betreffende de buitenlandse politiek van Nederland 1919-1945 3.5.2 (1917-1919)* (GS 117) (Nijhoff, Den Haag, 1964), no. 1060.

60 *Handelingen der Tweede Kamer* 1917-1918 (28 November 1917), 510.

61 Minutes 18 July 1918, report 30 August 1918, inv. no. 20, archive CVDV.

sert a plea for an adjudicatory court to be added to the proposed League.[62] Noting that the Scandinavian plans had not been received favourably in the United Kingdom, the Dutch government however refrained from publicly taking a position on the CVDV's recommendations.[63]

In March 1919, the Dutch government nevertheless had to express its views when the Allied powers invited the neutral states to Paris to discuss the draft League Covenant. The meeting in Hotel Crillon on 20-21 March seemed merely an act of courtesy from the great powers, whose League plans continued many aspects of pre-war concert politics.[64] Yet, the Allied powers deliberately sought to commit the European neutrals to the League, to counter the criticism that this new world organisation merely continued the wartime alliance.[65] In Paris, the delegates from the Netherlands, Switzerland and the Scandinavian states found their concerns and interests closely aligned. Apart from more general concerns on the impact of the mutual assistance clause on their neutral status and on the composition and role of the Council and the Assembly, the neutrals all insisted on further guarantees with regard to the envisaged court. In particular, they demanded sovereign equality with regard to its composition. Next to that, the Netherlands and Switzerland also argued in favour of compulsory arbitration.[66]

Afterwards, the Dutch delegate, the former Supreme Court judge Loder, reported disappointedly that the Allies had resisted most neutral demands.[67] Yet, the eventual League Covenant did show some amendments, especially with regard to the envisaged Permanent Court of International

---

62 Report 20 January 1919, inv. no. 20, archive CVDV.

63 Minutes 16 December 1918, inv. no. 20, archive CVDV; Remco van Diepen, *Voor Volkenbond en vrede. Nederland en het streven naar een nieuwe wereldorde, 1919-1946* (Bert Bakker, Amsterdam 1999), 34-36.

64 Marcus M. Payk, *Frieden durch Recht? Der Aufstieg des modernen Völkerrechts und der Friedensschluss nach dem Ersten Weltkrieg* (De Gruyter, Berlin/Boston 2018).

65 Karin van Leeuwen and Morten Rasmussen, 'A Political and Legal History of the Advisory Committee of Jurists' in P. Sean Morris (ed), *Transforming the Politics of International Law: The Advisory Committee of Jurists and the Formation of the World Court in the League of Nations* (Routledge, Oxon 2021), 69; on the Dutch critical reception of the Covenant see Remco van Diepen, *Voor Volkenbond en vrede. Nederland en het streven naar een nieuwe wereldorde, 1919-1946* (Bert Bakker, Amsterdam 1999), 36-42.

66 David Hunter Miller, *The Drafting of the Covenant* 2 (G.P. Putnam's Sons, New York/London 1928), 598-599, 623-625 and 628-629.

67 'Verslag der ALV der NVIR, 29 maart 1919', (1919) 12 *Mededeelingen NVIR*, 9 (20-24); on Loder's appointment see *Herinneringen en dagboek van Ernst Heldring (1871-1954) 1* (Historisch Genootschap, Utrecht 1970), 317-318.

Justice (PCIJ). And while most amendments had already been drafted between the Allies themselves, some aspects, such as the fact that the approval of the Court would be a matter of all members of the League and not merely the Council, reflected the Allied desire to bring the neutral powers into the League.[68] The Allied powers moreover decided that the elaboration of the Court Statute should not be delegated to the expert committee assisting all drafting work in Paris, but instead should involve a wider range of 'eminent jurists of great international reputation'.[69] This decision was most likely meant to accommodate the critical US Republican opposition to the League, but it also opened new ways for the small neutral states and in particular the Netherlands to be involved in the preparations for the PCIJ.

For the Netherlands, opportunities for having its demands heard in the new, temporary headquarters of the League of Nations Secretariat in London increased even further with the hiring of the Dutch lawyer Joost van Hamel (1880-1964) as the head of the Secretariat's Legal Section in June 1919. When accepting the job, Van Hamel had been promised the secretariat of the planned Advisory Committee of Jurists (ACJ) that was to advise on the PCIJ. Before the committee was even appointed, he was however forced to give up this position due to the arrival of the Italian jurist Dionisio Anzilotti (1867-1950) in the League Secretariat. Instead, Van Hamel secured a seat in the committee for the Dutch delegate at the Hotel Crillon meeting, his uncle Loder, referring to the status of the Netherlands as host of the PCA.[70] This placed the Netherlands in an exceptionally advantageous position, especially in comparison to other small neutral states. For, where on the various provisional lists of members that circulated in the League Secretariat the during the preparations for the committee there constantly were representatives from larger and/or Allied states such as Belgium, France, the UK, the U.S., Italy and Spain, the small neutrals

68 Karin van Leeuwen and Morten Rasmussen, 'A Political and Legal History of the Advisory Committee of Jurists' in P. Sean Morris (ed), *Transforming the Politics of International Law: The Advisory Committee of Jurists and the Formation of the World Court in the League of Nations* (Routledge, Oxon 2021), 69.

69 Drummond to Pichon, 14 June 1919, inv. no. 1299, 21.940.88, League of Nations Archive (LONA), Geneva.

70 Van Hamel to Drummond, 2 October 1919, LONA 1299 21.1345.88. For more details on the appointment of Anzilotti, see Morten Rasmussen, 'An Agent of International Law? The Legal Section of the General Secretariat, 1919-1926' in Haakon Ikonomou, Karin van Leeuwen and Morten Rasmussen (eds.), *The Cambridge Handbook of the League of Nations and International Law*(forthcoming, 2026).

were 'represented' only by one or two general members, whose names and nationalities constantly changed. Switzerland and Poland even had to settle for the appointment of 'expert secretaries'.[71] Meanwhile, Loder, knowing his committee membership was provided for, could start lobbying for Dutch proposals as well as for the Hague as the prospective court's seat – and the meeting place for the ACJ – at a relatively early stage.

That the somewhat 'tart' Loder thus became the most prominent Dutch voice in the establishment of the PCIJ had not been self-evident.[72] Born in 1849, Loder had long held a private practice in maritime law before joining the Supreme Court as a judge in 1908. He had represented Dutch interests within the *Comité Maritime International* (CMI) in the early 20th century, building on a 'phenomenal' mastery of four languages.[73] Loder's broader engagement with questions of international law had only emerged during the First World War, when he presided a committee of the Central Organisation for a Durable Peace (CODP) on international dispute settlement.[74] Loder then also became president of the International Intermediary Institute, an international desk for legal information established in early 1918 to restore the international reputation of the Netherlands.[75]

71 Memorandum Walters, 2 October 1919, inv. no. 1299 21.1064.88 LONA. More on the various configurations of the committee in Karin van Leeuwen and Morten Rasmussen, 'A Political and Legal History of the Advisory Committee of Jurists' in P. Sean Morris (ed), *Transforming the Politics of International Law: The Advisory Committee of Jurists and the Formation of the World Court in the League of Nations* (Routledge, Oxon 2021), 69.

72 The qualification of Loder's character comes from *Herinneringen en dagboek van Ernst Heldring (1871-1954) 2* (Historisch Genootschap, Utrecht 1970), 1145.

73 *Herinneringen en dagboek van Ernst Heldring (1871-1954) 2* (Historisch Genootschap, Utrecht 1970), 1145; on Loder's biography, see Freya Baetens and Veronica Lavista, '"Where Is Your Tribunal?" Bernard Loder (1849–1935) and the Quest for International Justice' in P. Sean Morris (ed), *The League of Nations and the Development of International Law. A New Intellectual History of the Advisory Committee of Jurists* (Routledge, Oxon 2021), 195.

74 B.C.J. Loder, *Règlement pacifique des conflits internationaux (Cour permanente d'arbitrage ; Cour permanente de justice internationale ; Conseil international d'enquête et de consiliation)* (The Hague, 1917).

75 Michael Riemens, *Een vergeten hoofdstuk: de Nederlandsche Anti-Oorlog Raad en het Nederlands pacifisme tijdens de Eerste Wereldoorlog* (Wolters-Noordhoff, Groningen 1995), 141.

Most likely, this personal engagement, as well as a change in private circumstances, paved the way to his 'diplomatic' career.[76] This regarded not only Loder's mission to the Paris Peace Conference, but also appointments into the CVDV and the Foreign Ministry's special Council of Assistance in Economic Matters, that was to assess claims regarding damages to Dutch citizens resulting from the war. And in late 1919, Loder was one of the three lawyers who advised the Dutch government on the legality of the asylum granted to the former German emperor. So, when Van Hamel presented his 'dear uncle' as the Dutch candidate for the ACJ in October 1919, both minister of Foreign Affairs Van Karnebeek and League of Nations Secretary General Eric Drummond (1876-1951) happily accepted Loder's candidacy.[77]

At the time, Dutch diplomacy with regard to the permanent court mostly focused on bringing the court to The Hague.[78] Dutch officials informed Van Hamel already in July 1919 that the Dutch government was willing to financially contribute to the establishment of the new court in The Hague – and repeated that message during an official visit to Drummond.[79] Unlike other small neutral states, the Dutch government moreover announced its unrestricted commitment to the League Covenant already in September 1919, in spite of many concerns and criticisms.[80] And to further illustrate its leadership on the issue, the Netherlands in autumn 1919 reached out to Denmark, Norway, Sweden and Switzerland to discuss common interests such as the Court during a neutral conference in The Hague.[81] Initially,

76 His niece mentions the death of Loder's wife and his close relation to the newly appointed minister of Foreign Affairs Herman van Karnebeek: Elisabeth Bryan Loder, *Herinneringen* (H.E. van Valkenburg-Lely, Utrecht 1980) 129.

77 Van Hamel to Van Karnebeek 21 October 1919 in inv. no. 137, Werkarchief H.A. van Karnebeek (2.05.25), NL-NA; Van Hamel to Loder 26 April 1920, Loder papers, Peace Palace Library (PPL), the Hague.

78 Remco van Diepen, *Voor Volkenbond en vrede. Nederland en het streven naar een nieuwe wereldorde, 1919-1946* (Bert Bakker, Amsterdam 1999), 39-40; *Herinneringen en dagboek van Ernst Heldring* 1 (1970), 323.

79 François to Van Hamel, 1 July 1919, *Documenten betreffende de buitenlandse politiek van Nederland 1919-1945 A.1 (1919-1920)* (GS 156) (Nijhoff, Den Haag 1976), no. 32/32a; Loudon to Van Karnebeek 6 October 1919, *Documenten* A.1 (1919-1920) no. 114.

80 *Handelingen Verenigde Vergadering* 1919-1920 (16 September 1919) 1; Remco van Diepen, *Voor Volkenbond en vrede. Nederland en het streven naar een nieuwe wereldorde, 1919-1946* (Bert Bakker, Amsterdam 1999), 43-45.

81 Van Karnebeek to Van Vredenburch 11 September 1919, *Documenten betreffende de buitenlandse politiek van Nederland 1919-1945 A.1 (1919-1920)* (GS 156) (Nijhoff, Den Haag 1976), no. 83; Notulen ministerraad 19 September 1919 *Documenten betreffende*

the other neutrals were reluctant to accept the invitation. The Scandinavian governments, who were already cooperating between themselves, still aimed at amending the Covenant.[82] Especially the Swedish government was keen to use the Dutch invitation as a cover for a more fundamental discussion of League membership among the neutrals – a discussion they felt was redundant once the Netherlands had ratified the Covenant in early 1920.[83] Yet, despite these different approaches of the European neutrals, the Dutch succeeded in assembling them in The Hague in February 1920.

The neutral conference and the proposal it produced highlighted both the similarities and the differences in the positioning of the neutral states. Under Loder's lead, the delegates deliberately refrained from negotiating a uniform draft for a court statute.[84] Yet, the 'five power proposal' drafted by Van Vollenhoven firmly committed to several core principles, such as the equality of states, the separation of arbitration and adjudication, the independence of judges from national influence, and the fact that the Court could not deny justice. These elements had in varying forms already featured in earlier Scandinavian, Swiss and Dutch drafts.[85] New elements that met with more contestation regarded, amongst others, the definition of jurisdiction and the question of compulsory jurisdiction.[86] The Dutch delegation for example insisted on individual standing and together with the Swiss diplomat Gaston Carlin (1859-1922) proposed to allow the Court to define its own competence – something the Swedish delegation feared would upset the Great Powers.[87] The end result disappointed some dele-

de buitenlandse politiek van Nederland 1919-1945 A.1 (1919-1920) (GS 156) (Nijhoff, Den Haag 1976), no. 95.

82 Van Vredenburgh to Van Karnebeek 4 October 1919, *Documenten betreffende de buitenlandse politiek van Nederland 1919-1945 A.1 (1919-1920)* (GS 156) (Nijhoff, Den Haag 1976), no. 110.

83 Sweerts de Landas to Van Karnebeek 3 January 1920, telegram Sweerts de Landas 23 January 1920, Hellner to Sweerts 28 January 1920, Sweerts de Landas to Van Karnebeek, 29 January 1920, all in inv. no. 1496, archive Ministry of Foreign Affairs 1814-1940 (2.05.03), NL-NA.

84 'Draft of a Convention', in *Documents presented to the committee relating to existing plans for the establishment of a Permanent Court of International Justice* (Den Haag 1920), 150; speech Loder in 'Séance de ouverture, 16 February 1920', Loder papers, PPL.

85 'Tableau synoptique des avant-project des pays suivants: Danemark, Norvège, Pays-Bas, Suède, Suisse', inv. no. E2001B#1000/1508#106*, Swiss Federal Archive (SFA), Bern. The national projects were also published in *Documents* (1920).

86 'Draft of a Convention', in: *Documents* (1920) 150.

87 Minutes 18 February 1920, inv. no. E2001B#1000/1508#106*, SFA.

gates, but others argued that the agreement was to be found in the further deliberations on a permanent court.[88] At the very least, the five power proposal was integrated in the collection of drafts prepared by the League Secretariat, and inspired the appendix the Secretariat drafted for the ACJ.[89] Moreover, it established close contacts between some neutrals, in particular between Loder and Carlin, who would gladly use Loder's membership of the ACJ to indirectly keep Switzerland involved in its deliberations.[90]

In the months that separated the neutral conference from the start of the ACJ, Loder actively lobbied for both the neutral proposal as well as the Dutch invitation to the committee to meet in The Hague.[91] Travelling to London and Paris, Loder visited the League Secretariat, future ACJ member Walter Phillimore, but also Cecil, Lord Reay and Bourgeois.[92] In parallel, he discussed both the neutral proposal and his own ideas on for example individual standing during the 1920 Portsmouth conference of the International Law Association.[93] With help of the League Secretariat, Loder's mission to bring the ACJ to The Hague soon bore fruit: a counter-proposal from the Belgian member Descamps, supported by the French and Japanese members, to have the committee meet in Brussels, was successfully suppressed.[94] Thus, by late May 1920, when invitations for the ACJ went out to its future members, 'The Hague' resumed its status as

88 Carlin to Bern 27 February 1920, inv. no. E2001B#1000/1508#106*, SFA. The Norwegian delegate Emil Huitfeldt was very disappointed: Haakon A. Ikonomou, Karin van Leeuwen and Morten Rasmussen, '"Calculate the limits of the possible". Scandinavian Legal Diplomacy & the Creation of the Permanent Court of International Justice (2023) 2 *Diplomatica*, 225.

89 'Memorandum presented by the Legal Section of the Permanent Secretariat of the League of Nations', in *Documents* (1920) 1.

90 Carlin to Bern 27 May 1920, 25 June 1920 and 16 July 1920, inv. no. E2001B#1000/1508#107*, SFA.

91 Invitation De Marees van Swinderen to the Secretary-General 14 April 1920, inv. no. 1299 21.3862.88 LONA.

92 Loder to Van Karnebeek, 15 April 1920 and 21 April 1920, inv. no. 136, Werkarchief H.A. van Karnebeek (2.05.25), NL-NA; also [Carlin], 'Extrait d'un rapport de la Haye', 29 April 1920, E2001B#1000/1508#107*, SFA.

93 Bernard Loder, 'Permanent Court of International Justice, The Second Day's Proceedings' (1920) *ILA Reports*, 144.

94 Van Hamel to Loder 26 April 1920, Loder papers, PPL; correspondence Loder-Van Karnebeek May 1920, inv. no. 136, Werkarchief H.A. van Karnebeek (2.05.25), NL-NA; Hammarskjöld's 'Report on voyage to Brussels', 9 May 1920, LONA 1299 21.4155.88; more details in Karin van Leeuwen and Morten Rasmussen, 'A Political and Legal History of the Advisory Committee of Jurists and the Foundation of the Permanent Court of International Justice' in P. Sean Morris (ed), *Transforming the*

capital of legal internationalism.[95] Moreover, Dutch and neutral ideas were firmly incorporated into the preparatory works of the Committee. It was up to Loder to capitalise on both.

D. 1920-1922: A New Court for The Hague

In early June, when Scott returned to the Netherlands to assist the US member of the ACJ, the famous Nobel Prize laureate Elihu Root, he finally found the Dutch firmly on his side in their unequivocal support for the court project. Dutch newspapers heralded the perspective of a PCIJ as 'one of the best opportunities for preserving peace and for the moral education of humankind', and would continue to fill their front pages with news from the ACJ during its roughly five weeks of session.[96] Meanwhile, the Foreign Office had ensured that the ACJ members would lack nothing - from private cars to telegraph connections - and even was prepared to take over the faltering committee secretariat until the League's legal section urged it to some restraint.[97] At the same time, Loder, who diplomatically refused the presidency of the ACJ, lobbied Root and Phillimore to get the latter elected to the chair - a position that to his regret eventually went to the Belgian veteran of international arbitration, Edouard Descamps.[98]

Within the ACJ, Loder presented himself on the one hand clearly as a representative of the neutrals, along with the Norwegian former politician and lawyer Francis Hagerup. That this representative role was a matter of communication as well as content was illustrated by the fact that Loder went to remarkable length to inform the Swiss ambassador Carlin about the committee's progress and to invite him for the teas and dinners with

---

Politics of International Law: The Advisory Committee of Jurists and the Formation of the World Court in the League of Nations (Routledge, Oxon 2021), 69 (84).

95 'Le Retour de La Haye', *Algemeen Handelsblad* (21 September 1920) cited from a contribution by De Lapradelle in *La vie des peuples* that argued precisely this.

96 'Internationaal Hof van Justitie', *De nieuwe courant* (14 June 1920) 1; for many more newspapers see delpher.nl

97 Van Kleffens to Van Eysinga, inv no 615, Van Eysinga family collection, Tresoar, Leeuwarden; Van Hamel to Van Karnebeek 4 June 1920, inv. no. 58, Werkarchief H.A. van Karnebeek (2.05.25), NL-NA; on the details of the preparations see the many documents in inv. no. 1496, archive Ministry of Foreign Affairs 1814-1940 (2.05.03), NL-NA.

98 Hammarskjöld report of June 12th on meeting with Van Karnebeek, L.175.500, Archive of Åke Hammarskjöld (AAH), Kungliga Bibliotek, Stockholm.

other ACJ members, on which Loder had insisted.[99] Carlin's reports to Bern subsequently provide valuable insight into how Loder defended some common interests. For example, Carlin approvingly reported how the ACJ's early decision to grant the seat of the new Court to the Hague – a decision that was gratefully received by the Dutch press – did not suffice to appease the Dutch delegate, as Carlin had feared.[100] Together with 'small state' members such as Rafael Altamira (Spain), Hagerup, but also with Albert Geouffre De Lapradelle (France) and Arturo Ricci Busatti (Italy), Loder vehemently defended the principle of sovereign equality with regard to the election of judges.[101] Eventually, the small state representatives had to make concessions on the issue in order to find a compromise – but so did the other side, Hagerup explained to Carlin.[102]

The election issue was far from the only question on which Loder defended the joint position of the neutral conference in the ACJ, or, where agreement had been lacking, the five-power proposal that he understood as such. For example, he also took a sharp stance against judges ad hoc, which the neutrals had felt would shift the new adjudicatory court back towards the model of arbitration. Although Loder's arguments found some willing ears, the ACJ eventually decided to allow for judges ad hoc in

99 Carlin was for example invited to a dinner hosted by Loder on 9 July: Carlin to Bern 16 July 1920, inv. no. E2001B#1000/1508#107*, SFA. For Loder's insistence on such informal meetings see Hammarskjöld, 'Report. Confidential, June 22nd 1920', L.175.480, AAH.

100 Carlin to Bern 29 June 1920, inv. no. E2001B#1000/1508#107*, SFA; for press see e.g. 'Laatste nieuws. Het int. Gerechtshof. Vestiging van den zetel in Den Haag' *De Telegraaf* (26 June 1920).

101 Advisory Committee of Jurists, *Procès-Verbaux of the Proceedings of the Committee: June 16th–July 24th 1920*, 102, 106, 119 and 127; also Ole Spiermann, '"Who Attempts Too Much Does Nothing Well": The 1920 Advisory Committee of Jurists and the Statute of the Permanent Court of International Justice' (2003) 1 *British Yearbook of International Law*, 187 (202).

102 Carlin to Bern 16 July 1920, Carlin to Bern 27 May 1920, 25 June 1920 and 16 July 1920, inv. no. E2001B#1000/1508#107*, SFA; also see Hagerup's own memorandum cited in Haakon Andreas Ikonomou and Morten Rasmussen, 'Scandinavian Legal Internationalism' in P. Sean Morris (ed), *Transforming the Politics of International Law: The Advisory Committee of Jurists and the Formation of the World Court in the League of Nations* (Routledge, Oxon 2021), 236 (256); and (on Loder's role) Freya Baetens and Veronica Lavista, '"Where Is Your Tribunal?"' in P. Sean Morris (ed), *The League of Nations and the Development of International Law: The Advisory Committee of Jurists and the Formation of the World Court in the League of Nations* (Routledge, Oxon 2021) 195 (204).

order to safeguard agreement on other vital issues.[103] Secondly, and more famously, Loder boldly initiated the discussion on compulsory jurisdiction. In a spirit of small state solidarity, and despite taking a more cautious position on the issue himself, Hagerup immediately backed Loder's rather undiplomatic initiative and refuted president Descamps' objections against raising the matter. That the ACJ ultimately included compulsory jurisdiction in its draft statute was however mostly due to the weight Root put in on the matter, as well as to the scheme Phillimore drafted with help from Hagerup: if Loder's radical memorandum on the issue had any merit, it was probably that it made the Phillimore scheme seem rather reasonable.[104] The weight Root and Phillimore pulled on compulsory jurisdiction was further illustrated by a third issue on which Loder defended the position of the neutral conference, now contrary to the position of Root and Phillimore. Regarding the competence of the court, Root and Phillimore favoured a limited understanding, while Loder argued for leaving this question fully to the court itself. Although Hagerup hesitantly supported Loder, Loder's expansionist idea of international law - common among leading Dutch scholars - was considered inopportune and thus omitted from the ACJ's recommendations.[105]

While generally following the lines set out by the five-power conference, Loder fought a lonelier battle on the issue of individual standing. This long-held Dutch desire had already separated the Dutch from the other delegations during the neutral conference. Although the French ACJ delegate and later rapporteur De Lapradelle firstly seemed to align with Loder's view

103 Advisory Committee of Jurists, *Procès-Verbaux of the Proceedings of the Committee: June 16th–July 24th 1920*, 169, 178, 531; on Carlin's lobby behind the scenes, see Carlin to Bern 19 July 1920, Carlin to Bern 27 May 1920, 25 June 1920 and 16 July 1920, inv. no. E2001B#1000/1508#107*, SFA.

104 Advisory Committee of Jurists, *Procès-Verbaux of the Proceedings of the Committee: June 16th–July 24th 1920*, 224-230, 249-251 (memorandum Loder). On Hagerup, see Haakon Andreas Ikonomou and Morten Rasmussen, 'Scandinavian Legal Internationalism' in P. Sean Morris (ed), *Transforming the Politics of International Law: The Advisory Committee of Jurists and the Formation of the World Court in the League of Nations* (Routledge, Oxon 2021), 236 (252).

105 Advisory Committee of Jurists, *Procès-Verbaux of the Proceedings of the Committee: June 16th–July 24th 1920*, 294, 307, 311; also Freya Baetens and Veronica Lavista, '"Where Is Your Tribunal?"' in P. Sean Morris (ed), *The League of Nations and the Development of International Law: The Advisory Committee of Jurists and the Formation of the World Court in the League of Nations* (Routledge, Oxon 2021), 195 (210).

on the issue, and Hagerup cautiously mentioned the precedent of the Prize Court, the majority firmly subscribed to the idea that private individuals before the court should always be represented by states. Hence, individual standing did not even appear in the ACJ's report.[106]

Upon the publication of the report in September 1920, the Dutch press eagerly repeated the official communication's framing of the report as a continuation of the work of the Hague Peace Conference of 1907.[107] While lauding the ACJ's 'ingenuous' compromise regarding the election of judges, commentators expressed concern on its 'bold' proposals for compulsory jurisdiction, which were held to put the entire project in great danger.[108] Nevertheless, when the League Council in October 1920 indeed proposed to remove compulsory jurisdiction from the draft Statute, Van Hamel turned to Dutch public opinion in order to mobilise support for the original ACJ's proposals.[109] Behind closed doors, the CVDV however took a more cautious position in its advice to the Dutch government. Prioritising the PCIJ's establishment as a major first step, the CVDV advised the government to not hold on to compulsory jurisdiction if that would jeopardise the court's establishment – even though the Dutch delegation also should not be the first to let it go.[110]

106 Advisory Committee of Jurists, *Procès-Verbaux of the Proceedings of the Committee: June 16th–July 24th 1920*, 205-217.

107 For example 'Het ontwerp voor een internationaal gerechtshof', *NRC* (16 September 1920), 1-2.

108 'Het Permanente Hof van Internationale Justitie' (1), *Algemeen Handelsblad* (19 September 1920), 1; De Louter, 'Het Internationaal Gerechtshof II', *De Nieuwe Courant* (28 September 1920), 1.
Critical on compulsory jurisdiction: 'Het Permanente Hof van Internationale Justitie' (2), *Algemeen Handelsblad* (24 September 1920), 1; De Louter, 'Het Internationaal Gerechtshof III'. *De Nieuwe Courant* (29 September 1920), 1 but cf. [Van Eysinga], 'Het Permanente Hof van Internationale Justitie' *NRC* (16 October 1920), 1

109 'De Volkenbondsraad. Het Internationaal Gerechtshof' *De Telegraaf* (27 October 1920); on Van Hamel's resistance also Karin van Leeuwen and Morten Rasmussen, 'A Political and Legal History of the Advisory Committee of Jurists and the Foundation of the Permanent Court of International Justice' in P. Sean Morris (ed), *Transforming the Politics of International Law: The Advisory Committee of Jurists and the Formation of the World Court in the League of Nations* (Routledge, Oxon 2021), 69 (94).

110 'Rapport 1 november 1920', inv. no. 31 archive CVDV. In a separate advice regarding possible amendments of the League Covenant, the CVDV had already demonstrated its attachment to the new court by proposing to give it competence over various additional subjects including resignation from the League (art 2.3 Covenant) and unjust war (art 16.1): 'Rapport 9 augustus 1920', *Documenten betreffende de buiten-*

In the First Assembly, this was precisely how the Dutch delegation positioned itself. As seemed common practice, the Dutch government chose to appoint its former ACJ representative Loder in its Assembly delegation to deal with the PCIJ Statute, thereby implicitly endorsing Loder's work in the ACJ. Although the Dutch delegate in the First Committee did support the discussion of the Scandinavian amendments to the Covenant – meant to insert a clear textual basis for compulsory jurisdiction – against an obvious majority, Loder, who represented the Netherlands in the Third Committee's discussion of the Court Statute, took a restrained position from the start, similar to the hesitant positions of the Scandinavian delegates.[111] After having corrected what he believed was a 'misunderstanding between the Jurists' committee and the Council' regarding the interpretation of the Covenant, which according to Loder permitted 'exactly the step forward' suggested by the ACJ, he made clear that he would support the proposals presented by the Council: 'In going further, there was the risk of bringing about disagreement between different Powers and thus of failing to achieve any result.'[112]

In subsequent committee and sub-committee meetings, Loder's contributions largely consisted of explaining the ACJ draft, and of emphasising that it was better left intact, even when the Brazilian representative Raul Fernandes (1877–1968) and the Swiss representative Max Huber (1874-1960) again tried to open the debate on compulsory jurisdiction.[113] Once the compromise seemed secured however, Loder took his chance to again state his position in the plenary Assembly. After declaring that the Netherlands 'gladly and with deep emotion' accepted the Court on its soil, and ensuring that it would protect the Court 'as a mother protects her child', Loder recalled what he considered 'the three essential principles' of the various schemes for the Court that had been discussed in various committees from

landse politiek van Nederland 1919-1945 A.2 (1919-1920) (GS 156) (Nijhoff, Den Haag, 1977) no. 37.

111 'Minutes of the First Committee 2 (22 November 1920)', *League of Nations, Records of the First Assembly* I (Geneva 1920) 8.

112 'Minutes of the Third Committee 3 (24 November 1920)', *League of Nations, Records of the First Assembly* I (Geneva 1920) 288.

113 Karin van Leeuwen and Morten Rasmussen, 'A Political and Legal History of the Advisory Committee of Jurists and the Foundation of the Permanent Court of International Justice' in P. Sean Morris (ed), *Transforming the Politics of International Law: The Advisory Committee of Jurists and the Formation of the World Court in the League of Nations* (Routledge, Oxon 2021), 69 (99-104).

the neutral conference onwards. The first two, the equality of states and the independence of the judge, now were about to be realised. However, the third principle, compulsory jurisdiction, had been 'eliminated', Loder evoked, because in the words of the British representatives, 'the time [was] not yet ripe'. While reassuring his audience that the Netherlands would not challenge the status quo at present, Loder warned: 'You are fighting against time; you will do so in vain.'[114]

E. Outlook: Land of Grotius, or..?

On December 16th, 1920, the Netherlands signed the Protocol for establishing the PCIJ. After clarifying that it did not cause any problems for its draft treaty with Belgium on the Scheldt, the Dutch government also accepted the optional clause in June 1921.[115] During the Second Assembly, the Dutch government succeeded in having Loder appointed to the new court.[116] And when he was also elected President at the very beginning of the PCIJ in 1922, it seemed as if the future indeed was approaching rapidly, as he had warned the Assembly in 1920.

Loder's appointment further strengthened the Dutch commitment to the PCIJ. As host of the Court, that commitment in the first place took the shape of technical assistance, for example with the arrangement of a postal office.[117] Loder, in his capacity of President, continued to regard the Court as 'work in progress', and for example in the famous 1927 *Lotus* case dissented in favour of a more expansive interpretation of the Court's jurisdiction.[118] Meanwhile, when in 1929 a reform of the PCIJ Statute was debated, Dutch representatives again took up the ambition to realise individual

---

114 'Twentieth plenary meeting (13 December 1920)', *League of Nations, Records of the First Assembly* I (Geneva 1920) 443-446.

115 *Staatsblad* 1921 no. 826; also Van Karnebeek to Council of Ministers 19 January 1921, *Documenten* A.2 (1920-1921), no. 220.

116 Michael Riemens, *De passie voor vrede. De evolutie van de internationale politieke cultuur in de jaren 1880-1940 en het recipiëren door Nederland* (De Bataafsche Leeuw, Amsterdam 2005), 194.

117 Hammarskjöld to Drummond 24 January 1922, inv no 1310 21/18840/18840 LONA; an attempt by Drummond to lure the Dutch government into also contributing financially however seems to have failed: Drummond to Van Karnebeek 30 January 1922, inv. no. 136, Werkarchief H.A. van Karnebeek (2.05.25), NL-NA.

118 The case of the S.S. "Lotus" (France v. Turkey) (1927), Judgment, PCIJ series A, no. 10, dissenting opinion by Loder; Freya Baetens and Veronica Lavista, '"Where Is

standing, next to pleading the case of compulsory jurisdiction.[119] Thus, Dutch government representatives and individual lawyers identifying with the Dutch cause continued their commitment to ideas and aims developed since the early 20th century.

As this chapter has aimed to demonstrate, these ideas and aims – and the interventions they inspired – typically relied on both a perceived exceptionalism building on the Dutch Grotian tradition and its hosting of the Hague courts and conferences, as well as on a sense of commonality that tied Dutch interests and ambitions to those of other small and/or neutral states during the early 20th century. Especially after the First World War, the Netherlands explicitly aligned with Switzerland and the Scandinavian states to amend the meagre plans for a Permanent Court concocted in Paris. Yet, in comparison to those other small states, the Dutch also held some rather distinctive positions, the most remarkable of which was its commitment to individual standing. This specific 'national tradition', combining ideals of a *ius gentium* that addressed an international community rather than states with the practical experiences of the merchant, continued to influence Dutch legal internationalism also beyond the establishment of the World Court.[120]

Your Tribunal?"' in P. Sean Morris (ed), *The League of Nations and the Development of International Law* (Routledge, Oxon 2021), 195 (212).

119 Willem van Eysinga, 'Het Juristencomité-1929 in zake het Permanente Hof van Internationale Justitie van den Volkenbond' (1929) 68-5 *Mededeelingen KNAW* B 89.

120 Karin van Leeuwen, 'On Democratic Concerns and Legal Traditions: The Dutch 1953 and 1956 Constitutional Reforms "Towards" Europe' (2012) 3 *Contemporary European History*, 357.

From Clóvis Beviláqua to Raul Fernandes: Brazilian (and Latin American?) Participation in the Drafting of the PCIJ's Statute

Lucas Carlos Lima

A. Introduction

The beginning of the 20th century was a particularly fruitful period for the development of international law in Latin America, as well as for the consolidation of the participation of Latin American states in major international meetings. Latin American states consolidated their independence processes, there were few territorial conflicts in the region, and a certain idea of pan-Americanism seemed to be solidifying. The Second Hague Peace Conferences represented a moment of increased participation in universal legal projects. At the end of the First World War Latin American states were interested in, for internal political purposes as well, sitting at the table with European states and join negotiations and decision-making processes. The same rings true in relation to the project of international justice.

This chapter focuses on the role of two Brazilian lawyers, Clóvis Beviláqua[1] and Raul Fernandes,[2] in drafting the Statute of the Permanente Court of International Justice (PCIJ). They participated in different mo-

1 Clóvis Beviláqua (1859-1944) served as professor of civil and comparative law at the Recife Law School in the capital of the state of Pernambuco – an important centre for legal training in imperial and early-republican Brazil. As the author of the Brazilian Civil Code of 1916, whose first draft was presented in 1899, and as its first commentator, Beviláqua is considered the founding father of Brazilian civil law scholarship. In 1906, he was appointed as Legal Advisor to the Ministry of Foreign Affairs of Brazil, position he held until his retirement in 1934. As Legal Advisor, Beviláqua was the author of several opinions on subjects such as progressive codification of international law, the organization of a 3rd Hague Peace Conference and the extradiction of nationals.

2 Raul Fernandes (1877-1968) served as Minister of Foreign Affairs of Brazil in two occasions: during the Post World War II administration of President Eurico Gaspar Dutra (1946-1951) and during the short administration of interim Presidents Café Filho and Carlos Luz (1954-1955). He also served as diplomatic representative for Brazil in several international conferences, such as the Paris Peace Conference (1919), the 6th Conference of the American Republics (1928) and the San Francisco Conference (1945).

ments of the long process which culminated in the Statute, and their respective contributions varied. Beviláqua was the legal adviser of the Brazilian Foreign Ministry and prepared a draft concerning the future organization of the PCIJ.[3] However, since Beviláqua decided not to partake in the work of the Advisory Committee of Jurists, the Brazilian Government sent jurist and politician Raul Fernandes to The Hague instead. Although Beviláqua's work is key to understanding the Brazilian position during the PCIJ's drafting, Raul Fernandes provides an important contribution from a practical point of view. The Brazilian lawyer coined the well-known "optional clause of compulsory jurisdiction" attributing jurisdiction to the Court – the highlight during his intervention at the Council of the League of Nations – a clause which is also known as the "Raul Fernandes' clause"[4] due to the influence of the Brazilian lawyer in coining it.

In Brazil, there is a very exhortatory literature idealizing the roles that three Brazilians played in the construction of the international judiciary: Clóvis Beviláqua and Raul Fernandes (in relation to the PCIJ) and Rui Barbosa (as the Brazilian delegate at the Second Peace Conference in The Hague).[5] This literature generally highlights the Brazilian contributions at certain conferences or in conceiving projects of international justice. In Brazil, the achievements of these three jurists are celebrated as fundamental inputs to the international legal order, although neither of them was trained as international lawyers or diplomats – as seems to be the case in the period for those participating in international law debates in Latin America.[6]

---

3 Clóvis Beviláqua, 'DRAFT for the organisation of the Permanent Court of International Justice' in Advisory Committee of Jurists, *Documents presented to the Committee relating to Existing Plans for the establishment of a Permanent Court of International Justice 1920*, 348.

4 Christian Tomuschat, 'Article 36' in Andreas Zimmermann et al. (eds), *The Statute of the International Court of Justice: A Commentary* (Oxford University Press, Oxford 2019), 712.

5 See Antônio Augusto Cançado Trindade, 'Latin America and the II Hague Peace Conference of 1907' in Paula Wojcikiewicz Almeida et al. (eds), *Latin America and the International Court of Justice* (Routledge, Oxon/New York 2017). See also: Albert G. De Lapradelle and Ellery C. Stowell, 'Latin America at the Hague Conference' (1908) 17 *The Yale Law Journal*, 270; Paulo Emílio Vauthier Borges de Macedo and Brenda Maria Ramos Araújo, 'A Man against a War' (2020) 23 *Journal of the History of International Law*, 282.

6 See Arnulf Becker Lorca, *Mestizo International Law* (Cambridge University Press, Cambridge 2015); and Juan Pablo Scarfi, *The Hidden History of International Law in the Americas* (Oxford University Press, Oxford 2017).

Barbosa, Beviláqua and Fernandes were politicians and lawyers involved in international matters due to circumstantial reasons only.

In Brazilian legal literature, Rui Barbosa is considered an unwavering defender of State equality in The Hague; Clóvis Beviláqua was considered one of the leading thinkers of international justice (particularly through his draft written as Legal Counsel to the Ministry of Foreign Relations concerning the League of Nations) and the architect of a Brazilian national legal identity; and Raul Fernandes was the mediator of interests between The Hague and Geneva. The Chapter's purpose is not to understand the role of each author in the construction of the first permanent Court, of Justice but to understand how their contributions could be identified as a national legal position and how this connects and represents some nuance of Latin-American regionalism. The phrase "regionalism" is employed here in a broader way, to mean expressions of ideas or practices that significantly diverged from European, North American, or other states that considered 'great powers' at the time.

This chapter focuses on identifying the distinctiveness of some of Barbosa's, Beviláqua's and Fernandes' ideas and how they connect with the debates on regionalism at the time. If it is true that every lawyer has a project in his or her mind, by reading their works and their arguments during the drafting of the PCIJ, I will identify if these projects correspond to a Brazilian, Latin American or American project.

This chapter is structured in four parts. First, it outlines contextual elements relevant to understanding the work of Beviláqua and Fernandes and shed light on the policy that Rui Barbosa had inaugurated during the Second Hague Peace Conference's debates on the creation of the Court of Arbitral Justice. Secondly, I analyse Beviláqua's project, his role as a policymaker and his adherence to the ideas of American international law. The focus will then shift to Raul Fernandes, the Brazilian delegate to the Advisory Committee of Jurists and the Council of the League of Nations. I conclude by arguing that the regionalism espoused by these three authors was a regionalism much more interested in a project of inserting Brazil in the international scene than an attempt to irrigate the nascent international court with elements of Latin American legal culture.

B. Brazil's Position in Relation to the Project of International Justice

There are three main considerations which clarify the actions of Beviláqua and Fernandes regarding the project of international justice. These elements also assist in the identification of whether their contribution represented regional or national traditions in their efforts to draft the PCIJ Statute at the time. The first consideration is Brazil's position in Latin America and its relationship with other Latin American states. The second is the perception of Brazilian elites that participation in international (and European) affairs was somehow recognized as a civilizational advance. These were times in which the notion of scientific progress, civilization, and development were common expressions ventilated in the public debate, and the acceptance of Brazil in these forums were sources of international and internal prestige.[7] Third, it is helpful to understand the profile of Brazilian international lawyers in the first twenty years of the twentieth century because this examination explains the legal background against which Beviláqua and Fernandes operated. Obviously, these three elements will be dealt with only to the extent that they contextualize the actions of Beviláqua and Fernandes.

The foreign policy literature of the period describes Brazil in the early years of the 20th century as a state seeking a spot among the great powers.[8] Brazil established its frontiers through negotiation and arbitration and participated actively in international and Pan-American conferences trying to project itself as a "civilized nation". Thus, Brazil claimed a certain regional leadership, in some moments connected with the Monroe Doctrine, claiming a leadership in the continent.[9]

Brazil was the only Latin American state to participate in the First World War and used this fact to gain visibility on the international scene and

---

7 See Lars William Janssen, *Law, Peace and Status: Brazil as a Middle Power during the Second Hague Peace Conference 1907* (Utrecht University Theses Repository, Utrecht 2020); Eugênio Vargas Garcia, 'Aspectos da Vertente Internacional do Pensamento Jurídico de Rui Barbosa' (1996) 4 *Textos de História,* 103 and Celso Lafer, 'Brazilian Identity and Foreign Policy: Past, Present and Future' (2000) 129 *Daedalus*, 207.

8 See Rubens Ricupero, *A diplomacia na construção do Brasil: 1750-2016* (Editora Contexto, São Paulo 2017), 330.

9 Juan Pablo Scarfi, 'In the Name of the Americas: The Pan-American Redefinition of the Monroe Doctrine and the Emerging Language of American International Law in the Western Hemisphere, 1898-1933' (2016) 40 *Diplomatic History*, 189 and E. Bradford Burns, *A Aliança Não-Escrita* (IPRI, Fundação Alexandre de Gusmão, Lisbon 2003).

increase its relations with the great powers. Additionally, Brazil also sent delegates to the 1919 Paris Conference. An interesting example in this regard is the fact that some diplomats defended the thesis of the "implicit mandate" in the League of Nations: in the absence of the United States from the League, it was Brazil that should take the place as the continent's interlocutor.[10] At the first meeting of the Council of the League, the Brazilian diplomat, Gastão da Cunha, expressly remarked that Brazil acted as a representative of the American continent.[11]

One of Brazil's strengths in this regard is precisely the role played as a representative and alleged defender of smaller nations and their Latin American counterparts, despite regional tensions. After declaring itself a republic, Brazil sought recognition by constructing new regional alliances. Brazil counted on the U.S. as a powerful ally to support Brazilian presence at the League. Brazil's presence in the League itself was a recognition of the ongoing process of a foreign policy aimed at participating in major global affairs. On the one hand, Brazil's presence was legitimized as a regional leadership, while on the other hand, it signalled to other nations that Brazil would be better positioned to establish dialogues than other states in the region. Thanks to U.S. support, Brazil gained a seat on the League Council. This institutional recognition crystalized the Brazilian foreign policy of participation that is highly connected with a particular discourse of progress and civilization.

One of the signs of progress and civilization present in the legal discourses of the period, which predate the 19th century, and are already present in the Pan-American Conferences, is Brazil's support of international arbitration. In the Panama Congress of 1826, the notion of arbitration emerged in American legal discourse. [12] The notion of arbitration was not only discussed universally at The Hague Conferences, but also regionally at the Pan American Conferences. At the later, legal discourse perceived interna-

10 Fernando Paulo de Melo Barreto, 'O Brasil e a Liga das Nações' in Raul M. da Silva and Clóvis Brigagão (eds), *História das Relações Internacionais do Brasil* (CEBRI, Rio de Janeiro 2019), 519.

11 Procès-verbal du Conseil de la Societé des nations, '*Minutes of the Council of the League of Nations 1st-15th sessions*', January 16th 1920. See also Paulo Emílio Vauthier Borges de Macedo, 'Clovis Beviláqua e a Justiça Internacional' (2017) 178 *Revista do Instituto Histórico e Geographico Brazileiro*, 210.

12 José Carlos Brandi Aleixo, *O Brasil e o Congresso Anfictônico do Panamá* (FUNAG, Brasilia 2000).

tional arbitration as a civilized process for resolving disputes.[13] This is a crucial point that characterizes the position of most Brazilian international lawyers: to reach a particular idea of civilization, it was necessary to do so through international arbitration and stress the rule of law over recourse to force. A significant indication of Brazil's position on international arbitration was its presence in the first constitution of the republic in 1891. Congress would have the power to authorize the Brazilian government to declare war if arbitration failed or could not be used.[14] Another notable example in this sense involved an arbitration between Brazil and Argentina over territory in the south of Brazil. In 1895, the arbitration was decided by President Glover Cleveland in favour of Brazil.[15] Other international arbitrations were used to settle Brazilian disputes.[16] Overall, Brazil's active participation in the debate on international arbitration was another sign of Brazil's intentions to participate in primary international debates on international justice. Therefore, it was possible to identify some national academic discussions regarding the contours of international justice.[17]

In this sense, one of the landmarks of Brazilian participation in the Second Hague Conference of 1907 was the presence of Rui Barbosa, sent to represent the Brazilian delegation at the conference due to his prestige as a national public figure. At the Hague, Barbosa became famous for the use of arbitration as an alternative to war, espousing pacifist tones which characterized Brazilian foreign policy at the time. One of the primary

---

13 Tereza Maria Spyer Dulci, *As Conferências Pan-Americanas (1889 a 1928)* (Alameida, São Paulo 2013).

14 Constitution of the United States of Brazil 1891.

15 *Brazil v. Argentina*, UNRIAA, Award for the settlement of disputes between Brazil and Argentina at Uruguay and Yguazu rivers of February 5th 1895, Vol. XXVIII, 277-282. See also José Tadeu Campos Araújo Filho, *Uma Análise Geopolítica da Questão de Palmas* (Kaygangue, Palmas 2009).

16 Mattos and Cruz, 'A Arbitragem na História da Política Exterior do Brasil' (2018) 11 *Territórios*, 256; Nelson, 'The Arbitration of Boundary Disputes in Latin America' (1973) 20 *Netherlands International Law Review*, 267; Woolsey, 'Boundary Disputes in Latin America' (1931) 25 *American Journal of International Law*, 324.

17 Clóvis Bevilaqua, *Principios Elementares do Direito Internacional Privado* (Editora Saraiva, São Paulo 1978); Clóvis Beviláqua, *Direito Público Internacional,* (Freitas Bastos, Rio de Janeiro1939); Francês Torres, *Vers la Paix* (Imprensa Nacional, Rio de Janeiro 1909); Rui Barbosa, *Problemas do Direito Internacional* (Truscott, London 1916); Rui Barbosa, *Os Conceitos Modernos do Direito Internacional* (Fundação Casa de Rui Barbosa, Rio de Janeiro 1983); Rui Barbosa, 'A Segunda Conferência de Paz da Haia' (2004) 16 *Revista dos Tribunais*, 399; Nabuco, *O Direito do Brazil: Primeira Memoria Apresentada em Roma a 27 de Fevereiro de 1903* (A. Lahure, Paris 1903).

reflections of Barbosa's presence at the conference was the fact that his passionate defence of the principle of equality stalled negotiations on the creation of a Court of Arbitral Justice, since his eloquence garnered support from other smaller states. Upon returning to Brazil, Barbosa was highly celebrated and his defence of equality crystallized as one of the main features of Brazilian legal foreign policy.[18] To other conference participants, such as Martens and Baron Marschall, Barbosa was responsible for the project's failure. Brazil's participation in the Second Hague Peace Conference was one of the moments of consolidation and formulation of legal foreign policy guidelines from which Brazil would continue later. Therefore, the positions of centrality of international justice permeated the national public debate and served as a guide for the future actions of Brazilian delegates and jurists at the birth of the Permanent Court of International Justice.

A final contextual element that should be emphasized is the fact that, at the beginning of the 20th century, Brazil did not have lawyers who dealt exclusively with international law issues. There is no space for us to discuss the foremost exponents here, but there is an emergent literature mapping Brazilian international lawyers at the time.[19] In short, the so-called international lawyers of the period were intricately linked to power, the Ministry of Foreign Affairs, or other disciplines such as public law or civil law. Barbosa was a lawyer and a politician, Beviláqua was a private lawyer and Raul Fernandes was a politician, member of the chamber of the representatives when he was summoned to participate in the Paris Conference. This background information seems relevant because some of the ways these men perceived international law comes from national references or a conception of global order coined from within national boundaries. Even the phenomenon of dialogue among Latin American countries was something recent.[20] However, it is possible to affirm that despite all the Pan-American initiatives of the period, the notion of American regional law

---

18 Paulo Emílio Vauthier Borges de Macedo, 'Clóvis Beviláqua e a Justiça Internacional' (2017), 178 *Revista do Instituto Histórico e Geographico Brazileiro*, 210; Celso Amorim, *A Diplomacia Multilateral do Brasil* (FUNAG, Brasilia 2007); Brenda Maria Ramos Araújo and Paulo Emílio Vauthier Borges de Macedo, 'Rui Barbosa' in George Rodrigo Bandeira Galindo (ed), *Direito Internacional no Brasil* (Lumen Juris, Rio de Janeiro 2021), 159.

19 George Rodrigo Bandeira Galindo, *Direito Internacional no Brasil – Vol. 1* (Lumen Juris, Rio de Janeiro 2021); George Rodrigo Bandeira Galindo, *Direito Internacional no Brasil – Vol. 2* (Lumen Juris, Rio de Janeiro 2021).

20 Juan Pablo Scarfi, *The Hidden History of International Law in the Americas* (Oxford University Press, Oxford 2017).

is not particularly received in Brazil, and this can be clearly identified in Clóvis Beviláqua's work.

C. Beviláqua's Project of International Justice as a Framework for Brazilian Action

During the Council of the League of Nation's meeting on February 12, 1920, a special commission of jurists was created to draft the Statute for the PCIJ in accordance with Article 14 of the Covenant. Brazil was granted a position on that commission. Clóvis Beviláqua was chosen to represent Brazil on the commission as an essential public figure responsible for the elaboration of the Brazilian Civil Code, among other things.[21]

From 1906 to 1934, Beviláqua was a legal advisor to the Ministry of Foreign Affairs, a position he held until 1934. Many of Brazil's legal positions in the period were articulated by Beviláqua, including Brazil's participation in the international justice debate. Beviláqua sent the Committee of Jurists a draft that was added to other proposals presented for discussion. Many of the Brazilian legal foreign policy positions were formulations arising from the legal opinions of Clóvis Beviláqua. The position of legal advisor of the Ministry of Foreign Affairs (also known as "O Itamaraty") continues to have profound influence within Brazilian State.[22]

Unsurprisingly, the project soon became a book in Brazil given the importance of its author.[23] To Beviláqua, the Court-to-be-created should have four main features: (a) permamency; (b) a composition that is not dependent on the choice of the litigant states, but an organ of the international society; (c) it must be composed of professional lawyers and not of politicians; (d) and finality, in the sense that decisions win the respect of all. It is not difficult to identify in Beviláqua's the strong influence of a

21 Roberto Dalledone Machado Filho, 'Entre a Imitação e a Criação' in George Rodrigo Bandeira Galindo (ed), *Direito Internacional no Brasil* (Lumen Juris, Rio de Janeiro 2021), 305; Arnaldo Sampaio De Moraes Godoy, *Clóvis Beviláqua Internacionalista e Pacifista* (Sérgio Fabris, São Paulo 2012); Antonio Celso Alves Pereira, 'Clóvis Beviláqua e o Direito Internacional' (2017) 473 *Revista do Instituto Histórico e Geographico Brazileiro*, 249.

22 See in this regard George Rodrigo Bandeira Galindo, 'Imunidade de Jurisdição dos Estados e Poder Executivo Brasileiro: Os Pareceres dos Consultores Jurídicos do Itamaraty' (2021), 18 *Revista de Direito Internacional*, 162.

23 Clóvis Beviláqua, *Projet d'Organisation d'Une Cour Permanente de Justice Internationale* (Besnard Frères, Paris 1921).

continental idea of tribunal transposed to the international realm. However, it is possible to identify several references to the Supreme Corte of the United States of America in Beviláqua's project.

It is worth mentioning that Beviláqua sincerely believed in the project of international justice that the Permanent Court represented. In his words

> The Court, by which an ancient human aspiration is realised - that of finding a peaceful method of solving international conflicts - is intended to accomplish a two-fold task: to bring to an end disagreements between States, and to render clearer and more certain the idea of the unity of international law as well as of the Society of States which that law is to organise[24]

The reference to international law's unity is made purposefully. Beviláqua did not participate in the debate of an American International Law inaugurated by the Chilean lawyer Alejandro Alvarez.[25] Beviláqua was a good reader of another Brazilian that confronted Alvarez's ideas, Manuel de Sá Viana, who wrote a book called "*De la non existence d'un droit international américain*"[26]. Beviláqua opposed the idea of a regional international law because he viewed solidarity as the ultimate foundation of international law.[27] This solidarity privileges a universal conception of international law. Beviláqua even states "those who advocate the formation of European or American international law are opposed to the evolutionary march of

24 Advisory Committee of Jurists, *Documents presented to the Committee relating to existing plans for the establishment of a Permanent Court of International Justice 1920*, 359.

25 Alejandro Alvarez, 'Latin America and International Law', (1909) 3 *American Journal of International Law*, 269; Juan Ignacio Arias Krause and Mariela Cecilia Avila, 'Las Bases del Derecho Internacional Americano em la Obra de Alejandro Alvarez', (2021) 34 *Revista Derecho Valdivia*, 153; Liliana Obregón, '¿Para qué un derecho internacional latinoamericano' in René Urueña (ed), *Derecho internacional. Poder y límites del derecho en la sociedad global* (Universidad de Los Andes, Colombia 2015).

26 Manoel Alvaro de Souza Sá Vianna, *De la Non Existence d'un Droit International Américain*, (L. Figueiredo, Rio de Janeiro 1912); See in this regard Liliana Obregón, 'Identity Formation, Theorization and Decline of a Latin American International Law' in Paula Wojcikiewicz Almeida and Jean-Marc Sorel (eds), *Latin America and the International Court of Justice* (Routledge, London 2017), 3; See also Fabia Fernandes Carvalho and Patrícia Ramos Barros, 'Universalismo à Brasileira', in George Rodrigo Bandeira Galindo (ed), *Direito Internacional no Brasil* (Lumen Juris, Rio de Janeiro 2021), 333.

27 Clóvis Beviláqua, *Direito Público Internacional* (Freitas Bastos, Rio de Janeiro1939).

international law towards universalism, which is its ideal".[28] This may lead to the conclusion that the Beviláqua's project should not be viewed as a Brazilian national contribution, but as contribution to a universalist project of international justice made by a Brazilian lawyer

The Beviláqua project has many of the common points that were later adopted by the Permanent Court. There are many references to U.S. practice and the U.S. Supreme Court as a model court. However, some distinctions are interesting to analyse because they demonstrate novel ideas that reveal the author's perception of the ideal court for safeguarding international peace. This is the case because Beviláqua believed states would be morally deprived of reasons to instigate war with a Court decision. He believed the creation of a caselaw, a jurisprudence from a Court, League of Nation's judicial power would exercise a profound and beneficial influence on individual conscience.[29]

Two suggestions present in the project stand out. The first regards the judges of the Court and their election. For Beviláqua, judges should only be elected by the Assembly of the League of Nations and would then be elected by the judges themselves. According to Beviláqua, to ensure the full equality of States, the first elected judges should be responsible for selecting the following judges, therefore keeping the choice in the hands of a technical body rather than in the hands of politics and power. In this matter, Beviláqua's project differed from those of Descamps, Ricci-Busatti, and Philimore because it did not provide for the representation of the great powers. Beviláqua sought to solve the problem of national representation: the Court would be an independent organization, which would reproduce itself without State influence. In this way, the project reflected Rui Barbosa's ideas and the position of Brazilian foreign policy at the time. In Beviláqua's words:

> For the first nomination, it was necessary to have recourse to a different process. The choice could be entrusted to the Assembly or to the Council. The Assembly represents, in the most complete manner, the League of Nations. Chosen by it, the judicial power will be designated by the Society itself, in an indirect election, no doubt, but in which all the States will have really cooperated. But once constituted, the Tribunal

28 Clóvis Beviláqua, 'Sociedade das Nações' (1920) XXXIV *Revista Forenze Doutrina Legislação e Jurisprudência*, 252.

29 Ibid, 253.

> must be detached from the other organs of the League of Nations, in order to move freely in its orbit and better represent human thought, in its aspiration towards justice, in its ceaseless march towards future enlightened by the truth of the mind, which is science, and not the truth of the heart, which is goodness.[30]

However, as noted in Brazilian scholarship[31], Beviláqua's project strongly differed from that of Rui Barbosa because it did not strongly advocate for compulsory jurisdiction. Strongly connected with the defence of Brazilian interests and the logic of arbitration, Beviláqua's view of international justice relied on the principle of self-limitation. This principle says states are free to choose which disputes to submit to the international judge.[32] This position can be perceived as contradictory because it imposes a limitation on this freedom. For Beviláqua, the judicial institution was necessary for society's progress, hence the need to choose judges and reinforce their impartiality. However, jurisdiction remained optional.

A third interesting feature of the project concerns which rules the Court should apply. According to Article 24 of Beviláqua's project "The Court should apply the rules of international law, whether laid down in the Treaties which have to be applied or interpreted, or in General Treaties. In any cases not covered by either general or special Treaties, the Court shall apply principles recognised by the doctrine" (*consacrés par la doctrine*, in the French original version). Then it continues, "if such principles

30 Advisory Committee of Jurists, *Documents presented to the Committee relating to existing plans for the establishment of a Permanent Court of International Justice 1920*, 366. From the original in French: "Pour la première nomination, il a fallu avoir recours à un autre procédé. Le choix pouvait être confié à l'Assemblée ou au Conseil. L'Assemblée représente, de la manière la plus complète, la Société des Nations. Choisi par elle, le pouvoir judiciaire sera désigné par la Société elle-même, dans une election indirecte, sans doute, mais dans laquelle tous les Etats auront réellement, coopéré. Mais une fois constitué, le Tribunal doit se détacher des autres organes de la Société des Nations, afin de se mouvoir, librement, dans son orbite et représenter mieux la pensée humaine, dans sons aspiration vers la justice, dans sa marche incessante vers l'avenir éclairé par la vérité de l'entendement qui est la science, et pas la vérité du coeur, qui est la bonté."

31 Paulo Emílio Vauthier Borges de Macedo, 'Clovis Beviláqua e a Justiça Internacional' (2017) 178 *Revista do Instituto Histórico e Geographico Brazileiro*, 210.

32 Article 30 of Beviláqua's Project. Advisory Committee of Jurists, *Documents presented to the Committee relating to existing plans for the establishment of a Permanent Court of International Justice*, 353. See also Clóvis Beviláqua, 'A Liga das Nações e a soberania dos Estados', (1919) *Jornal do Commercio*, May 6.

are lacking or in doubt, it shall deliver judgment in conformity with the general principles of law and equity".[33] Interestingly, Beviláqua does not include customary law as a possible applicable law. While there seemed to exist a certain reluctance to customary law in Latin America at that time, Beviláqua explains its reasons, which has more to do with its close connection with German legal literature. To Beviláqua, "The doctrine is the scientific statement of customary law".[34] While the position seems in accordance with Latin American authors that cast doubt on customary international law, the reasons here are more aligned with the author's conception of law.

The project can be perceived as a manifestation of Brazil's will to participate in the international debate with one of the great minds of the newborn Republic rather than a specific manifestation of a regional perception. In fact, when one identifies the authors referred to be Beviláqua in the explanation of the project, it will verify that he seems more interested in establishing a dialogue with European authors (Scelle, Descamps, Nyholm) and American authors (James Brown Scott, Elihu Root and others). Additionally, Beviláqua seems interested in mentioning Rui Barbosa and Alberto Torres in his work. Beviláqua likely made this decision to highlight Brazilian authors and political leaders because who have somehow participated in discussions of international justice, Beviláqua might have been paying tribute to a certain Brazilian juridical-diplomatic tradition, emphasizing his country's position as a producer of individuals capable of influencing ideas in the field – alongside with the North Americans.

Although Beviláqua was chosen to represent Brazil and formulate the proposal of an international court, a personal obstacle prevented him from participating in meetings at the Hague and he never left the country. Thus, his representative on the Committee of Jurists became Raul Fernandes. As mentioned, Fernandes was a member of the Brazilian delegation to the Peace Conference, which represented Brazil in the reparations commission of the Treaty of Versailles. Upon analyzing Raul Fernandes' dual role, elements of Latin Americanisms start to emerge.

Fernandes participated in the entire Advisory Committee of Jurists debate without the right to vote. It was not until July 19, 1920, that he finally replaced Beviláqua due to decision-making deadlock between Committee

33 Advisory Committee of Jurists, *Documents presented to the Committee relating to existing plans for the establishment of a Permanent Court of International Justice*, 353.

34 Ibid, 371.

members. According to Spiermann, Dionisio Anzilotti, a leading Italian international law scholar who would become a PCIJ judge in the near future, played a role in this movement.[35] However, Fernandes would also be on the first committee of the League Council, responsible for adopting the Statute and there he would formulate his optional clause of compulsory jurisdiction.

D. From The Hague to Geneva: Raul Fernandes and the Latin American Representation

The impasse concerning the optional clause of compulsory jurisdiction represents a tension between those who desired a permanent judicial institution with compulsory jurisdiction over all States and those who paid tribute to a voluntarist conception somewhat connected to the arbitral practice.[36] Within the third Committee of the League, which was responsible for the final work on the Statute of the Court, Raul Fernandes paved the way for the intermediate solution.[37] This is undoubtedly a significant contribution. However, another aspect of Fernandes' performance during those years is even more interesting to examine. At the beginning of the century, he positioned himself not only as a representative of Brazilian interests, but as a representative of the American continent during the production of the Statute of the Permanent Court of International Justice.

Being the only delegate from Latin America in the Advisory Committee of Jurists (ACJ), Raul Fernandes sometimes relied on his role as a regional "representative" to enhance the authority of his views. A practical consequence of this situation implies an adherence and defence of the principle of equality of States – something previously articulated by Barbosa in the Second Hague Conference but somewhat shared as a Latin-American pos-

35 Ole Spiermann, '"Who Attempts Too Much Does Nothing Well": The 1920 Advisory Committee of Jurists and the Statute of the Permanent Court of International Justice', (2002) 73 *British Yearbook of International Law*, 235.

36 Nicolas Politis, *La Justice Internationale* (Librairie Hachette, Paris 1924).

37 Advisory Committee of Jurists, *Documents presented to the Committee relating to existing plans for the establishment of a Permanent Court of International Justice 1920*, 222, 228. See also Larissa Ramina, 'Raul Fernandes' in George Rodrigo Bandeira Galindo (ed), *Direito Internacional no Brasil* (Lumen Juris, Rio de Janeiro 2021), 419.

ition.[38] It is interesting to note that one of his functions at the ACJ was to defend the Beviláqua project that represented the official Brazilian position in foreign policy.

Regarding one of the critical points of the project, which was the election of judges, Fernandes supported the Root-Phillimore proposal, that established a simultaneous election carried out by both the Council and the Assembly. This proposal ensured, as a conciliatory measure, an equitable participation of the two bodies in the composition of the Court. By supporting this point, Fernandes contradicted Beviláqua's position, which, at least in theory, should have been defended by the Brazilian representative due to Beviláqua's highest rank and him being the inventor of the idea. This raises the question of whether adherence to the Root-Phillimore proposal relates to personal beliefs or alliance issues in foreign policy.

During the Advisory Committee's debates, Fernandes sometimes played the "Latin American" card to promote ideas connected to the Brazilian Foreign policy and Beviláqua's project.[39] For instance, Fernandes clearly reminded Committee members that Brazil was a member of the Council of the League of Nations and that some proposals would never receive the votes from Latin American states. Fernandes made this reminder to support the Root-Phillimore project. It was the 5th of July, and the Committee members were discussing which project of Court structure should be worked on. After several discussions and some defence for the different projects, Raul Fernandes explained he thought "that he should present Brazil's point of view which in his opinion was the same as Latin America's in general".[40]

38 Antônio Augusto Cançado Trindade, 'The Presence and Participation of Latin America at the II Hague Peace Conference of 1907' in Yves Daudet (ed), *Actualité de la Conférénce de la Haye de 1907: Deuxième Conférence de la Paix* (Académie de Droit International/Martinus Nijhoff Publishers, Leiden/The Hague 2008); Antônio Augusto Cançado Trindade and Alfredo Martínez Moreno, *Doctrina Latinoamericana del Derecho Internacional – vol. 1* (Inter-American Court of Human Rights, San José of Costa Rica 2003), 5.

39 Within the Advisory Committee, Fernandes had developed some innovative ideas that were never explored. For instance, Fernandes strongly defended the idea of imposing penalties to parties which did not respect provisional measures and was very reticent in relation to the exhaustion of diplomatic means as a condition for submitting a dispute to the Court.

40 Advisory Committee of Jurists, *Documents presented to the Committee relating to existing plans for the establishment of a Permanent Court of International Justice 1920*, 365.

In a drastic turn to pragmatism and realism, Fernanes continued pointing out that the principle of equality of States is the test the Court should follow. Still, at the same time, "consideration must be had for undeniable realities, namely that a Court on which the said Powers was not represented would necessarily be impracticable". Here, reality supersedes the notion of equality. To Fernandes, "[i]n a given case the responsibility [of great Powers] and their interests are more deeply affected, since it would be necessary in order to enforce the execution of a sentence that they take coercive measures of a military and economic character. (...) The majority of Members of the League of Nations are immutably opposed to any rule involving disregard for this principle", and finished with a veiled threat: "If the proposals which he objected to were accepted by the Committee, Brazil, in agreement with the majority of States interested, when the time came, would without fail, vote against the project, thus causing the fall of the institution which the whole world wished to see powerful and lasting".[41]

At first glance, one might infer a legal dimension in Fernandes' role in invoking the principle. However, the principle of equality of States seemed rather adaptable as a test for the efficiency of the Court. These excerpts appear to demonstrate that Fernandes was guided by four different considerations: first, the need to uphold the principle of legal equality of States; second, the practical requirements of formulating a compelling project for an international court trying to balance the different interests within the Committee; third, the desire to defend Beviláqua's draft; and fourth, the importance of observing Brazil's interests as a member of the League in the Council and in the Assembly. While it is possible to identify Fernandes support for the Root-Phillimore project in the Advisory Committee, due to the proximity between Brazil and the United States, Beviláqua's project was also invoked as a solution when thorny issues emerged.

A year later when writing about the nascent Court, Fernandes once again defended the compliance of the Court with the principle of the legal equality of States:

> There has always been a division into large and small states: it is the strength of the great powers that it is a question of overcoming. Small nations feel that their lives are in danger if the reign of justice is not secured. The Court will dominate the great and protect the little ones. Therefore, all nations are not in the same situation in the face of the

41 Ibid, 365-367.

> current problem: the great powers make great sacrifices, the small ones sacrifice almost nothing, but they obtain a protection that the great States do not need.[42]

E. Conclusion: Which Regionalism Did Fernandes and Beviláqua Defend?

It is difficult to argue that Beviláqua or Fernandes' performances demonstrated a purely regional or Latin American approach that influenced the Permanent International Court project. It is more accurate to suggest both Beviláqua and Fernandes provided an approach that reflected Brazilian debates and interests in a broader context. The ideas of Beviláqua and Fernandes, as well as those of many others, are articulations of paths that could have been followed by ideas of international justice. The Beviláqua project, although it was little explored in practice, served as a mould for Fernandes' performance at the Advisory Committee of Jurists. Therefore, it is exceedingly difficult to understand one without the other.

Finally, Raul Fernandes' performance can be described as one trying to accommodate a certain idea of compulsory jurisdiction and the tribute of State consent (which was also defended by Beviláqua). To the extent that this tension was also reflected among other authors and authorities in the continent, one can speak of a regional dimension. However, theses discussion also existed beyond Latin America.

In different ways, both lawyers displayed some inclination or affinity for the United States' interests. An examination of the authors' works reveals Fernandes was a Francophile and Beviláqua a Germanophile. However, their inclination towards the U.S. could be explained by virtue of Brazil's foreign policy and the historical proximity of the two countries. In the end, Gastão da Cunha was right because Brazil represented America as a whole, not only Latin America. This illustrates how the principle of legal equality of States was a shield and a sword for espousing the interests of different powers in America

---

42 Raul Fernandes, 'O Princípio da Igualdade Jurídica dos Estados na Atividade Internacional Depois da Guerra' (1921) *Jornal do Commercio*, 17: "Houve sempre uma divisão em grandes e pequenos Estados: é a força das grandes potências que se trata de abater. As pequenas nações sentem que a sua vida está em perigo se o reinado da justiça não for assegurado. A Corte dominará os grandes e protegerá os pequenos. Portanto, todas as nações não estão na mesma situação em presença do problema atual: as grandes potências fazem grandes sacrifícios, as pequenas não sacrificam quase nada, mas obtêm uma proteção de que os grandes Estados não têm necessidade."

Beviláqua's strong ideas and the conciliatory role performed by Fernandes' solutions represent an extension of Brazilian legal foreign policy that articulated a position of centrality of Brazil in the League. In 1926, Brazil got involved in the controversy surrounding Germany's entry into the League and followed the U.S.'s lead by exiting the organization. Within the Brazilian domestic legal system, it was Clóvis Beviláqua who gave the legal opinion justifying the withdrawal of Brazil from the League. To Beviláqua, it was a mere administrative act, an act of self-limitation of the Brazilian state.[43] Beviláqua's vision based on state sovereignty would ultimately prevail, and Brazil would then be officially out of League of Nations.

43 Clóvis Beviláqua, 'Saída do Brasil da Sociedade das Nações e da Corte Permanente de Justiça Internacional' in Antonio Paulo Cachapuz de Medeiros (ed), *Pareceres dos Consultores Jurídicos do Itamaraty – vol. II* (Coleção Brasil 500 Anos/Senado Federal/FUNAG, Brasília 2000), 343.

The Empire of the Rising Sun and the Permanent Court of International Justice – Japan's Role in the Formation Stage

Itai Apter

A. Introduction

The Advisory Committee of Jurists (ACJ) met, on 16-24 July, 1920 in the Peace Palace in the Hague), to discuss the establishment of a Permanent Court of Justice (PCIJ) pursuant to Article 14 of the League of Nations (LoN) Covenant. Mineichirō Adachi, the Japanese delegate, "was certain on his arrival at the Hague, that the Committee would not succeed".[1] Nevertheless, Adachi was very involved in the Committee's discussion, providing important space for a previously lacking Asian perspective on international law and adjudication of international disputes. These dimensions were significant at the time and are relevant today, and should be the focus of future research and consideration by scholars and policy makers alike interested in the design of international dispute resolution mechanisms and a workable and pragmatic international rule of law.

As known, the LoN entrusted the Advisory Committee of Jurists (ACJ) with setting up the PCIJ. The Committee included representatives and delegates of mostly European states. This composition reflected the European origins of the emerging law of nations and the prominence of European scholars, like Hugo Grotius and others, in forming early international law in the centuries before World War I. Japan, represented in the ACJ by Adachi, was one of the three non-European states represented (alongside Brazil and the United States). Despite presenting a different approach to international law and the future operation of the PCIJ, Japan's influence on the PCIJ Statute was significant.

Some scholarly work discusses Japan's positions and contributions to the establishment of the PCIJ in a general context. However, there are

1 Advisory Committee of Jurists, *Procès-Verbaux of the Proceedings of the Committee: June 16th–July 24th 1920*, 542.

relatively few texts which specifically focus on Japan's contribution.[2] The present chapter aims to fill this gap, exploring how Japan's positions related to the PCIJ's subsequent functions, focusing on case law relevant to Japan, the approaches of Japanese PCIJ justices, and related positions that are of contemporary and future relevance to international dispute resolution.

The chapter begins by exploring the place of Imperial Japan on the world stage in the decades preceding the establishment of the PCIJ (section 2). This part of the analysis highlights the shift in the policy of Japanese rulers from isolation to internationalism. Most relevant to the PCIJ's formation, this opening section also considers Japan's participation in the 1899 and 1907 peace conferences and Japan's role in WWI. The most important legal developments of the period discussed hereafter (section 2) are the formation of the Permanent Court of Arbitration (PCA) and the drafting of the LoN Covenant. The paper's second section highlights Japan's role in the constitution of the PCA and the LoN from a legal perspective, including a consideration of some PCA administered proceedings. Proceeding on the basis of earlier findings, the chapter next analyses Japan's positions in the PCIJ Stature negotiations in the temporal legal-political framework (section 3). Setting the scene for what follows, the analysis emphasizes positions concerning the national composition of the bench, the Court's physical location, the standing of the parties before it, and the PCIJ's jurisdiction (section 4). The discussion here also considers Japan's position in respect of the PCIJ's jurisdiction over criminal acts. In respect of jurisdiction, the chapter pays special attention to Japan's approaches on compulsory versus consent-based jurisdiction. In some cases, the Japanese positions have been explained by referring to Japan's unique cultural, social, political and legal characteristics. The debate relates to this type of reasoning, based on the unique characteristics of Japan at that period, interlinking it to the temporal background. The chapter finally explores how the Japanese ideas contributed to achieving the expressed goals of the PCIJ, and how these were reflected in the functioning of the PCIJ until its demise in 1940 (section 5).

2 For a relatively recent example see Tetsuya Toyoda, 'A Civilizational Pluralist and Inegalitarian: Miniechiro Adachi (1869-1934)' in P. Sean Morris (ed), *The League of Nations and the Development of International Law: A New Intellectual History of the Advisory Committee of Jurists* (Routledge, Oxon 2022), 74.

B. Japan in the pre-PCIJ Era – The Peace Conferences and WWI

Until the mid-19th century, Japan was considered as a territory largely isolated from the global order, far away from most of the international community. Japan's trade relations were mostly limited to geographically close China and Korea, and to cooperation with the Dutch and the Portuguese. This was part of the isolation policy that Japan's rulers proclaimed three centuries before. The policy was termed as 'Sakuko' (the closed country). Sakuko aimed at protecting the regime and the Japanese way of life from outside religious and political, and foreign influences.[3]

Under this 'closed state' governance system, external trade was severely limited, combined with measures directed at preserving the regime in place. The aim was to avoid conflicts with foreign powers, and to minimize external cultural influences.[4] The causes of this isolationist policy were associated with the creation of a class feudal based society, based on ancient principles.[5] In practice this meant that Japanese society was immune to international developments elevating the status of individual rights. The development of such rights featured prominently on the legal stage around the world, following the French Revolution, and was also slowly making its way to the law of nations that was gradually taking shape.[6]

This isolationist trend was somewhat transformed in the mid-19th century. Japanese leaders in the Meiji Era identified the potential of utilizing international law to cement Japan's standing in the global legal order of the period. In 1868 the Meiji leaders declared that Japan would conduct its foreign relations in accordance with public international law. This was especially challenging as international law was considered generally applicable only between Christian nations.[7] This step by Japan's rulers could be viewed as an important, and courageous, move towards Japan's integration

3 Tessa Morris-Suzuki, *The Technological Transformation of Japan: From the Seventeenth to the Twenty-First Century* (Cambridge University Press, Cambridge, 1994), 15-18.

4 This was done through what is termed as 'edicts' on contacts with foreigners including respect of trade (with some exceptions). Michael S. Laver, *The Sakuko Edicts and the Politics of Tokugawa Hegemony* (Cambria Press, New York 2011), x.

5 Jackie Hogan, *Gender, Race and National Identity: Nations of Flesh and Blood* (Routledge, New York 2009), 40.

6 For a counterclaim, including the assertion that was rioting in Japan at the same time as the French Revolution see Jordan Sand, 'Megacity One' (2021) 43 *London Review of Books*, 1 (11).

7 Susumu Yamauchi, 'Civilization of International Law in Japan During the Meiji Era (1868-1912)' (1996) 24 *Hitotsubashi Journal of Law and Politics*, 1 (2-3).

into the international law community, despite the challenges posed by its European orientation and origin.

Eminent Japanese scholars believed that Japan could employ international law to claim its independence and sovereignty as state equal to all other states in the international community.[8] The embracing of international law by the Meiji regime did not stop there. Japan took an important step further and declared it was committed to the laws of nations in the conduct of hostilities against China in the Sino-Japanese war of 1894.[9] This declaration was echoed by a leading Japanese international legal academic who stated that "it was the earnest intention of the Japanese government to do everything in accordance with international law".[10] Yamauchi argues that the purpose of this declaration was two-fold: first, avoiding a pretext for intervention of European powers, and second, emphasizing the characterization of Japan as a civilized nation.[11] The purported adherence to international law by Japan also featured in the Russia-Japan war of 1904-1905. Some historians argued that Japan was "(...) taking no liberties with accepted international practice (...)".[12] The declarations by the Meiji regime indicated that Japan was ready to subject itself to restrictions imposed by international law (the laws of war) and not to merely pay lip-service to general principles of international law.

The laws of war were at the time was only at their embryonic stage. In 1863, guidance was developed for Union soldiers in the American Civil War termed as the Lieber Code, based upon earlier notions of laws aimed at regulating 'just war' theories.[13] The Lieber Code focused on the basic

8 Ibid.

9 For an analysis of Japan's conduct during the war in accordance with this declaration, with some notable exceptions, see Douglas Howland, 'Japan's Civilized War: International Law as Diplomacy in the Sino-Japanese War (1894-1895)' (2007) 9 *Journal of the History of International Law*, 179.

10 Rune Svarverud, *International Law as World Order in Late Imperial China: Translation, Reception and Discourse 1847-1911* (Brill, Leiden/Boston 2007), 62.

11 Susumu Yamauchi, 'Civilization of International Law in Japan During the Meiji Era (1868-1912)' (1996) 24 *Hitotsubashi Journal of Law and Politics*, 10.

12 As quoted in Rune Svarverud, *International Law as World Order in Late Imperial China: Translation, Reception and Discourse 1847-1911* (Brill, Leiden 2007), 64.

13 For elaboration see Patrik I. Labuda, 'Lieber Code' in Frauke Lachenmann and Rüdiger Wolfrum (eds), *The Law of Armed Conflict and the Use of Force. The Max Planck Encyclopedia of Public International Law* (Oxford University Press, Oxford 2017), 663.

principles of distinction between combatants and non-combatants.[14] The Code reflected a somewhat precedential codification of protections of non-combatants while recognizing military necessity.[15] This was followed by more expansive provisions in the first 1864 Geneva Convention, the 1874 Brussels Declaration, and the 1880 Oxford Manual on the Laws of War.[16] The Meiji regime still choose to adopt the modern notions of the laws of war despite their restrictive manner, highlighting its willingness to become part of the international community even if this came at a price.

The first Hague Peace Conference took place in 1899. In the years before the Conference, Japan joined various international treaties, cementing its position in the international community.[17] Japanese officials were keenly aware that the main aim of the Conference was to promote peace amongst European nations. Nevertheless, they still saw merit in participating. This might be explained by their understanding that the declared aim was achieving a global cessation of hostilities, or out of a possible premonition that the Conference was a starting point for creating a modern system of international adjudication of disputes by peaceful means. [18]

Alongside discourse on disarmament, the main idea discussed in the 1899 Conference was establishing a permanent court for resolving conflicts between nations. The Conference discussions brought forth the first signs of the emergence of both the Hague Permanent Court of Arbitration (the PCA) and the Permanent Court of International Justice (PCIJ).[19] Japan seemed to have supported these constructs, including a compulsory arbitration mechanism to resolve international conflicts between states.[20]

14 The Lieber Code was considered as one of the first attempts to codify the laws of war, including the principle of distinction. J. Martin Rochester, *The New Warfare: Rethinking Rules for an Unruly World* (Routledge, New York 2016), 55.

15 Hugo Slim, 'Civilians, 'Distinction and the Companionate View of War' in Haidi Willmot et al. (eds), *Protection of Civilians* (Oxford University Press, Oxford 2016), 15.

16 Judith Gail Gardam, *Non-combatant Immunity as a Norm of International Humanitarian Law* (Martinus Nijhoff, Dordrecht/Boston/London 1993), 18-19.

17 Klaus Shlichtman, 'Japan, Germany and the Idea of the Hague Peace Conferences' (2003) 40 *Journal of Peace Research*, 377 (379).

18 Ibid, 382.

19 For an analysis of the discussion on international adjudication during the 1899 Conference see David D. Caron, 'Symposium: The Hague Peace Conferences, War and International Adjudication: Reflections on the 1899 Conference' (2000) 94 *The American Journal of International Law*, 4.

20 Klaus Schlichtmann, 'Japan, Germany and the Idea of the Hague Peace Conferences' (2003) 40 *Journal of Peace Research*, 377 (384).

Interestingly, both the Japanese government and some sections of the Japanese public supported the idea of a mediation and arbitration convention, including the noted mandatory mechanisms, to promote international peace.[21] After the Conference, in 1900, Japan acceded to the 1899 Hague Convention (which did not include a binding adjudication mechanism). Japan also nominated one Japanese judge and one foreign jurist to represent it in the envisioned court.[22]

In 1907, Japan participated in the second Hague Peace Conference. The 'covert' participation of a Korean delegation in the Conference posed a challenge for Japan (the Secret Emissary affair).[23] Unsurprisingly, the conference again discussed the option of imposing an obligation on states to accept arbitration for the resolution of disputes with other states.[24] Recognizing that that the question of compulsory or voluntary subjection to arbitration to resolve disputes was a mainly European affair, Japan was reluctant to take sides.

At the same time, because of Japan's troublesome experience with an arbitration proceeding in 1905, the Japanese delegation was supposed to object to compulsory arbitration. However, upon further consideration, Japan abstained in the vote on the issue, due to pressures by the French delegation.[25] Schlichtmann argues that Japan's participation in the Peace Conferences reflected its willingness to take an active part in the formation of the global legal order at the time. However, Japan's involvement in the 1907 Conference stopped short of an express and explicit legal undertaking

21 Ibid.

22 Ibid.

23 Klaus Shlichtman, 'Japan, Germany and the Idea of the Hague Peace Conferences' (2003) 40 *Journal of Peace Research*, 377 (388). Delegates from Korea suddenly appeared at the Hague Conference at the end of June 1907 (during the conference which lasted from 15 June to 18 September 1907) claiming they were representing the Korean Emperor. The delegates made allegations against Japan's conduct towards Korea. According to news reports the Korean Emperor claimed that these delegates forged their credentials and did not represent him. This event is referred to as the Secret Emissary Affair, Chung Kweon-hyun, 'The Heroes of the Hague Secret Emissary Affair', Chosun Ilbo, http://english.chosun.com/m/news/article.amp.html?contid=2007060761009.

24 A. van Blankenstein, 'Enforcement of an Arbitral Award against a State: With Whom are You Dealing?' (1993) 6 *Leiden Journal of International Law*, 353 (373).

25 Klaus Shlichtman, 'Japan, Germany and the Idea of the Hague Peace Conferences' (2003) 40 *Journal of Peace Research*, 377 (390).

to be bound by international arbitration for resolving international disputes with other states.[26]

Japan's role in WWI was limited, although it joined the Allied forces as part of its 1902 alliance with Great Britain, responding to the requests by the British for assistance in the Pacific war arena.[27] Japan again made clear, in its declaration of war on Germany, that it would "attain its national aim within the limit of the law of nations".[28] This once again highlighted Japan's trust at the time in international regulation of relationships between states, including when it came to hostilities.

C. Japan, the PCA and the League of Nations

In 1905, the PCA (then known as the International Court of Arbitration) ruled against Japan in the Japanese House Tax Decision in respect of exemptions from taxation in regards to land held by foreign investors.[29] Despite this loss, Japan still did not hesitate to join the PCA. Japan ratified the Convention on the establishment of the Permanent Court of Arbitration in 1912.[30] It saw the importance of adhering to international frameworks even if the price to be paid might be high.

In 1912, Japan was involved in a dispute with the state of California in respect of legislation preventing Japanese ownership of land. According to at least one source, Japan considered submitting the dispute to be resolved by the PCA, on the basis of an arbitration treaty concluded in 1908 between

26 Ibid, 391.

27 Christina L. Davis, 'Linkage Diplomacy: Economic and Security Bargaining in the Anglo-Japanese Alliance, 1902-1923' (2008-2009) 33 *International Security*, 143 (147).

28 Coleman Phillipson, *International Law and the Great War* (T. Fisher Unwin, London 2005), 62.

29 *Germany, France and Great Britain v. Japan*, PCA Case No. 1902-2 (21 May 1905). For an analysis of the case, the decision and its impacts see Douglas Howland, 'The Japan House Tax Case, 1899-1905: Leases in Perpetuity and the Myth of International Equity', (2015) 75 *Zeitschrift für ausländisches öffentliches Recht und Völkerrecht*, 413.

30 PCA website, Member States, https://pca-cpa.org/en/about/introduction/contracting-parties.

the US and Japan.[31] However, Japan decided no not pursue action in the PCA, possibly due to its previous bad experience with the Court.[32]

Following WWI, the Allied forces decided to hold the 1919 Paris Peace Conference, which would result in the establishment of the LoN. The five prominent global powers, including Japan, attended the conference.[33] The inclusion of Japan in the conference, as a 'latecomer' reflected the perception in the international community that it was one of the winning states of WWI.[34] At the same time, as Smith has pointed out, the decision to include Japan corresponded with the Wilsonian approach to international relations. This could be understood from Wilson's speeches highlighting the idea that Japan would join the other great powers not only in the material sense, but also in the 'moral' one.[35] According to Smith, Wilson was mainly motivated by Japan's status before the war as a regional power, including its close alliance with Great Britain), and his expectation that Japan would be the main power in Asia.[36]

The Wilsonian approach chimed well with the renewed shift in the Japanese administration towards internationalism and cooperation with the West, following disappointing outcomes of military conflicts, especially concerning China and Manchuria. This policy, based on economic diplomacy, was termed 'Shidehara diplomacy', turning away from Machiavellian and aggressive approaches to economic cooperation, peace and justice as tenants of foreign Japanese foreign policy.[37] The basic precepts of Shidehara diplomacy were reflected in the composition of the Japanese delegation to

31 The agreement was signed following a period of tension between the two countries. Thomas A. Bailey, 'The Root-Takahira Agreement of 1908' (1940) 9 *Pacific Historical Review*, 19 (21).

32 Klaus Schlichtman, *Japan in the World: Shidehara Kijūrō, Pacifism, and the Abolition of War, Volume 1* (Lexington Books, USA 2009), 242.

33 Leonard V. Smith, *Sovereignty at the Paris Peace Conference* (Oxford University Press, Oxford 2018), 23.

34 Thomas W. Burkman, *Japan and the League of Nations – Empire and World Order, 1914-1938* (University of Hawaii Press, Honolulu 2008), xii; Naoko Shimazu, 'Japan at the Paris Peace Conference of 1919: A Centennial Reflection', (2019) 3 *Japan Review*, 10 (13).

35 Leonard V. Smith, *Sovereignty at the Paris Peace Conference* (Oxford University Press, Oxford 2018), 23-24.

36 Ibid.

37 Sadao Asada, 'Between the Old Diplomacy and the New, 1918–1922: The Washington System and the Origins of Japanese-American Rapprochement' (2006) 30 *Diplomatic History*, 211 (228-229).

the 1919 Peace Conference, which included pro-Western internationalists and diplomats with ties to the Ministry of Foreign Affairs.[38]

The Japanese attitude towards the establishment of the LoN was somewhat reluctant and suspicious. This resulted from concerns that the LoN would develop policies dominated by Western powers seeking their own interests, while ignoring the interests of countries in other regions, including Japan.[39] At the same time, if the LoN was to be established, Japan wanted to be a part of it. Thus, the main aim was to direct efforts to design the PCIJ's structures as to mitigate any harmful outcomes to Japan from its operations.[40]

This was the basis for the 'racial equality proposal', the major policy initiative submitted by Japan to the Covenant of the LoN.[41] The original proposal read as follows:

> The equality of nations being a basic principle of the League of Nations, the High Contracting Parties agree to accord as soon as possible to all alien nationals of states, members of the League, equal and just treatment in every respect making no distinction, either in law or in fact, on account of their race or nationality.[42]

While the proposal received some support, Australia vehemently opposed it, and the British Delegation objected as well.[43] Due to this objection, Japan had to be satisfied with the proposal being recorded in the minutes of the Conference.[44]

Following this defeat, some members of the Japanese delegation recommended the government not to join the Treaty of Versailles. Nevertheless,

---

38 Naoko Shimazu, *Japan, Race and Equality: The Racial Equality Proposal of 1919* (Psychology Press, London 2009), 19.

39 Thomas W. Burkman, *Japan and the League of Nations – Empire and World Order, 1914-1938* (University of Hawaii Press, Honolulu 2008), 23.

40 Burkman argues that this shift reflects the fact that the Japanese delegation to the Paris Conference abandoned its initial obstructionist approach it displayed in at the outset of the Paris Conference and adopted a more constructive approach to the negotiations. Thomas W. Burkman, *Japan and the League of Nations – Empire and World Order, 1914-1938* (University of Hawaii Press, Honolulu 2008), 46.

41 Ibid.

42 For an extended analysis see Naoko Shimazu, *Japan, Race and Equality: The Racial Equality Proposal of 1919* (Psychology Press, London 2009).

43 Thomas W. Burkman, *Japan and the League of Nations – Empire and World Order, 1914-1938* (University of Hawaii Press, Honolulu 2008), 46.

44 Ibid.

once again overcoming initial resistance at joining or adhering to mostly European-led international initiatives, Japan decided to sign, and join the LoN as one of the four Charter founding members and League Council members (a Japanese national was also appointed to the role of Under-Secretary-General).[45] This reflected the positive attitude of senior officials in the Japanese political establishment, also reflected in the negotiations which led to the establishment of the PCIJ.

D. Japan and the PCIJ Statute Negotiations

As a League Council member, Japan nominated a representative to the ACJ. The representative appointed, after the initial nomination fell through, was the aforementioned Mineichirō Adachi, a prominent international law Japanese scholar and diplomat who served as the Japanese Ambassador to Belgium.[46] It is difficult to know whether the Japanese approach would have been different if the Adachi was not chosen to replace the originally envisaged delegate to the ACJ.

Adachi regularly updated Tokyo on the progress of the various stages of the discourse and expressed opinions which reflected the unique nature of the characteristics of Japan and the Far-Eastern world. Adachi was the sole representative of the region who participated in the meetings.

The *first* issue where Adachi voiced a strong view concerned the composition of the PCIJ judiciary. He empathically stressed that if all kinds of civilizations would not be represented, this would undermine the legitimacy of the court in the eyes of the world (beyond the Great Powers).[47] Moreover, Adachi made it clear that if Japan, despite its distance from the center of European activity, would not be represented, the Japanese people would never subject themselves to its jurisdiction.[48] This is very much akin to contemporary ideas in international law-making about "nothing about us without us", which seem to have been a mainstay in Adachi's position

45 Tosh Minohara, Shusuke Takhara, Ryota Murai, 'The Great War and Shifting Relations' in Makto Iokibe and Tosh Minohara (eds), *The History of US-Japan Relations: From Perry to the Present* (Springer Singapore, Singapore 2017), 43.

46 Roy Hidemichi Akagi, *Japan's Foreign Relations, 1542-1936: A Short History* (Hokuseido Press, Tokyo 1936), 460.

47 Advisory Committee of Jurists, *Procès-Verbaux of the Proceedings of the Committee: June 16th–July 24th 1920*, 136.

48 Ibid.

throughout the deliberations. Responding to this proposal, Hagerup, the representative of Norway to the ACJ, first noted the validity of the position by Root (the US representative) that great powers would not wish to submit their will to secondary states. At the same time, he agreed with Adachi's views that if the PCIJ project was to succeed, it would be important to have the support of the publics of all states involved. According to Hagerup this could be achieved by allowing secondary states to also be represented in the court.[49]

After some discussion, it was Adachi who proposed the language for the text of the relevant article in the PCIJ Statute, which stated that each LoN member would have the right to nominate a permanent judge (alongside other judges to be appointed by the LoN Assembly).[50]

Continuing down the path of rationalizing his views by reference to Japan and the Far East, Adachi pointed out that if judges would not be provided with permanent positions, this would make it almost impossible for those which did not reside in Europe to take up positions.[51] Loder, the representative of the Netherlands, and Ricci-Busatti, the representative of Italy, agreed with the idea posed by Adachi and shared his concerns, but both raised questions about whether the anticipated workload of the PCIJ would justify providing permanent positions for judges. They noted that this would be dependent upon the question of the competence of the court and whether it would allow standing for individuals and not only to states.[52]

It was also very important to Adachi that, if a state is party to a dispute before the PCA, a judge of its nationality would also sit in on the proceedings. Adachi explained that after consulting with European and Asiatic friends and colleagues, he concluded that this would contribute to an efficient resolution of cases brought before the PCIJ.[53] He later explained that, because of the unique nature of different societies (including societies from the Far East like Japan, not based on Christianity but rather on ideas related to Buddhism, Shintoism and Confucianism), it would be important that a judge coming from such a background explain decisions to domestic audiences utilizing concepts familiar to them.[54] Phillimore, the representative of

49 Ibid, 137-138.
50 Ibid, 165.
51 Ibid, 187.
52 Ibid, 188-189.
53 Ibid, 168.
54 Ibid, 529-530.

the UK, agreed with Adachi's views on the need for a national judge if the party in question is not represented by a judge.[55] Loder, on the other hand, argued that appointing a national judge would not increase confidence in the PCIJ, although he did agree that national assessors can be appointed to preform advisory functions.[56]

At a later stage in the discussion, Adachi again highlighted the importance of Japanese involvement in selection of the judges, wholeheartedly endorsing the view that candidates would be elected by governments, and not by justices of the PCA.[57] Other members, including Ricci-Busatti, De Lapradelle, questioned this position.[58] Ricci-Busatti noted the importance of a non-political process of nomination,[59] while De Lapradelle noted that there would not be a real difference between election by the PCA justices and governments, as the justices would in any case be heavily influenced by the governments which nominated them.[60]

The *second* issue Adachi was interested in concerned the physical location of the PCIJ. Adachi supported the placement of PCIJ in the Hague Peace Palace, and not at the seat of the LoN (i.e. Geneva). He explained that, in addition to the advantage of separating the political body of the LoN from its judicial arm, this would reflect the perception of Asiatic countries. Adachi added that "in Japan, when Hague is mentioned, this means peace and justice".[61] This position was supported by various members of the AJC, with only De Lapradelle noting that he might have reservations. Loder expressed gratitude for this position, assuring the ACJ that "Holland" would do its best to serve as the host country for the PCIJ.[62]

The *third* important issue in respect of which Adachi chose to voice an opinion was which actors would have access to the Court. This question came up in the context of the discussion of whether minorities should be afforded access to the PCIJ. This question was part of overall thematic

55 Ibid, 169.
56 Ibid.
57 Ibid, 414.
58 Ibid, 416, 418-419.
59 Ibid, 416.
60 Ibid, 414.
61 Ibid, 203.
62 Ibid, 203.

discourse of the dilemmas surrounding the approach the LoN should take with respect to protection of minorities following WWI.[63]

Adachi supported limiting access to the PCIJ only to states, asserting that if states would wish to take upon issues of their subjects to the Court, they could have the opportunity to so.[64] Unlike Adachi's positions so far discussed, this time he did not provide an explanation that linked his position to Japanese or Asiatic notions. It could be that he was thinking about the Korean aspiration for independence from Japan (the Secret Emissaries case discussed above).[65] Alternatively, Adachi might have linked this idea to diplomatic protection, which considered states as representatives of their nationals in international disputes with other states.[66] Altamira, the representative of Spain, and Hagerup of Norway, supported Adachi's views. Altamira explained his views by referring to the basic notion of diplomatic protection.[67] De Lapradelle and Loder objected. The former argued that individuals should be allowed access to the PCIJ in cases of denial of justice between individuals and states.[68] The latter cautioned that limiting competence to inter-state disputed would be contrary to the basic ideas of the LoN.[69]

In respect of a different aspect of this question, Adachi supported wide access for any state wishing to utilize the PCIJ for dispute resolution, including those who were not members of the LoN.[70] All members of the ACJ who voiced an opinion on this issue agreed with Adachi's view.[71] Root noted in particular that the purpose of the LoN was to prevent war, associating this goal with the need to allow every state access to the PCIJ.[72]

---

63 Antônio Augusto Cançado Trindade, 'Some Reflections on the Forthcoming Centenary of the Statute of the Hague Court' in Giuliana Ziccardi Capaldo (ed), *The Global Community Yearbook of International Law and Jurisprudence 2019* (Oxford University Press, Oxford 2020), 3 (9).

64 Advisory Committee of Jurists, *Procès-Verbaux of the Proceedings of the Committee: June 16th–July 24th 1920*, 204-205.

65 See footnote 23 and the accompanying text.

66 Advisory Committee of Jurists, *Procès-Verbaux of the Proceedings of the Committee: June 16th–July 24th 1920*, 220.

67 Ibid, 205.

68 Ibid.

69 Ibid, 206.

70 Ibid, 221.

71 Ibid, 222.

72 Ibid, 223.

The *fourth* matter which Adachi expressed views on was the question of the jurisdiction of the Court. Adachi first and foremost addressed the question of whether it would be necessary that both states parties to the litigation would be required to consent to the jurisdiction of the PCIJ. Adachi was adamant that the PCIJ would only be able to adjudicate disputes where both parties agreed to its jurisdiction.[73] He based his views on the legal framework of the LoN.[74] Adachi explained that if one state would be allowed to force litigation in the PCIJ onto the other, this could pose significant obstacles to the progress of the Court.[75] At some point in the discussion of the ACJ, there seemed to have been much support for the PCIJ to expand its jurisdiction beyond the consent of parties. This was explained by Descamps, the representative of France and the chair of the ACJ, as reflecting what was agreed upon in the 1907 Hague Conference.[76] Adachi was concerned about this direction. He delivered a passionate speech warning ACJ members that establishing such expansive jurisdiction would be detrimental to its success, which he considered vital.[77] Surprisingly, Adachi's arguments in opposition to compulsory jurisdiction were different from those voiced by other members of the ACJ. Arguments by other members focused on differences in approaches towards international law between common law systems and other legal traditions; failures to reach agreement on compulsory jurisdiction in the context of naval warfare (Root); and concerns that weaker states would impose litigation on the stronger states and off-set economic and military advantages.[78] Again, Adachi did not provide a 'Japanese' or an 'Asiatic' explanation for his objections to the compulsory jurisdiction of the PCIJ. However, his approach seems to chime well with the earlier reluctance of Japan to join the PCA and its suspicious attitude towards internationalism in the decades before the PCIJ negotiations. This position also fits with the Japanese aim, in respect of the LoN, to make sure that its interests would be protected from European compulsion.

73 Ibid, 225.

74 Ibid. Adachi referred to Article 14 of the LoN Statute.

75 Ibid.

76 Ibid, 228.

77 Ibid, 541-543.

78 Sara McLaughlin Mitchell and Emilia Justyna Powell, *Domestic Law Goes Global: Legal Traditions and International Courts* (Cambridge University Press, Cambridge 2011), 131-132; Advisory Committee of Jurists, *Procès-Verbaux of the Proceedings of the Committee: June 16th–July 24th 1920*, 286.

When it came to the question of endowing the Court with jurisdiction over international crimes, possibly as a court which would be separate from the PCIJ, Adachi voiced support. However, Adachi pointed out that the ACJ did not have a mandate (or the time) to explore this option.[79] Similarly, Ricci-Busatti, Loder, Fernandes (the representative of Brazil), expressed sympathy for the idea of PCIJ jurisdiction for international crimes, yet pointed out various procedural and substantial difficulties with this idea, referring to concerns associated with definitional issues and the mandate of the ACJ.[80]

The analysis in the foregoing presents an interesting snapshot of Japanese views on the design of the PCIJ. These ranged from positions clearly associated with an Asian perspective, to advance ideas and approaches which seemed to have been absent at times from the discussions. Even when the positions were not manifestly associated with the regional perspective, or ultimately rejected, they influenced the discussions and ultimate outcomes in ways which would impact its future operations.

E. The Japanese Positions and their Impact on the PCIJ

I. The Composition of the Court

Starting with the *composition of the Court*, the impact of the Japanese approach may be self-evident. At the end of the day, after much discussion and following several more comments made by Adachi on the importance of representation of all members of the LoN,[81] a relatively complicated system of appointment of judges to the PCIJ was devised.[82] Most relevant to the positions stated by Adachi, the PCIJ Statute stipulated that

> At every election, the electors shall bear in mind that not only should all the persons appointed as members of the Court possess the qualifica-

79 Advisory Committee of Jurists, *Procès-Verbaux of the Proceedings of the Committee: June 16th–July 24th 1920*, 502.

80 Ibid, 504-510.

81 Ibid, 384-385.

82 Articles 2-15 PCIJ Statute.

> tions required, but the whole body also should represent the main forms of civilization and the principal legal systems of the world.[83]

Scholarship hailed this as a major achievement of Japan in impacting the functioning of the PCIJ, defined as "plurality of civilizations" (also embodied in the ICJ Statute).[84] This achievement was an important one, and very far from the original 'Sekuko' policy of isolation.

The PCIJ was the first court in history which was considered a 'World Court', or the "first selective representation international court".[85] This term can be associated with many factors related to the origins of the Court, but also with the decision by the ACJ to ensure a universal composition of the court with representatives of various and diverse legal and political cultures.

The variety of the nationalities and cultural backgrounds of the PCIJ justices, alongside their distinct fields of expertise and knowledge of international law and other fields of law, brought to the fore different approaches to the resolution of cases.[86] The combination of the different specialisations and judicial temperaments contributed to a balance in decision-making and process that underlay the judgements issued by the PCIJ. This was because the justices applied different views and approaches to the issues brought before the Court.[87] Such an outcome can be directly associated with Adachi's push for "plurality of civilizations".

As could be expected, the varieties of the background of the justices caused some difficulties to the operation of the PCIJ, as was the case for example in respect of the first Japanese justice on the bench. Yorozu Oda serving on the court between 1922-1930, was not an international law expert and had problems following deliberations due to language issues (he had only a basic knowledge of French).[88] He was also purported to have wide knowledge of Chinese and Japanese classical literature, thus realizing the

83 Article 9 PCIJ Statute.

84 Tetsuya Toyoda, 'Japan's Early Challenge to Eurocenterism' in Felix Rösch and Atsuko Watanabe (eds), *Modern Japanese Political Thought and International Relations* (Rowman & Littlefield Publishers, Lanham 2018), 43 (45).

85 Ruth Mackenzie et al., *Selecting International Judges* (Oxford University Press, Oxford 2010), 13.

86 Robert Kolb, *The Elgar Companion to the International Court of Justice* (Edward Elgar Publishing, London 2014), 136.

87 Ibid.

88 Ibid, 138.

early visions of Adachi in the negotiations of the PCIJ Statute.[89] Alongside Oda, later replaced by Adachi himself (serving from 1930-1934), it is also worth mentioning the other Asian justice from China, Wang Chung-hui (serving from 1931-1936). The latter boasted an educational background from almost all leading societies of the time, including China, Japan, England, Germany and the US.[90]

Adachi's proposal of national judges sitting *ad hoc* on cases before the PCIJ, where their nation state was a party, also had an important impact on decision-making in the PCIJ. This approach and its outcome is also viewed as the "original approach" to the issue, later duplicated by the ICJ and other international tribunals.[91] In most of such cases (with some notable exceptions), national judges vote in support of the arguments of their states.[92] Despite this tendency for bias on behalf of the appointing state, some commentators argued at the time that this process has practical merits. These commentators argue that the *ad hoc* national judges have been able to represent the legal systems of the parties to the disputes before the Court, and "have increased confidence of nations in the tribunal [the PCIJ]".[93]

However, it is important to note that judges did not always support the positions of their states. In the *SS Wimbledon* case, Anzilotti, the Italian judge, voted against Italy's position before the Court.[94] This phenomenon of national judges not supporting the positions of their government was highlighted by Oda, referencing another example, as an important manifes-

89 Ibid.

90 Ibid.

91 For an argument that this "original approach" does not reflect present day realities see Tom Dannenbaum, 'Nationality and the International Judge: The Nationalist Presumption Governing the International Judiciary and Why it Must Be Reversed' (2012) 45 *Cornell International Law Journal*, 77 (183).

92 Charlotte Ku, 'International Court of Justice' in Thomas G. Weiss and Sam Daws (eds), *The Oxford Handbook on the United Nations* (2nd edn, Oxford University Press, Oxford 2018), 190 (194).

93 Shigeru Oda, 'What the International Court Has Done' (1928) 3 *Pacific Affairs*, 17 (18).

94 Wilhelm Georg Grewe and Michael Byers, *The Epochs of International Law* (De Gruyter, Berlin/Boston 2013), 615. This example is often provided to highlight that national judges in the PCIJ (or the ICJ) did not always vote in favor of their nominating state. However, at least according to this source, no real Italian interest was at stake, as Italy was only formally part of the case, making this example less significant.

tation of the impartiality of international justice.[95] Others, like former ICJ Justice Schwabel, noted the following:

> While national judges in the large majority of cases have voted consistently with the position of their countries, this is not so in a significant minority (...) In a number of other cases, judges of the Permanent Court (...) have voted contrary to the submissions of their own country, among them, Lord Finlay, Judge Weiss (...)[96]

In 1929, PCIJ President Dionisio Anzilotti also referred to Lord Finlay's decisions as exceptions to the inclination of national judges to adopt the positions of the countries which nominated them.[97]

II. The Physical Location of the PCIJ

The PCIJ's Hague Peace Palace location was preserved for almost the entirety of the period of its functioning. This was until its eventual brief relocation to Geneva in 1940, due to the invasion of Germany to the Netherlands, before completely ceasing operations in light of WWII.[98]

It is questionable whether Adachi's reasoning that physical separation from the LoN seat in Geneva would result in judicial independence from the LoN's political sphere proved to be correct. According to some commentators, the answer was in the negative. According to Amr, the PCIJ was part of the machinery of the LoN in its aim to promote peaceful resolution of disputes.[99]

---

95 Shigeru Oda, 'What the International Court Has Done' (1928) 3 *Pacific Affairs*, 17 (18).

96 Stephen M. Schwabel, 'National Judges and Judges Ad Hoc of the International Court of Justice' (1999) 48 *International Comparative Law Quarterly*, 889 (893).

97 See for example Tom Dannenbaum, 'Nationality and the International Judge: The Nationalist Presumption Governing the International Judiciary and Why it Must Be Reversed' (2012) 45 *Cornell International Law Journal*, 77 (136).

98 From 1940 onwards the PCIJ did not really function and this move of the location of the President of the PCIJ and its Registrar was likely only a formality. Malgosia Fitzmaurice and Christian J. Tams, 'Introduction' in Malgosia Fitzmaurice and Christian J. Tams (eds), *Legacies of the Permanent Court of Justice* (Martinus Nijhoff, Leiden/Boston 2013), 1 (2).

99 Mohammed Sameh M. Amr, *The Role of the International Court of Justice as the Principal Judicial Organ of the United Nations* (Brill, London/Boston 2003), 15.

Looking back, bearing in mind that the collapse of the LoN did coincide with the PCIJ's closure of operations, it did not seem to be the case that its functions could have been considered as "organic" to the LoN,[100] and that its operations were very much dependent on the "political bodies to which it was affiliated".[101] Others offer a more balanced and nuanced view, noting the role played by the PCIJ in providing advisory opinions to the LoN. According to this balanced approach, as long as the global political climate was peaceful, the relationship (particularly on the administrative and financial side) between the PCIJ and the LoN benefitted the latter; but in times of global crisis the close ties between the institutions placed obstacles on its substantive work,[102] ultimately leading to its demise.

III. Standing before the PCIJ

Limiting the standing before the PCIJ to states, an aspect with regard to which Adachi's positions in the ACJ were accepted as well, proved to be an important element of the Court's operation. This was because it had an impact on the accessibility of parties to the PCIJ and the cases brought for its adjudication. Nevertheless, it is difficult to assess whether the limitation of standing to the PCIJ only to states did not limit its sphere of influence. In this respect, while states did turn to the Court to resolve disputes, based on express consent or on the basis of reference in existing agreements, the tendency was to only refer disputes of relatively technical nature to adjudication, rather than disputes of a much more complicated and controversial manner. [103]

Clarifying his reluctance to a more expansive standing, Adachi explained that states can make the case for their own nationals, and they did resort to this option in several cases. Indeed, PCIJ case law highlighted that when states act in such a manner they are asserting their own rights under inter-

100 Ibid, 18.

101 Judith Resnik and Dennis Edward Curtis, *Representing Justice: Invention, Controversy, and Rights in City-states and Democratic Courtrooms* (Yale University Press, Connecticut 2011), 260.

102 Shabtai Rosenne, *The Law and Practice of the International Court, 1920-2005* (Brill, London/Boston 2006), 97-101.

103 Christian J. Tams, 'The Contentious Jurisdiction of the Permanent Court' in Christian J. Tams and Malgosia Fitzmaurice (eds), *Legacies of the Permanent Court of Justice* (Martinus Nijhoff, Leiden/Boston 2013), 27.

national law, as an injury caused to a national of a state can be considered an injury to the state itself.[104]

As noted, Adachi also considered it important that non-LoN members would have access to the PCIJ. As cases involving Germany and Poland have demonstrated, non-LoN members did participate in proceedings, and the underlying legal framework did not place obstacles on such participation.[105]

IV. Compulsory Jurisdiction of the PCIJ

On the PCIJ's jurisdiction, as noted, Adachi advocated for a consent requirement and against compulsory jurisdiction. Despite his objection to compulsory jurisdiction, Adachi himself tried, in 1930, to convince the Japanese government to accept such jurisdiction by the PCIJ. His efforts did not bear fruit.[106]

At the end of the day, the ACJ included a provision allowing states to provide the PCIJ with compulsory jurisdiction under certain circumstances, in the context of bilateral and multilateral treaties, which could be termed the "optional clause of compulsory jurisdiction".[107] Despite the fact that this mechanism did not compel states to subject themselves to the PCIJ jurisdiction, Adachi strongly objected to it, emphasizing the potentially dangerous consequences and diversion from the mandate provided to the Commission by the LoN.[108]

From a substantive perspective, it is difficult to tell whether the consent requirement and compulsory jurisdiction contributed to the success of the PCIJ (at least until 1940), or rather caused it to fail. According to some contemporary scholars, while the PCIJ did make important contributions

104 *Mavrommatis Palestine Concessions Case (Greece v. United Kingdom)* 30 August 1924, PCIJ, Series A, No. 2 (1924); *Panevezys–Saldutiskis Railway Case (Estonia v. Lithuania)*, 28 February 1939, PCIJ, Series A/B No. 76 (1939), para. 65.

105 Andreas Zimmermann et al., *The Statute of the International Court of Justice: A Commentary* (Oxford University Press, Oxford 2012), 626.

106 Tetsuya Toyoda, 'A Civilizational Pluralist and Inegalitarian: Miniechiro Adachi (1869-1934)' in P. Sean Morris (ed), *The League of Nations and the Development of International Law: A New Intellectual History of the Advisory Committee of Jurists* (Routledge, Oxon 2022), 74.

107 Article 36 PCIJ Statute.

108 Advisory Committee of Jurists, *Procès-Verbaux of the Proceedings of the Committee: June 16th–July 24th 1920*, 541-542.

to international law, its non-compulsory jurisdiction was one of the reasons for its failure to fulfill its role as a guardian of peace (or "the hope of the ages").[109] Others opined that despite this lack of fulfilling its promise, overall, it did serve as an important judicial body during the inter-war period. Seemingly, these commentators point out that even if the lack of compulsory jurisdiction meant fewer cases, states have agreed in advance in numerous treaties to its jurisdiction in dispute resolution clauses. These scholars argue that when the PCIJ did function, its work demonstrated the utility of peaceful resolution of disputes between states by international adjudicative bodies.[110]

V. PCIJ Jurisdiction in Respect of Crimes against Humanity

Unlike Adachi's position on the issue of compulsory jurisdiction, his view on precluding PCIJ jurisdiction in respect of crimes against humanity was eventually accepted. The PCIJ Statute did not include a reference to jurisdiction over international crimes. It is difficult to assess what would have been the result of PCIJ jurisdiction in respect of crimes against humanity in practice.

Following the discussions in the ACJ, there were various inter-war period attempts (until WWII) to establish a specific court to address international crimes; a reference in a treaty on the crime of aggression to PCIJ jurisdiction; and a treaty to establish the content of international crimes.[111] Each of these efforts failed. In 1923, the LoN established a special committee which proposed that its organs could determine if a state engaged in a "real act

109 Gary Born, 'A New Generation of International Adjudication' (2012) 61 *Duke Law Journal*, 775 (800-803).

110 Christian J. Tams, 'Peace through International Adjudication: the Permanent Court of International Justice and the Post-war Order' in H. Ruiz Fabri et al. (eds) *Peace Through Law: The Versailles Peace Treaty and Dispute Settlement After World War I* (Nomos, Baden-Baden 2019), 217 (227-229).

111 Jessica Lynn Corsi, 'An Argument for Strict Legality in International Criminal Law' (2018) 49 *Georgetown Journal International Law*, 1321 (1379-1380); Matthew Lippman, 'The History, Development and Decline of Crimes Against Peace' (2004) 36 *George Washington International Law Review*, 957 (972-973); Mark A. Lewis, 'The History of the International Association of Penal Law, 1924-1950: Liberal, Conservative or Neither' in Morten Bergsmo et al. (eds), *Historical Origins of International Criminal Law* (Torkel Opsahl Academic EPublisher, Brussels 2015), 599 (616-628).

of aggression". The Soviet Union, Britain, Germany and the United States objected to the proposal.[112] In 1926, the ADIP (*Association de Detroit Penal*), a civil society organization, suggested a plan for an international criminal court. The LoN at the time was preoccupied with other matters, including the revision of the PCIJ Statute, and did not consider this proposal.[113] In a similar manner, states did not adhere to an attempt by the LoN to establish such am international criminal court in 1937. Scholars at the time noted that "practically and politically such a court was unattainable".[114] This failure to arrive at a consensus for establishing a court with jurisdiction over international crimes demonstrates that Adachi's view and position on the issue, reflecting an approach based on realism, were in line with that of the international community at the time.

F. Conclusions

The idea of establishing a system of international adjudication to resolve global disputes reflected a Euro-centric approach which can be traced to the 1899 and 1907 Hague Peace conferences. Japan participated in these conferences, but its impact was relatively limited. It was clear from the outset that Japan did not look favorably at a global institution that would be inherently Western and display European leanings. When Japan had the opportunity to face "international justice" in mechanisms created as result of these conferences, it lost.

Considering this background, it might be surprising that Japan, through Adachi, was not only very involved in the design of the PCIJ, but significantly impacted its operation. Some of the basics, like the appointment of judges and the need for consent jurisdiction (which found their way to the ICJ and to other contemporary tribunals) originated almost exclusively from Adachi's views. This was the case even when there was almost unanimity amongst members of the ACJ against his views, which were only later accepted when the work on the PCIJ Statute was completed.

112 Matthew Lippman, 'The History, Development and Decline of Crimes Against Peace' (2004) 36 *George Washington International Law Review*, 957 (972-973).

113 Mark A. Lewis, 'The History of the International Association of Penal Law, 1924-1950: Liberal, Conservative or Neither' in Morten Bergsmo et al. (eds), *Historical Origins of International Criminal Law* (Torkel Opsahl Academic EPublisher, Brussels 2015), 599 (618).

114 Jessica Lynn Corsi, 'An Argument for Strict Legality in International Criminal Law' (2018) 49 *Georgetown Journal International Law*, 1321 (1379).

Seemingly, amongst the members of the Committee, his views were more in line with those of the international community, taking a realist view of the functioning of international adjudication at its early stages.

Both elements (compulsory jurisdiction and nomination of judges) still feature today in discussions on the establishment of new international courts, such as the envisioned global investment court.[115] In the framework of these discussions, as well as scholarly debates on the history of the PCIJ, it could be useful to take into account Adachi's views, which reflected Japanese perceptions of international adjudication. This could be done by conducting further research into his positions, and the linkages to historical events, in comparison to positions expressed by other members. Hopefully, such inquiries will result in bringing the Japanese approaches closer to the forefront of contemporary international legal scholarship, which so far mostly focused on the majority opinions expressed by representatives of the US and European countries in the ACJ, or their countries' attitudes towards the drafting of the PCIJ Statute.[116] Historical inquiries into the views expressed by Adachi and other positions of non-Western origin might well produce a different line of thinking towards contemporary adjudication of international disputes. This could be especially relevant for those tasked with structuring new dispute resolution mechanisms. Importantly, such an approach could demonstrate that the early ideas of the Empire of the Rising

115 For one of the drafts for the proposed court published by UNCITRAL (United Nations Commission on International Trade Law) see Possible reform of investor-State Dispute Settlement (ISDS) – Pertinent Elements of Selected Permanent International Courts and Tribunals. UNCITRAL Website, https://uncitral.un.org/sites/uncitral.un.org/files/media-documents/uncitral/en/030222_pertinent_elements_of_selected_international_courts_final.pdf.

116 See for example: Yilin Wang, 'The Origins and Operation of the General Principles of Law as Gap Fillers' (2022) 13 *Journal of International Dispute Settlement*, 560 (564-568) (discussing views expressed by ACJ members from the US, UK, France and the Netherlands); Lorna Loyd, 'A Springboard for the Future: A Historical Examination of Britain's Role in Shaping the Optional Clause of the Permeant Court of International Justice' (1985) 79 *American Journal of International Law*, 28; Saskia Millmann, 'Making the Case for Arbitration – Edouard Descamps's Long Advocacy for Peaceful Dispute Resolution' in P. Sean Morris (ed), *Transforming the Politics of International Law: The Advisory Committee of Jurists and the Formation of the World Court in the League of Nations* (Routledge, London 2022), 134-149 (focusing on the contribution of the Belgian member); Juliette McIntyre, 'Revisiting the International Court of Justice Procedure for the Rrevision of Judgements' (2021) 42 *Michigan Journal of International Law*, 479 (498) (focusing on the position of the member from the Netherlands).

Sun about how such systems should function are of continuous validity and relevance for the next century.

PART II
The Permanent Court in Operation

Proceedings before the Permanent Court of International Justice: Design and Early Developments of the Procedure and Working Methods of a World Court

Antoine Ollivier[*]

The establishment of the World Court, as the first international permanent court with a general and potentially universal jurisdiction, could be viewed as experimental. As the President of the Advisory Committee of Jurists noted during the preparation of the Statute of the future Permanent Court of International Justice (PCIJ), "it had not to be forgotten that this [was] still a trial period" ("*période d'essai*").[1] Nevertheless, the work carried out in the early years of the PCIJ exercised a lasting influence on the development of the judicial settlement of international disputes. The foundations laid down at the time of the PCIJ do not only represent an historical reference point, but also form the very basis on which the current World Court, the International Court of Justice (ICJ), continues to operate in many respects. This is indeed directly reflected in the ICJ's Statute, which is, as mentioned in the Charter of the United Nations (UN), "based upon the Statute of the Permanent Court of International Justice" (Article 92 of the UN Charter). However, this legacy extends beyond the general principles on which the current Court's organization, functions and competence were modelled in its Statute. In shaping many of the procedural and practical aspects of the

* The author should like to thank Mr. Philippe Couvreur, who authorized him to make use for the present contribution of some research and information provided in Philippe Couvreur, 'Regards sur la Cour permanente de Justice internationale' in M. Cherif Bassiouni et al. (eds), *The Global Community Yearbook of International Law and Jurisprudence: Global Trends: Law, Policy and Justice. Essays in Honour of Professor Guiliana Ziccardi Capaldo* (Oxford University Press, Oxford 2013), 101. The views expressed by the present author remain strictly personal.

1 Advisory Committee of Jurists, *Procès-Verbaux of the Proceedings of the Committee: June 16th–July 24th 1920*, 195. See also e.g. ibid, 543 (Adachi advising "to go gently with the infant, to watch it for some time and to see the strength of its vitality before giving it more nourishment"). The *Procès-Verbaux*, as well as all PCIJ publications hereinafter referred to in the footnotes (PCIJ Series A, B, A/B, D and E), are available on the ICJ website, https://icj-cij.org/pcij.

Court's functioning, the PCIJ's approach proved also and continue to be of crucial importance.

In this regard, the task faced by the first judges of the PCIJ when designing and developing its procedure and working methods was unprecedented. Indeed, the experience drawn from the practice of international arbitration was of a certain relevance for several procedural questions. Thus, the provisions regulating the Court's procedure contained in the PCIJ Statute were largely taken over from similar provisions which had been set out in the Hague Conventions for the Pacific Settlement of International Disputes of 1899 and 1907. The Advisory Committee of Jurists considered that the principles drawn from the arbitral procedure called for limited adjustments in the context of the PCIJ.[2] Nonetheless, the objective of establishing a 'World Court', as a judicial body resembling more closely to national courts,[3] and to bring the settlement of international disputes a step further than the model of arbitration as it was then known, did raise novel issues.

As far as the procedure and working methods of the Court were concerned, these issues were to a large extent left out of the Statute, and were to be settled by the Court itself. Such issues included both practical matters and aspects of a more fundamental character, ranging from the concrete administration of the proceedings to the ways in which the Court, as a body of judges representing the "main forms of civilization and (...) the principal legal systems of the world" (Article 9 of the Statute), should perform a truly universal, international judicial function.

The newly established Court first addressed these issues in drafting the Court's Rules of procedure. While the judges considered many of the questions at hand extensively in this context, a degree of caution prevailed similar to that during the drafting of the Statute itself. More specifically, room was left for the empirical development of the procedural rules on the basis of the future Court's practice and experience of adjudication. Consequently, the foundational work of the PCIJ, at its preliminary session in 1922 (30 January–24 March 1922), when it adopted its first set of Rules, was progressively developed through the application and successive revisions of these Rules in 1926, 1927, 1931 and 1936.

---

2 Advisory Committee of Jurists, *Procès-Verbaux of the Proceedings of the Committee: June 16th–July 24th 1920*, 44, 247.

3 See B. Schenk von Stauffenberg, *Statut et Règlement de la Cour permanente de Justice internationale. Eléments d'interprétation* (Carl Heymanns Verlag, Berlin 1934), 12-13.

The present chapter considers a few aspects of the early developments of the Court's Rules and practice, and how they profoundly and lastingly marked the work and functioning of the World Court. First, it will address the initial plans and organization of the Court's work, and how the Court's permanence was considered in practical terms (I). Second, it will focus on the development of the Court's procedural rules (II). Thirdly, a series of remark will be made on the progressive elaboration of a procedure for the internal deliberations of the Court (III). Finally, a general overview of some of the main aspects of the conduct of the proceedings in the practice of the PCIJ will be provided (IV).

A. The Permanence of the Court: Organisation of the Court's Sessions and Composition of the Bench

One of the first practical issues regarding the organization and work of the PCIJ, both during the elaboration of the Statute and in the early years of the Court's functioning, concerned the very meaning of its "permanent" character as provided for by Article 14 of the Covenant.[4]

Different views were expressed in this respect in the initial drafts and among the members of the Advisory Committee of Jurists. However, the principle which was finally set out in the Statute was that the Court should convene for one annual, ordinary session, beginning on 15 June each year, to deal with the cases on its docket. The convening of "extraordinary sessions" was also provided for in the Statute, with a view to dealing with possible urgent cases, but no detailed consideration was given to such possibility during the Statute's drafting.

The system originally envisioned in the Statute was mainly justified by the uncertainty as to the work which would actually be required from the Court, if not by the belief that in fact the Court would have little work[5]. In light of the Court's unforeseeable workload, another consideration among the drafters of the Statute was the potential difficulty of finding judges pre-

4 A detailed account of the historical development of the relevant provisions of the Statute and Rules is provided in Antoine Ollivier, 'Article 23' in Andreas Zimmermann et al. (eds), *The Statute of the International Court of Justice. A Commentary* (Oxford University Press, Oxford 2017), 508-525.

5 See e.g. Dionisio Anzilotti, PCIJ, *Modification of the Rules (1931)* (Series D, No. 2, 2nd Add., 1931), 60.

pared to establish themselves permanently in The Hague and consequently, to abandon other occupations they had in their home countries.[6] In this regard, the principle of the Court's annual sessions was in line with other provisions in the original Statute which did not contemplate an absolute incompatibility of the position of member of the Court with other professional occupation, but only with the exercise of political or administrative functions (Article 16 of the Statute).

Hence, the Court's "permanence" was originally not meant in a literal sense with all judges constantly present at the seat of the Court. Instead, the Court's permanence rather meant that its composition should remain unchanged (subject to the nomination of "national (*ad hoc*) judges"), and referred to the fact that the Court and its members should render themselves available at all times to deal with the cases submitted, if necessary by means of extraordinary sessions[7]. The Statute provided that the President and the Registrar should reside at the seat of the Court, and several powers were entrusted consequently to the President in the Rules of Court, should the latter not be sitting.[8] In view of the possible absence of some judges, the Statute also provided for the election of deputy-judges to replace those who could not attend the Court's meetings.[9]

---

6 See Advisory Committee of Jurists, *Procès-Verbaux of the Proceedings of the Committee: June 16th–July 24th 1920*, 186-189.

7 See e.g. PCIJ, *Modification of the Rules (1931)* (Series D, No. 2, 2nd Add., 1931), 62 (Altamira).

8 In addition to certain procedural powers to be exercised by the President when the Court was not sitting, the original Rules of Court provided for the power of the President to indicate provisional measures. In 1931, the Court revised its Rules on this point, considering that the Statute only provided for the indication of provisional measures by the Court itself (Article 41 of the Statute). Provisions were added to the effect that the President should convene the Court without delay to deal with a request for provisional measures, or could convene *proprio motu* a meeting of the Court to examine the opportunity of indicating such measures.

9 The PCIJ was initially to be composed of eleven judges and four deputy-judges, with the possibility for the Assembly, upon proposal of the Council of the League of Nations, to later on increase these numbers to a total of 15 judges and 6 deputy-judges (Art. 3 of the 1920 Statute). See the Report of the Advisory Committee, in Advisory Committee of Jurists, *Procès-Verbaux of the Proceedings of the Committee: June 16th–July 24th 1920,* 711: "[T]his is only the beginning. Later on those States which are, for the time being, outside the League of Nations, will enter it: as and when this takes place, the Assembly (...) may increase the number of judges. As, however, too large a body cannot administer justice satisfactorily, the composition of the Court must not exceed 15 judges and 6 deputies."

Given the PCIJ's particularly busy first years, the system of ordinary sessions did not work as contemplated. Indeed, the PCIJ adopted the course of convening between two ordinary sessions to deal with cases ready for hearing. Therefore, extraordinary sessions were held throughout the year[10] and the Court's functioning tended to be permanent in a practical sense.[11]

However, this state of practice led to undesirable consequences which became a matter of ongoing concern.[12] This practice impacted on the Court's actual composition. Judges residing in countries most distant from the seat of the Court, in particular those from South America, faced difficulties travelling to attend extraordinary sessions, especially during winter. Therefore, recourse was often to be had to the deputy-judges, and among them, to those who resided in Europe and were more readily available than other belonging to other continents.[13]

This situation whereby European judges enjoyed a privileged position in the actual composition of the Court prompted the Statute's revision in 1929.[14] It was then decided to end the system of sessions and to provide that the Court should "remain permanently in session". The position of deputy-judges was also abolished and the number of judges increased to 15. This revision also included changing the regime of incompatible activities for judges to prohibit them from any other professional occupation during their term of office. The corresponding provisions in the revised Statute

10 From 1922 to 1935, the Court held thirty-five sessions, fourteen were ordinary sessions and twenty-one extraordinary, *cf.* PCIJ, *Sixteenth Report* (Series E No. 16), 67-8; Manley Ottmer Hudson, *The Permanent Court of International Justice, 1920-1942: a treatise* (The Macmillan Company, New York 1943), 334. Nevertheless, the PCIJ's caseload remained irregular, with the Court adjourning sessions depending on the status of the cases, see B. Schenk von Stauffenberg, *Statut et Règlement de la Cour permanente de Justice internationale. Eléments d'interprétation* (Carl Heymanns Verlag, Berlin 1934), 112-124.

11 As soon as 1926, it was felt that the whole question of sessions would have to be reconsidered at some point, PCIJ, *Revision of the Rules of the Court (1926)* (Series D, No. 2, Add., 1926), 45, 50 et seq.

12 Manley O. Hudson, *The Permanent Court of International Justice, 1920-1942: A Treatise* (The Macmillan Company, New York 1943), 337.

13 See 'Report on the Work of the Committee submitted by Fromageot and Politis' in PCIJ, *Minutes of the Committee of Jurists on the Statute of the Permanent Court of International Justice* (1929), 11.

14 The other major modifications to the Statute during its revision consisted in incorporating provisions, previously made in the Rules of Court, on advisory proceedings.

and in the Rules (which were revised in 1931 and 1936)[15] were taken over in the Statute and the Rules of the International Court of Justice after its establishment in 1945 and continue to form the general basis for the organization of its work.

B. The Proceedings before the Court: the Development of an International Judicial Procedure

As indicated at the outset, the drafting of the PCIJ Statute did not prompt extensive discussions on procedural matters. It was thought that the Advisory Committee should not outline the procedure in too much detail in the Statute and that it was for the "Court itself (...) to formulate these rules in its internal regulations"; the procedural rules to be included in the Statute itself, and to be submitted as such to the States' approval, should therefore only deal with fundamental points.[16] Accordingly, the Statute's provisions were both general and mainly drawn from the arbitral procedure.

In this regard, however, the establishment of a permanent judicial body likely entailed several distinctive procedural consequences compared to the model of international arbitration. Indeed, the Court's power to adopt its Rules of Procedure (Article 30 of the Statute) and thereby provide a pre-established, binding procedural framework for future parties to cases departed from the general approach in the context of international arbitration, where procedural rules shall be agreed between the parties.[17] Furthermore, the elaboration and application of such Rules would reflect the respective role of the Court and the parties in the conduct of the proceedings. Although some may have viewed the Court's role and importance as justifying a certain preeminence of the latter over the parties in procedural

15 The 1929 Revision Protocol only entered into force in 1936. As already provided for in the original Statute, the Assembly took the step of electing 15 members, and four deputy judges, at the 1930 elections, pending the entry into force of the revised Statute. Further to the invitation made by the Assembly, the Court undertook to adapt its Rules, in 1931, to adopt, in practice, the principle of the permanent functioning of the Court.

16 Advisory Committee of Jurists, *Procès-Verbaux of the Proceedings of the Committee: June 16th–July 24th 1920*, 248 (Baron Descamps).

17 See also Article 51 of the Hague Convention on the Peaceful Settlement of International Disputes, which rules are only dispositive and subject to any agreement between the parties to the dispute.

matters,[18] a distinct balance was established in the Rules and early practice of the Court.

The first Rules of Court, adopted in 1922, were generally meant to provide a procedural framework sufficiently detailed to offer to potential States parties to cases the required predictability and legal security, and, at the same time, sufficiently general to allow for some flexibility in its application.[19] This approach was not only justified by practical considerations or expediency. It was also a way to establish, as much as possible, a general procedural framework that would accommodate the domestic procedural systems or legal traditions which were mainly represented within the Court (or within the Advisory Committee, during the elaboration of the Statute), namely the Continental/Civil law and the Anglo-American/Common law systems. The need to elaborate a compromise between these legal traditions — or avoid favoring one over the other — arose in some discussions concerning the administration of evidence,[20] the respective role of the Court and the parties, or the conduct of the oral phase of the proceedings.[21]

Another consideration explaining the cautious approach by the drafters of the first Rules of Court was linked to the novelty of the jurisdiction to be vested in the Permanent Court. Remarkably, the 1922 Rules of Court did not contain detailed provisions addressing the procedural aspects of the Court's compulsory contentious jurisdiction, or the proceedings regarding the Court's advisory jurisdiction (for which no precedents at the international level could be of use). Thus, some proposals have been left out of the first Rules adopted by the PCIJ. The question of advisory proceedings was addressed in 1922, but it was agreed that it should be settled in connection

18 Dionisio Anzilotti described the prevailing tendency in 1922 to "regard the will of the Parties as of secondary importance, in view of the Court's role and importance", PCIJ, *Modification of the Rules (1931)* (Series D., No. 2, 2nd Add., 1931), 166-167 (with reference to the question whether the Court should be bound by time-limits agreed between the parties). Reference was made in this regard to the control of the procedure entrusted to the Court under Article 48 of the Statute ("The Court shall make orders for the conduct of the case, (...) and make arrangements connected with the taking of evidence"). See further below (footnotes 24 and 25).

19 See e.g. PCIJ, *Preparation of the Rules of Court of January 30th 1922* (Series D, No. 2, 1922), 58 (Finlay), 60 (Oda).

20 See e.g. ibid, 142; see also PCIJ, *Revision of the Rules* (Series D, No. 2, Add., 1926), 117 et seq., 124-126, 132.

21 PCIJ, *Preparation of the Rules of Court of January 30th* (Series D, No. 2, 1922), 81-82, 147, 209 et seq.

with particular cases as they arose.[22] Likewise, the procedure to deal with possible objections by a respondent State to the Court's compulsory jurisdiction invoked by the applicant State, albeit the subject of discussions at the preliminary session, was eventually omitted in the Rules of 1922.[23] Specific provisions have thus only been progressively set out in the subsequent revisions of the Court's Rules, on the basis of the Court's practice.

Finally, regard had been had to the special nature of the parties to the cases, as States, and to the need to accommodate to a certain extent their will in the rules and the conduct of the proceedings. This led to the inclusion of provisions in the Rules of Court recognizing the possible influence to be exercised by the parties on the rules of procedure applicable in a given case (by proposing modifications or additions to certain provisions of the Rules of Court), or on the exercise of certain of the Court's powers (such as the fixing of time-limits).[24] In this connection it was emphasized that "it was in the interest of the Court that the rules should not be so rigid as to prevent States having recourse to it".[25] Notwithstanding the fact that proper consideration must be given to the interests of States parties to a

22 Ibid, 98. The original Rules contained only three general provisions dealing with advisory opinions.

23 Ibid, 77-78, 148, 201, and 213-214. The matter, in particular the question whether the objection to the jurisdiction should be decided upon by the Court separately from and prior to the discussion of the merits of the case, was dealt with for the first time by the Court in the *Mavrommatis* case, Judgment of 30 August 1924, (Series A, No. 2), 9. A specific provision dealing with the proceedings concerning a preliminary objection was first introduced in the Rules in 1926.

24 See the discussions on articles 32 and 33 of the Rules of Court (1922), in PCIJ, *Preparation of the Rules of Court of January 30th 1922* (Series D, No. 2, 1922), 52-54, 57-61, and PCIJ, *Modification of the Rules (1931)* (Series D., No. 2, 2nd Add., 1931), 165-171.

25 PCIJ, *Preparation of the Rules of Court of January 30th 1922* (Series D, No. 2, 1922), 58 (Anzilotti). See also ibid, 59-60 (Weiss): "it must not be forgotten that the litigants would be sovereign States, and that the institution of a too rigid procedure might prevent them from having recourse to the Court, so that there would be a danger that the Court would never be made use"); and 60 (Huber): "the ideas of "droit public" and "fixed rules" must be set aside in so far as concerned the procedure of the Permanent Court, which was an international Court; in international proceedings the fundamental principle was the free-will of the parties"; "practical examples drawn from his own experience [demonstrated] the danger of establishing a too rigid procedure for the Court such as might arouse the susceptibilities of sovereign States"). With respect to the flexibility to be left to the parties, including in the framing of the *compromis* regarding modifications to be proposed to the Rules of Court, time-limits, or other procedural questions, see also PCIJ, *Elaboration of the Rules of Court of March 11th 1936* (Series D, No. 2, 3rd Add., 1936), 64-65.

case in the conduct of the proceedings, the limits to the prerogatives and influence to be left to them in this regard, including those limits resulting from the provisions of the Statute,[26] as well as the powers of the Court in procedural matters, were recalled on several occasions. More generally, as summarized in its *dictum* in the *Mavrommatis* case, the Court retained the ability, in the absence of rule in its Statue or the Rules of Court regarding the procedure, "to adopt the principle which it considers best calculated to ensure the administration of justice, most suited to procedure before an international tribunal and most in conformity with the fundamental principles of international law".[27]

C. The Deliberations of the Court: The Progressive Elaboration of the PCIJ's Internal Judicial Practice

The internal working methods of the PCIJ and the procedure to be followed for drafting decisions were the subject of extensive discussions among the judges of the Permanent Court.

First, at its preliminary session, devoted to the adoption of the Rules of Court, the Court rejected proposals to appoint a judge who should act as "Rapporteur" by studying the case and drafting the decision.[28] Lord Finlay warned that such a system "would not have been easily accepted from the perspective of the Anglo-Saxon countries"[29]. The principle of collegial

26 PCIJ, *Free Zones of Upper Savoy and the District of Gex*, Order of 19 August 1929 (Series A, No. 22), 13.

27 PCIJ, *Mavrommatis Palestine Concessions (Objection to the Jurisdiction of the Court)*, Judgment of 30 August 1924 (Series A, No. 2), 16.

28 PCIJ, *Preparation of the Rules of Court of January 30th 1922* (Series D, No. 2, 1922), 78, 419; see the proposals of the Secretariat, ibid, 263 (art. 37), 266 (art. 49), 269 and 270 (art. 61-63), as well as the preliminary draft presented by Altamira, 278, 280. It was nonetheless understood that the Court remained free to decide, in a particular case, to entrust one of its members with the task of preparing a draft judgment, ibid, 78. This was the case at the Court's first session, where a single member was entrusted with the preparation of a draft opinion based on the Court's deliberations, see PCIJ, *Second Report* (Series E, No. 2), 170.

29 PCIJ, *Preparation of the Rules of Court of January 30th 1922* (Series D, No. 2, 1922), 78 ("Lord Finaly remarked that if the Court adopted the *rapporteur* system, this would have a deplorable effect on opinion in legal circles in Anglo-Saxon countries. He proposed that no provision regarding the drawing up of a report or the nomination of a rapporteur should figure in the Rules. This would not however prevent the Court, if it considered it desirable in a special instance, from appointing one of its

work was mainly explained by reference to Article 9 of the Statute and the necessity of ensuring, through the equal participation of all judges in the drafting of the decisions, the representation of the principal legal systems at every stage of the Court's deliberations. Accordingly, "all members of the Court should in effect be rapporteurs".[30]

The PCIJ also refrained from committing itself to a precise procedure for its deliberations by way of provisions in its Rules. Thus, this matter was left to the progressive development of the Court's practice.[31] This approach was justified by the fact that it concerned an internal matter, but also by the wish here again to retain a degree of flexibility.

Initially, the practice of the Court involved, after the closure of the oral proceedings in a case, holding first deliberations. Following these deliberations, a drafting committee, selected by secret ballot, would prepare the draft judgment or opinion to be submitted to the Court for discussion and adoption. From 1925 onwards, the practice has been to appoint two members of the Court, with the President being member *ex officio*, to form such drafting committees.[32]

The initial approach of first holding oral deliberations in the "*Chambre du conseil*" was later superseded by the distribution of written notes by the judges prior to the general discussion of the case.[33] In this respect, concerns that written notes would limit the freedom of the Court's deliberations were counterbalanced by the argument that the prior expression in writing

members to draw up a draft judgment, as was done in England and in the US, but any decision left to the Court").

30 PCIJ, *Modification of the Rules (1931)* (Series D, No. 2, 2nd Add., 1931), 223. See also PCIJ, *Revision of the Rules of the Court (1926)* (Series D, No. 2, Add., 1926), 249.

31 See PCIJ, *Annual Report 1926-1927* (Series E, No. 3), 214, where the deliberation process was first described and summarized, with the following introduction: "The present practice of the Court as regards deliberation upon judgments and advisory opinions has been adopted as the result of the experience so far gained, but various systems have been tried and the Court is in no way committed to any particular method. The present practice (...) is therefore liable to variation (...)".

32 PCIJ, *Annual Report 1925-1926* (Series E, No. 2), 170-171.

33 Ibid, 171. The system of written notes, adopted in some early cases on an exceptional basis, was eventually adopted in 1925, under the Presidency of Max Huber; it was agreed at that time, and the practice has been uniformly followed since then, that such notes should be anonymized and distributed simultaneously to all judges. On the very initial practice of purely verbal deliberations, see the account given by the Registrar in PCIJ, *Modification of the Rules (1931)* (Series D, No. 2, 2nd Add., 1931), 223-224.

of their individual opinions on the case would better ensure the equality between the Court's members.[34]

The balance and sequence between the written phase, carried out individually by each judge, and the collective phase of deliberations continued, however, to be a matter of debate within the Court. Therefore, several adjustments were made to the internal judicial practice over time. For example, the Court adopted the practice of holding a preliminary exchange of views, after the conclusion of the oral proceedings and prior to the distribution of the judges' written notes. This was done "for the purpose of bringing out the questions of most importance from the point of view of the judgment or opinion to be delivered".[35] The orderly conduct of the deliberations[36] and the requirements of time efficiency,[37] were among the factors which were also taken into account in this regard.

After further debates within the Court,[38] the practice of the Court was consolidated for the first time in a resolution adopted in 1931[39]. Various views were expressed on this occasion, including on: the necessity of holding more substantive deliberations before the judges could or should expose their individual views in writing;[40] the compulsory character of the

34 See PCIJ, *Revision of the Rules of the Court (1926)* (Series D, No. 2, Add., 1926), p. 57 (Anzilotti): written notes "are intended to establish a certain equality between members, some of whom were using their own language and other a language strange to them".

35 PCIJ, *Annual Report 1926-1927* (Series E, No. 3), 214.

36 PCIJ, *Modification of the Rules (1931),* Series D, No. 2, 2nd Add., 218 (Anzilotti): the method of written notes "had been instituted by M. Huber to enable judges to better understand each other and to shorten deliberations".

37 The length of the deliberations was the subject of some criticisms from members of the Court, see Manley Ottmer Hudson, *The Permanent Court of International Justice, 1920-1942: A Treatise* (The Macmillan Company, New York 1943), 581. See also e.g. PCIJ, *Modification of the Rules (1931)* (Series D, No. 2, 2nd Add., 1931), 226 (Count Rostworowski). See further section IV below.

38 Ibid, 218-226, 231-234, 235-243, 244-251. Following the discussion on an initial proposal from Hurst and Altamira (ibid, 292), a draft resolution ("*Projet de résolution concernant la pratique de la Cour en matière judiciaire*") was prepared by Fromageot, ibid, 300.

39 PCIJ, *Modification of the Rules (1931)* (Series D, No. 2, 2nd Add., 1931), 267, 300-301.

40 Reflecting the aims pursued by Hurst and Altamira, the 1931 Resolution put an emphasis on the first "deliberation" of the Court after the closure of the oral proceedings (and after sufficient time is allowed to judges to study the oral arguments of the parties), which should serve "the purpose of collectively examining the case as it presents itself after the hearing, bringing out the questions to be solved and discussing them severally. The President ensures that all questions called to notice

submission of such written notes (and the non-committing character of the opinion so expressed);[41] and the mode of composition of the drafting committees. The Court also considered the President's distinct role in carrying out the conduct of the deliberations, and in particular in drawing up the questions to be put to the discussions and vote in a case.[42]

The initial resolution was adopted on an experimental basis,[43] and it was not immediately officially published by the Court.[44] Following the Resolution's revision in 1936,[45] it was eventually issued with the indication that the Court "was entirely free to suspend [its] application in a given case, if it held that the circumstances of the case justified that course".[46]

As illustrated by the discussions about the PCIJ's internal judicial practice and the caution with which it adopted its Resolution on this matter, the Court progressively established its working methods. These methods stood

---

either by himself or by the judges have been discussed and that each judge has made known his impressions in regard to them", ibid 300 (English text in PCIJ, *Annual Report 1935-1936* (Series E, No. 12), 196).

41 "At a suitable interval of time after this deliberation, each judge expresses his personal view in writing in the form of a note, without committing himself to a definite opinion" (Point 4 of the 1931 Resolution).

42 See e.g. Anzilotti's reference to the presidency of Max Huber, and the latter's practice of preparing detailed questions, which had "given rise to difficulties" and led Anzilotti, when President, to "generally confin[e] himself (...) to preparing a plan of discussion, drawn up in very general terms, which the Court was at liberty to supplement or amend", PCIJ, *Modification of the Rules (1931)* (Series D, No. 2, 2nd Add., 1931), 240-241. See also ibid, 222 ("M. Anzilotti, speaking from experience, explained how onerous and complex was this task. (...) A President however impartial, was always afraid of being led to consider questions from his own personal standpoint"). In this regard, the 1931 Resolution provided that the President, on the basis of the notes of each judge, prepares and submits to the Court a "plan of discussion provisionally determining the order and the terms of the question on which the Court must give its opinion", which remains subject to the freedom of the Court to subsequently modify the order of its discussion and the terms of the questions (ibid, 301).

43 Ibid, 267, 300-301.

44 PCIJ, *Annual Report 1930-1931* (Series E, No. 7), 297-298.

45 This revision mainly consisted in: i) including provision setting out the elaboration of a preliminary draft by the drafting committee, to be submitted to the judges for possible written amendments (first reading), and the submission of a revised draft for discussion by the Court (second reading); and ii) incorporating a provision for the submission by the judges, after the first reading and before the second reading, of the text of the separate or dissenting opinions which they intended to attach to the decision of the Court. Former provisions of the 1931 Resolution, dealing with the questions to be put to representatives of the parties at the hearing, were removed in the 1936 Resolution, after such provisions were incorporated in the Rules of Court.

46 PCIJ, *Annual Report 1935-1936* (Series E, No. 12), 197.

the test of time, and the general economy of the PCIJ Resolution, provisionally adopted by the ICJ in 1946, was not modified when the latter adopted and revised its own Resolution.[47] Although several changes and additions were made on these occasions, compared with the practice followed by the PCIJ,[48] the Resolution generally reflects the constant concern of the Court to ensure the equal and active participation of all judges in the examination of the case, and that the judgment or advisory opinion constitute a collective decision by the Court as a whole.[49] Moreover, by retaining its freedom to depart from provisions of the Resolution in particular circumstances, and by avoiding to set out details for every aspects of its internal methods (and in its Rules), the Court afforded itself sufficient flexibility to further adapt and develop its practice.[50]

---

47 On 5 July 1968, the ICJ adopted the Resolution concerning its internal judicial practice. It revised it only once, in 1976 (Resolution adopted on 12 April 1976), and a new article was inserted in the resolution in 2020; see ICJ, *Acts and Documents* (No. 8, 2024), 176 *et seq.* As indicated in the preamble, the Court "remains entirely free to depart from the present Resolution, or any part of it, in a given case, if it considers that the circumstances justify that course".

48 In the 1968 Resolution, one of the most significant differences with the PCIJ 1931/1936 Resolution concerned the first meeting of the Court after the closure of the hearing, which should be strictly confined to a preliminary examination of the questions to be decided in the case, without proposing or discussing any possible solutions. The 1976 Resolution however contemplates the possibility for the President to also invite judges "to indicate their preliminary impressions" during this first deliberation. Similarly to the debates and evolution at the time of the PCIJ, as noted above, this modification may have been prompted by the preference of some judges to have collective discussions at an early stage, and before individual views might become "frozen" in a written note, see Geneviève Guyomar, 'La révision par la Cour internationale de Justice de sa résolution visant la pratique interne en matière judiciaire', (1976) 22 *Annuaire français de droit international*, 116, referring to André Gros, "Observations sur le mode de délibération de la C.I.J.", (1975) 14 *Communicazioni e studi*, 385.

49 Geneviève Guyomar, 'La révision par la Cour internationale de Justice de sa résolution visant la pratique interne en matière judiciaire', (1976) 22 *Annuaire français de droit international*, 116; Joan E. Donoghue, 'A View of the Court from Within', Speech of H.E. Judge Joan E. Donoghue, President of the International Court of Justice, to the Sixth Committee of the General Assembly, 28 October 2022 (https://icj-cij.org/sites/default/files/press-releases/0/000-20221028-STA-01-00-EN.pdf), 9.

50 On the further developments of the Court's working methods at the time of the ICJ, in light of its increasing caseload, see below section IV.

D. The Conduct of the Proceedings before the Court: General Overview of the PCIJ's Practice

The general procedural framework established in the Rules contributed to the remarkable efficiency with which the PCIJ conducted its proceedings in practice. On average, the length of the proceedings on the merits of a case, from the institution of the proceedings to the reading of the judgment, lasted between one and one and a half year, which also often included preliminary or other incidental proceedings.[51] Several requests for advisory opinions, often submitted as urgent by the Council of the League of Nations, were even dealt with within a few months, and for the very first requests, within a few weeks.[52] Over its first decade of existence (1922-1931), the PCIJ delivered between three to seven judgments or advisory opinions every year.

This was achieved, first, by the organization of the written phase of the proceedings in relatively short timeframes, generally not exceeding a few months.[53] The Rules of Court provided that in principle, for the cases submitted by special agreement, each party would submit within the same time-limits three written pleadings (case, counter-case, and reply). For cases submitted to the Court by means of a unilateral application, the Rules of Court provided for the successive submission of two written pleadings by each party (case and reply for the applicant; counter-case and rejoinder for the respondent). Although the respective merits of each of these methods, for the States concerned and for the Court, were already noted and considered at the time of the PCIJ,[54] they did not appear to cause significant practical difference in the overall length of the proceedings.[55] The PCIJ

---

51 See the particulars for each case provided *in* PCIJ, *Annual Report 1939-1945* (Series E, No. 16), 92 *et seq.*

52 During the first session of the Permanent Court, in 1922, three advisory opinions (relating to questions which arose at the International Labour Organization) were given within three months (at a time where no written phase was contemplated by the Court for advisory proceedings).

53 The extension of time-limits by the Court, at the request of the parties, were usually limited to a few days or weeks at most. See the Court's practice in its first years, reported in PCIJ, *Annual Report 1926-1927* (Series E, No.°3), 206-208; *Annual Report 1927-1928* (Series E, No. 4), 274-278; and *Annual Report 1928-1929* (Series E, No.°5), 242.

54 PCIJ, *Preparation of the Rules of Court of January 30th 1922* (Series D, No. 2, 1922), 72-75, 125 *et seq.* (137), 207; see also PCIJ, *Revision of the Rules of the Court (1926)* (Series D, No. 2, Add., 1926), 98.

55 With the rather short time-limits fixed for the submission of the written pleadings, and the short intervals (of one to one and a half months) when pleadings had to

did not significantly modify the relevant provisions in its Rules during its successive revisions of 1931 and 1936. This is, by contrast, a matter where some significant developments occurred in the Rules and practice of the ICJ. In particular, after having faced extensive and prolonged proceedings in the *Barcelona Traction* case,[56] the ICJ introduced a provision in its Rules (in 1972) to the effect that "time-limits should be as short as the character of the case permits".[57] The ICJ also revised its Rules to provide for the submission, in principle, of only one written pleading by each party in cases submitted by means of a unilateral application.[58] In cases submitted by means of a special agreement, it provided for only two pleadings.[59] The ICJ took later on other initiatives, either by amending its Rules or by another means, with a view to avoid unnecessary delays in the proceedings.[60]

---

be submitted consecutively by each party, no difference ensued for cases submitted by a unilateral application (with in principle four consecutive pleadings) compared to those submitted by a special agreement (with, in principle, three simultaneous pleadings).

56 The Court considered necessary to make reference "to the unusual length of the present proceedings, which ha[d] been due to the very long time-limits requested by the Parties for the preparation of their written pleadings and in addition to their repeated requests for an extension of these limits. The Court did not find that it should refuse these requests and thus impose limitations on the Parties in the preparation and presentation of the arguments and evidence which they considered necessary. It nonetheless remains convinced of the fact that it is in the interest of the authority and proper functioning of international justice for cases to be decided without unwarranted delay." *Barcelona Traction Light and Pwer Company (Belgium v. Spain) (New Application)*, Judgment of 5 February 1970, ICJ Reports (1971), 30-31 (27).

57 Article 48 of the Rules of Court (1978). See also the addition that, in making orders to determine the number and the order of the filing of the pleadings and the time-limits within which they must be filed, any agreement between the parties "which does not cause unjustified delay" shall be taken into account by the Court (Article 44 (2), of the Rules of Court, 1978).

58 In cases begun by means of an application, the Court may still authorize or direct the submission of additional pleadings (Reply and Rejoinder) if the parties are so agreed, or if the Court decides *proprio motu* or at the request of one of the parties, that these pleadings are necessary (Article 45 (2)).

59 The Rules were also revised in 1972, providing that, subject to the special agreement or any subsequent agreement of the parties, only two pleadings shall be filed by each party (Memorial and Counter-Memorial, within the same time-limits); the Court "shall not authorize the presentation of Replies unless it finds them to be necessary" (Article 46 (3)).

60 In 2001, the Court amended its Rules to provide that preliminary objections to the jurisdiction of the Court or to the admissibility of the application, or other objection the decision upon which is requested before any further proceedings on the merits,

On the other hand, the organization of the hearing caused some debates at the time of the PCIJ.[61] Oral proceedings, similarly to the written phase, were held in short time-frames, contributing to the quick pace with which the cases were dealt with by the PCIJ. The latter usually held hearings shortly after the closure of the written procedure,[62] and they did not, at least in the early practice of the Court, last more than eight days[63]. Yet, PCIJ judges expressed concerns about the prolonged duration of hearings and sought ways to further shorten it. In this regard, the Court not only considered the practical aspects of the conduct of the hearings,[64] but also the specific character and purpose of

---

"shall be made no later than three months after the delivery of the Memorial" (and thus no longer within the time-limit fixed for the delivery of the Counter-Memorial; see Article 79 (1) of the Rules of Court). The Court also adopted several "Practice Directions for use by States appearing before it", including with the aim of accelerating proceedings on preliminary objections (see Practice Direction V).

61 On the equal importance attached by the drafters of the Statute to the written and oral phases of the proceedings, as opposed to the past model of arbitration and the 1899 and 1907 Hague Conventions, see Advisory Committee of Jurists, *Procès-Verbaux of the Proceedings of the Committee: June 16th–July 24th 1920*, p. 737, and B. Schenk von Stauffenberg, *Statut et Règlement de la Cour permanente de Justice internationale. Eléments d'interprétation* (Carl Heymanns Verlag, Berlin 1934), 323-325.

62 See PCIJ, *Elaboration of the Rules of Court of March 11th, 1936* (Series D, No. 2, 3rd Add., 1936), 117.

63 The *Legal Status of Eastern Greenland case* was rather exceptional, with 31 sittings being held between 21 November 1931 and 7 February 1933, Judgment of 5 April 1933 (Series A/B No. 53), 25. See also the following cases, in which the hearing of witness experts added to the average duration of the oral proceedings, PCIJ, *Certain German Interests in Polish Upper Silesia (Merits),* Judgment of 25 May 1926 (Series A, No. 7), 8, 13; PCIJ, *Free Zones of Upper Savoy and the District of Gex,* Judgment of 7 June 1932 (Series A/B, No. 46), 101; PCIJ, *Phosphates in Morocco,* Judgment of 14 June 1938 (Series A/B, No. 74), 21; PCIJ, *Diversion of Water from the Meuse,* Judgment of 28 June 1937 (Series A/B No. 70), 9.

64 See the proposals made, with a view to saving the time required for their consecutive interpretation in the other official language of the Court, to abandon the interpretation of the oral statements of the parties' representatives at the hearing (and to rely only on the written, and more complete and reliable translations which in practice were always prepared), PCIJ, *Revision of the Rules of the Court (1926)* (Series D, No. 2, Add., 1926), 108-110 (and proposal from Altamira, p. 264). See also PCIJ, *Modification of the Rules (1931)* (Series D, No. 2, 2nd Add., 1931), 114-115, 251-252, 291 (note from Altamira). In rejecting these proposals, the PCIJ noted that the principle of bilingualism serves the interests of the judges, parties, and the press and the general public, see PCIJ, *Annual Report 1932-1933* (Series E, No. 9), 163. The PCIJ nevertheless adopted, in 1933, a resolution providing that it could decide in a particular case to dispense itself from the interpretation during the hearing, and decided so in a few cases, ibid, 153, and PCIJ, *Annual Report 1933-1934* (Series E, No. 10), 140 et seq.; PCIJ, *Annual Report 1934-1935* (Series E, No. 11), 142, and PCIJ, *Annual Report 1935-1936* (Series E, No. 12), 185.

the oral proceedings before the Court. Within the short time frame allocated to the hearings, limited time was given for the parties' counsel to prepare oral replies. The PCIJ attempted to maintain the purely oral nature of the pleadings early on. The Court expected the parties' counsel to arrive fully prepared at the hearings and promptly reply to the other party's counsel.[65] Additionally, the Court repeatedly expressed the view that the "reading of prepared written statements [was] contrary to the principle underlying oral proceedings", a practice which several judges complained of.[66] Nevertheless, the PCIJ equally recognized the importance of protecting the freedom required for States appearing before it, and for their agent and counsel, to present their arguments in the most appropriate manner. In this connection, several views were expressed in the early debates within the PCIJ regarding the methods for judges to put questions to counsel at the hearing, on the nature of the cooperation to be expected between an international Court (composed of 15 or more judges of different nationalities and legal training) and the agent and counsel representing a State during such hearings, and the related requirements.[67] Many of these questions and considerations continue to be relevant in the practice of the current Court, and in terms of the assessment of the role

65 "In the case of the Minority Schools in Upper Silesia, at the Thirteenth (Extraordinary) Session, the Court granted the German Agent one clear day for the preparation of his oral reply, but the view was expressed at the private meeting held to consider the point that agents should come into Court fully prepared", PCIJ, *Annual Report 1927-1928* (Series E, No. 4), 287. See also PCIJ, *Annual Report 1929-1930* (Series E, No. 6), 296.

66 PCIJ, *Annual Report 1929-1930* (Series E, No. 6), 296: "Theory and practice as regards granting of time for preparation of oral arguments during hearings. As regards the granting of requests by Agents or Counsel for the time to prepare their oral arguments, replies and rejoinders, the Court has repeatedly expressed itself as of opinion that Agents, etc., should come before it fully prepared to argue the case, and that the reading of prepared written statements is contrary to the principle underlying oral proceedings. Accordingly, when requested to grant time for the preparation of a reply or rejoinder, the Court has very frequently curtailed the amount of time sought and as a general rule is averse to granting more than half a day, or sometimes, in the case of replies to very lengthy speeches, one day. In every case, however, the Court regards such grants of time as a special concession to the Parties and not as a right which they may claim".

67 See PCIJ, *Modification of the Rules (1931)* (Series D, No. 2, 2nd Add., 1931), 212-215. For a recent overview of the practice and calls for enhanced questions from the bench, including early directions from the Court on the points or issues to be addressed during the hearing (in accordance with Article 61 of the Rules), see Alina Miron, Working Methods of the Court (2016) 7 *Journal of International Dispute Settlement*, 371 (387-388).

and importance of the oral proceedings before a World Court and the degree of control and direction that the Court may exercise.[68]

Regarding the third and final phase in a case before the Court, the PCIJ usually proceeded to deliberations shortly after the oral proceedings. On average, the time between the end of the hearings and the reading of the judgment was about one month. As indicated in section III, the PCIJ considered in detail the adequate means of conducting deliberations, and developed empirically and progressively its internal judicial practice. However, the flexible approach followed by the PCIJ in setting out its methods of work was predicated on the potential increase of its caseload, with a view to any potential future need to adapt such methods.[69] This did not occur for the PCIJ and its docket remain relatively stable over the years, with even a slight decrease in the number of cases during its second decade of activities (1931 to 1939).[70] The ICJ, on the other hand, faced a completely different situation and a substantial increase of its docket over time. This lead the Court, *inter alia*, to revise some of its working methods to expedite the examination of contentious cases.[71]

---

68 Further provisions concerning the oral proceedings were added in the Rules of the ICJ, during its revision in 1972, and other initiatives have been taken since then in practice, with a view to exercise further control over the oral pleadings.

69 See e.g. the remark from Loder pointing out, in 1926 (with regard to the inclusion of provision in the Rules concerning the number of judges which should compose the drafting committee), that "[t]he Court had probably not arrived at a final conclusion as regards its method of work. And if it had several cases to deal with at the same time, it would be absolutely necessary to change it", PCIJ, *Revision of the Rules of the Court (1926)* (Series D, No. 2, Add., 1926), 171.

70 From 1922 to 1930, the PCIJ delivered 35 judgments or advisory opinions (3 to 7 by year). From 1931 to 1939, it delivered 24 judgments or advisory opinions (1 to 6 by year).

71 Regarding its deliberations, the Court decided in 1997, first on an experimental basis, to proceed without written notes for its judgments concerning preliminary phases of the proceedings (preliminary objections). A number of other measures were taken, in particular with a view to reduce the length of the written pleadings submitted by the parties, see "The International Court of Justice revises its working methods to expedite the examination of contentious cases", ICJ Communiqué No. 98/14 (6 April 1998), https://www.icj-cij.org/files/press-releases/0/000-19980406-PRE-01-00-EN.pdf. See also R. Higgins, 'Respecting Sovereign States and Running a Tight Courtroom', (2001) 50 *International and Comparative Law Quarterly*, 121; Ronny Abraham, 'L'amélioration des méthodes de travail de la justice internationale – Le point de vue de la Cour internationale de Justice' in *The Contribution of the International Tribunal for the Law of the Sea to the Rule of Law: 1996-2016* (Brill Nijhoff, Leiden/Boston, 2016), 223; Alina Miron, 'Working Methods of the Court' (2016) 7 *Journal of International Dispute Settlement*, 371; Joan E. Donoghue, "A View

As indicated at the outset, the PCIJ felt the experimental nature of designing rules and procedures concerning its work in its early years. Notwithstanding the gradual development of its rules and working methods over time, the Court proved largely successful in this endeavor. It not only laid down the principles and rules most suited to the proceedings of an international Court and the fundamental principles of international law, which continue to a large extent to govern the proceedings today before the ICJ. It also left room for their flexible and efficient application, and for further developments and improvements as the context and requirements changed over time.

It is also remarkable how the themes regularly addressed today when considering the procedure and working methods of the Court[72] echo some of the questions faced and thoroughly considered by the PCIJ in establishing and revising its Rules and practice. In matters where the debate is sometimes framed as one where "loyalty to tradition competes with the spirit of reform"[73], the legacy of the first World Court, hundred of years after its establishment, remains undoubtedly of great significance.

---

of the Court from Within", Speech of H.E. Judge Joan E. Donoghue, President of the International Court of Justice, to the Sixth Committee of the General Assembly, 28 October 2022 (https://icj-cij.org/sites/default/files/press-releases/0/000-20221028-STA-01-00-EN.pdf).

72 See e.g. Shabtai Rosenne, 'Some Reflections on the 1978 Revised Rules of the International Court of Justice', (1981)19 *Columbia Journal of Transnational Law*, 235 (238); *Report of the Study Group established by the British Institute of International and Comparative Law to examine the efficiency of procedures and working methods of the International Court of Justice*, 45 *International and Comparative Law Quarterly* (1996), 1; ICJ, *A Dialogue at the Court. Proceedings of the ICJ/UNITAR Colloquim held on the occasion of the Sixtieth Anniversary of the International Court of Justice* (ICJ/UNITAR, 2006), 18-31; and the references above in footnote 71.

73 Alina Miron, 'Working Methods of the Court' (2016) 7 *Journal of International Dispute Settlement*, 371, 371. See also: 'Speech of H.E. Judge Joan E. Donoghue, President of the International Court of Justice, on the occasion of the seventy-fifth anniversary of the Court', 18 April 2021 (https://icj-cij.org/sites/default/files/press-releases/0/000-20210419-STA-01-00-EN.pdf), 2.

The Concept of International Law in the Early Advisory Opinions of the Permanent Court of International Justice, 1922–1930

*P. Sean Morris**

A. Introduction

When Jeremy Bentham introduced 'international law' as a term in legal literature, it is commonly held he was doing so in part to find an alternative expression that was acceptable to the English speaking person, as opposed to the term 'law of nations', which was widely used in Continental legal literature.[1] Throughout the 17th and 18th centuries, the law of nations concept was predominantly employed by Continental writers to refer to a 'system of rules' in relation to how nations and peoples regulated their relations with each other.[2] Despite its Continental roots, English writers such as William Blackstone embraced the term law of nations, understood as consisting of rules of natural law, 'mutual compacts, treaties, leagues, and arrangements' among peoples and states.[3] This description is similar to what we nowadays call international law. Yet, for English and Continental writers in these centuries, there was no such concept as international law – at least, not until it was introduced by Bentham to the world.[4]

* I am indebted to Henri de Waele and Christian Tams for their comments and suggestions on an earlier draft of this chapter. I would also like to thank John Morss for a careful reading of the final version. All other mistakes or omissions are the author's.

1 Jeremy Bentham, *An Introduction to the Principles of Morals and Legislation* (Clarendon Press, Oxford 1907). Note that this work, initially published, in 1789 has been reprinted several times.

2 See works such as Emer de Vattell, *The Law of Nations* (1758), translated by Joseph Chitty (Sweet, Stevens and Sons, London 1834) x; Christian Wolff, *Jus Gentium Methodo Scientifica Pertractratum*, Vol. 2, the translation, by Joseph Drake, republished in James Brown Scott (ed), *The Classics of International Law* (Clarendon Press, Oxford 1934).

3 See Mark Janis, 'Jeremy Bentham and the Fashioning of "International Law"' (1984) 78 *American Journal of International Law*, 405 (406).

4 Bentham, *An Introduction to the Principles of Morals and Legislation* (1907), 328.

In the Preface to *Principles of Morals and Legislation*, Bentham wrote:

> Part the 7th. Principles of legislation in matters betwixt nation and nation, or, to use a new though not inexpressive appellation, in matters of international law.[5]

This is significant, and worth pondering for a moment. As we can see, Bentham offered a summary of Part Seven of the work, and while doing so, he introduced a new word that essentially captured and summarised his thoughts. From this point of view, the concept of international law was purely, to use Bentham's words: 'new though not inexpressive appellation.'[6] Had he been writing around the same time as this chapter was penned, he would have been chastised for introducing new terms the reader was not prepared for, or arbitrarily experimenting with the English language. But Bentham was writing in the 1770s (the work was initially printed in 1780 and published in 1789),[7] scoring a first victory for what is still an intellectual pursuit for many writers trying to find answers to the question what *is* international law.

In his *magnum opus*, Bentham identified what he meant by international law, which included 'circumstances that have given rise to the principal branches of jurisprudence.'[8] It should be noted that Bentham's depiction of the concept of international law juxtaposed between notions of jurisprudence as practiced in both England and Continental Europe. Bentham nevertheless went on that the idea of international law is connected to various factors such as political quality of individuals. Bentham explains that:

> These may, on any given occasion, be considered either as members of the same state, or as members of different states; in the first case, the law may be referred to the head of *internal*, in the second case, to that of *international* jurisprudence.[9]

---

5 Ibid, viii.

6 Ibid.

7 Ibid, ii (a note explains that: 'The First Edition of this work was printed in the year 1780; and first published in 1789'). It is presumed that the difference is as stated, the work was printed as written or what we in the 2020s would refer to as self-published before it was put under the imprint of a reputable publisher in 1789.

8 Ibid, 324.

9 Ibid, 326.

Two particular things must be noted about the preceding clauses. The first is that Bentham identified a certain political quality or 'persons whose conduct is the object of the law'.[10] The use of political-quality connotates, at least to the present author's view, state-linkage as one of the features of international law. The second feature, perhaps his core definition of international law, was hidden in a footnote in which he explained the shifting conception of the law of nations. Here he posited the following:

> The word international, it must be acknowledged, is a new one; though, it is hoped, sufficiently analogous and intelligible. It is calculated to express, in a more significant way, the branch of law which goes commonly under the name of the *law of nations*: an appellation so uncharacteristic, that, were it not for the force of custom, it would seem rather to refer to internal jurisprudence. The chancellor D'Aguesseau has already made, I find, a similar remark: he says that what is commonly called *droit des gens*, ought rather to be termed *droit entre les gens*.[11]

It is a reasonable assumption that Bentham familiarised himself with a variety of sources on the law of nations, and was cognisant with the term's explicit meaning.[12] The overarching question may well be: what motivated him? Did he sincerely believe this new *appellation* of international law was more suited to describe law of nations, or was there something jurisprudential or doctrinal to the term, separating it from the law of nations? Given Bentham's familiarity with the 'law of nations' concept, encountered in Blackstone's work[13] or French legal literature (evident from his reference to Henri François D'Aguesseau, 1668–1751),[14] he likely intended to shift the paradigm to the coined word of international law.

In the present author's view, the features of the law of nations can be set out in two forms. The first may be referred to as a 'jurisprudential mode', wherein the doctrinal approach to the law of nations remained theoretical, without any iterations of positive law being understood. This mode would persist until the major shifts in the early 20th century. The second form is that of representing 'mutual transactions' for the purpose of international

10 Ibid.

11 Ibid.

12 See also Mark Janis, 'Jeremy Bentham and the Fashioning of "International Law"' (1984) 78 *American Journal of International Law*, 405 (408–409).

13 Ibid, 405.

14 Ibid, 409 noting that '[i]t may be that reading D'Aguesseau sparked Bentham's creation of the term "international"'.

adjudication, while embracing a shift toward positive law.[15] It should be noted that both these terms appeared in Bentham's work,[16] but are used here in a different context and to different purposes. The contention is that these two forms, modalities or propositions can adequately capture the rise of the World Court in the early 1920s, and its first decade of adjudication. There are of course always pitfalls when using new language to develop and defend an argument. To be sure, the analysis that follows remains a modest one, focusing on the framing of these notions of 'jurisprudential mode' and 'mutual transactions', without delving more deeply into the extensive literature on the law of nations or (the genealogy of) 19th century international law.[17]

B. Conceptualisations of the Law of Nations

It is well known that legal luminaries of the 17th and 18th centuries such as Christian Wolff (1679–1754) and Emer de Vattel (1714–1767), among others, characterised the law of nations as a form of legal 'science' in which peoples and states regulated their relations with each other. For example, in formulating the law of nations as a science, Wolff stated that:

> [W]e understand the science of that law which nations or peoples use in their relations with each other and of the obligations corresponding thereto.[18]

---

15 This chapter hereby merely suggests that the law understood in the context of the law of nations contained sources that were non-formal before a shift or acceptance of positive law; see also Mark Janis, 'Jeremy Bentham and the Fashioning of "International Law"' (1984) 78 *American Journal of International Law*, 405; Edgar Bodenheimer, 'The Notion of Positive Law' (1978) 26 *American Journal of Comparative Law Supplement*, 17; Roscoe Pound, 'Natural Law and the Positive Natural Law' (1960) 5 *National Law Forum*, 70.

16 Jeremy Bentham, *An Introduction to the Principles of Morals and Legislation* (Clarendon Press, Oxford 1907), 326–327, noting 'international jurisprudence' and 'mutual transactions between sovereigns' for presumably the settlement of an international dispute.

17 See generally, David Kennedy, 'International Law and the Nineteenth-Century: History of an Illusion' (1996) 65 *Nordic Journal of International Law*, 385; Robert Schütze, 'German Idealism after Kant: Nineteenth-Century Foundations of International Law' (2023) 25 *Journal of the History of International Law*, 105.

18 James Brown Scott (ed), *The Classics of International Law* (Clarendon Press, Oxford 1934), 9. A similar approach was developed in Emer de Vattel, *The Law of Nations* (1758), translated by Joseph Chitty (Sweet, Stevens and Sons, London 1834), x.

A similar reasoning exists in Vattel's formulation that sees the law of nations as a

> science which teaches the rights subsisting between nations or states, and the obligations correspondent to those rights.[19]

Both characterisations proceed from the same conception of science, as well as the rights and obligations of states. What should be understood is that both stood the test of time and held sway in the doctrinal legal discourses taking place in academia, and to some extent even the practice of law.[20] As a framework for the intellectual structure of the law of nations, the literature up to the turn of the twentieth century would continue to refer to these conceptual frameworks.[21] As initially exemplified by Vattel and Wolff, they articulated a tradition that sought to maintain a unity in the scientific approach, which subsequently proved important for the jurisprudential mode to attract a wider legal community. As pointed out earlier, certainly Bentham seems to have been tempted to embrace it. He however appears to have merely substituted the term 'law of nations' with his new 'international law' appellation.

The law of nations (and its jurisprudential mode) identified rights of states, peoples and obligations in order for them to interact and relate to one another. Meanwhile, the idea of promoting peace fostered a need for pacific settlement of international conflicts. Some of the major conflicts of the nineteenth century such the Franco-Prussian War (1870–1871) and the Russo-Turkish War (1877–1878) nurtured a dream among states, activists and international lawyers to establish a World Court.[22] Such debates flour-

19 Emer de Vattel, *The Law of Nations* (1758), translated by Joseph Chitty (Sweet, Stevens and Sons, London 1834), iv.

20 See Mark Janis, *America and the Law of Nations 1776–1939* (Oxford University Press, Oxford 2010).

21 E.g. James Lorimer, *Institutes of the Law of Nations: A Treatise of the Jural Relations of Separate Political Communities* (William Blackwood and Sons, Edinburgh 1884); Cornelis van Vollenhoven, *The Three Stages in the Evolution of the Law of Nations* (Martinus Nijhoff, Den Haag 1919).

22 The ideas for a world court varied but certainly there have been various epochs where peace activists, states and international lawyers dreamt of a world court prior to the twentieth century, see e.g., Sandi Cooper, *Patriotic Pacifism: Waging War on War in Europe, 1815–1914* (Oxford University Press, Oxford 1991); Paul Laity, *The British Peace Movement 1870–1917* (Oxford University Press, Oxford 2002); Martin Ceadel, *Thinking About Peace and War* (Oxford University Press, Oxford 1987); C. Wilfred Jenks, *The Prospects of International Adjudication* (Stevens and Sons, London 1964).

ished from the 1870s on, whereby many authors expressed concern that the creation of a body without compulsory jurisdiction would be unable to promote the rule of law.[23] Even prior to the 1870s, it is well-known that writers such as Vattel expressed similar arguments. Hence, the idea of international justice, whether in the form of arbitration or a permanent judicial body, has been fundamental to how important aspects of international adjudication came to evolve. In fact, when the Jay Treaty of 1794 was signed between the US and Great Britain, it was assumed that Vattelian notions of justice influenced the negotiators who decided to include specific methods of arbitration.[24]

What then did the law of nations mean in this context? The rise of arbitration and other methods of dispute settlement, which culminated in the founding of the PCIJ in the 1920s, reflected the interrelationship between adjudication and arbitration as 'mutual transactions' for the pacific settlement of disputes. The early outlook to the peaceful settlement of international disputes for example, taking into account principles such as equity and justice, meant that the law of nations contains the same features. This is because the peaceful settlement of disputes reflects the ability to preserve equity and justice, while at the same time representing methods for *enforcing* international law. These methods can allow for successive tribunals to perform their role as a pillar of international society. Article 7 of the Jay Treaty, inter alia, allowed for the appointment of commissioners to adjudicate claims involving violations of the law of nations. These commissioners had to consider 'justice, equity and the law of nations'. Exactly this test, in my view, seems to conform to the idea of 'mutual transactions' in the settlement of international disputes. According to one observer, 'the law of nations is founded on justice, equity, [and] convenience'.[25] The law of nations demonstrates how such mutual transactions are carried out. In

23 C. Wilfred Jenks, *The Prospects of International Adjudication* (Stevens and Sons, London 1964), 13, stating that: 'From the Geneva Arbitration of Award of 1872 until 1930 there appeared to be a long-term trend towards the acceptance of a larger measure of compulsory jurisdiction.'

24 Treaty of Amity, Commerce and Navigation, between His Britannic Majesty; and the United States of America, signed at London 19 November 1794 ("Jay Treaty"). See moreover Alexis Keller, 'Inter-State Arbitration in Historical Perspective' in Thomas Schultz and Federico Ortino (eds), *The Oxford Handbook of International Arbitration* (Oxford University Press, Oxford 2020), 843 (845), note 6, suggesting that Jay relied on Vattel's modern theory of arbitration that was modelled on the Cantons of Switzerland.'

25 Frederick Pollock, *Essays in the Law* (Macmillan, London 1922), 64.

this context, they may be said to represent rights, justice, and equity before an international tribunal. For individuals or entities that appear before such tribunals, they would have a right to justice that is fair and equitable, based on, arguably, the rule of law as developed in the law of nations. At the same time, in face of a World Court with compulsory jurisdiction, states will wish to share the same treatment of justice, fairness and equity.

These theoretical conceptions of the law of nations do not tell the full story. They do rather help to identify ways in which the law of nations shifted from the 18th and 19th to the 20th century. It was during the latter century that the World Court became a reality, and Bentham's notion of international law began to materialise. Where, moreover, taking into account the rise of the scholar-jurist active in the international judiciary, mutual transactions occur also where the output of such an individual serves a source of jurisprudence (legal theory) and a practical source of law.[26] In recent times, similar observations were expressed in a review of the role of international dispute settlement:

> [A] focus of dispute settlement gives higher priority to solving bilateral problems than to vindicating other kinds of community interest. It has tended also to encourage legal-positivist scholarship that emphasizes materials already generated by recognized sources of law (treaties, the custom-creating legal practice of relevant actors, judicial decisions, scholarly opinions, and so on), and strictly separates statements of the *lex lata* from suggestions for reform *de lege ferenda*.[27]

Such views allow one to rethink the rise of the PCIJ in the 1920s, and muse on whether the scholar-jurist who wrote scholarly opinions or sat on the bench had knowingly or unknowingly embraced Bentham's notion, or at least the positive international law the new institutions and World Court found themselves dealing with. This leads on to the question of what the early Advisory Opinions of the Court – as a genre considered

26 See for example Freya Baetens and Veronica Lavista, "'Where is Your Tribunal?' Bernard Loder (1849–1935) and the Quest for International Justice' in P. Sean Morris (ed), *The League of Nations and the Development of International Law* (Routledge, Oxon 2022), 195.

27 Benedict Kingsbury, 'The International Legal Order' in Mark Tushnet and Peter Cane (eds), *The Oxford Handbook of Legal Studies* (Oxford University Press, Oxford 2005), 272.

more academically oriented than rulings on contentious cases[28] – can tell us about its dominant philosophy, and the possible reorientation (in a theoretical and jurisprudential sense) of the international legal system. That this was already happening off the bench is made clear, for example, by the writings of early 20th century publicists such as those by Lassa Oppenheim (1858–1919).[29]

C. The Permanent Court of International Justice and its Advisory Opinions, 1922–1930

The PCIJ was set up in 1920 after the Advisory Committee of Jurists (ACJ) drafted its Statute, subsequently adopted by the Council and Assembly of the League of Nations.[30] The Court was fully operational in 1922, having spent the previous year on administrative matters, by then receiving the first requests for Advisory Opinions. In the summer of 1922, it issued its

28 The focus of this paper are the Advisory Opinions up to 1930 in the PCIJ, and the connection they had with legal scholarship and the scholar-jurist or publicists in fashioning a concept of international law. While it may be tempting to discuss contentious cases, they are not the object of this chapter. Given that the PCIJ operated for eighteen years, it handled only sixty-six applications, of which thirty-eight constituted contentious cases and the remaining twenty-eight were advisory opinions (see Shabtai Rosenne, *The World Court: What It Is and How It Works* (Oceana Publications, New York 1962), 217 listing judicial statistics in Appendix 4). But see Christian J. Tams, 'The Contentious Jurisdiction of the Permanent Court' in Christian J. Tams and Malgosia Fitzmaurice (eds), *Legacies of the Permeant Court of Justice* (Martinus Nijhoff, Leiden/Boston 2013); Marika Giles Samson and Douglas Guilfoyle, 'The Permanent Court of International Justice and the "Invention" of International Advisory Jurisdiction' in Christian J. Tams and Malgosia Fitzmaurice (eds), *Legacies of the Permanent Court of International Justice* (Martinus Nijhoff, Leiden/Boston 2013). See also, Leland Goodrich, 'The Nature of the Advisory Opinions of the Permanent Court of International Justice' (1938) 32 *American Journal of International Law*, 738, (740–743) (discussing in particular developments in the rules regarding contentious procedure).

29 Lassa Oppenheim, *International Law: A Treatise, Vol. 1 – Peace* (Longmans, Green and Company, London 1905), 4.

30 See generally e.g. Willem-Jan van der Wolf and Donja de Ruiter (eds), *The Permanent Court of International Justice: Its History and Landmark Cases* (International Courts Association, Den Haag 2011); P. Sean Morris, *Transforming the Politics of International Law: The Advisory Committee of Jurists and the Formation of the World Court in the League of Nations* (Routledge, Oxon 2021); P. Sean Morris, *The League of Nations and the Development of International Law: A New Intellectual History of the Advisory committee of Jurists* (Routledge, Oxon 2021).

very first response, and by 1930 had published a total of eighteen such documents.[31] We may turn to these Advisory Opinions to look for answers to the question to what extent the Court engaged with legal scholarship, and international law as a concept in the normative sense. In what follows, an attempt is made to ascertain how the aforementioned jurisprudential mode explains the dominant philosophy, treating it either as a form of reasoning or as purely doctrinal approach. Alternatively, it is very possible that the Advisory Opinions more represented the mutual transactions model mentioned earlier.

31 *Designation of the Workers' Delegate for the Netherlands at the Third Session of the International Labour Conference*, Advisory Opinion, 31 July 1922, PCIJ Series B no 1 (1922); *Competence of the International Labour Organization in regard to International Regulation of the Conditions of the Labour of Persons Employed in Agriculture*, Advisory Opinion, 12 August 1922, PCIJ Series B no 2 (1922); *Competence of the International Labour Organization in regard to International Regulation of the Conditions of Labour of Persons Employed in Agriculture*, Advisory Opinion, 12 August 1922, PCIJ Series B no 3 (1922); *Nationality Decrees Issued in Tunis and Morocco (French Zone) on November 8th, 1921 (Great Britain v France)*, Advisory Opinion, 7 February 1923, PCIJ Series B no 4 (1923); *Status of Eastern Carelia*, Advisory Opinion, 23 July 1923, PCIJ Series B no 5 (1923); *Questions relating to Settlers of German Origin in Poland*, Advisory Opinion, 10 September 1923, PCIJ Series B no 6 (1923); *Questions Concerning the Acquisition of Polish Nationality*, Advisory Opinion, 15 September 1923, PCIJ Series B no 7 (1923); *Delimitation of the Polish-Czechoslovakian Frontier (Question of Jaworzina)*, Advisory Opinion, 6 December 1923, PCIJ Series B no 8, (1923); *Question of the Monastery of Saint-Naoum (Albanian Frontier)*, Advisory Opinion, 4 September 1924, PCIJ Series B no 9 (1924); *Exchange of Greek and Turkish Populations (Greece v Turkey)*, Advisory Opinion, 21 February 1925, PCIJ Series B no 10 (1925); *Polish Postal Service in Danzig (Poland v High Commissioner of the League of Nations and Free City of Danzig)*, Advisory Opinion, 16 May 1925, PCIJ Series B no 11 (1925); *Article 3, Paragraph 2, of the Treaty of Lausanne (Frontier between Turkey and Iraq)*, Advisory Opinion, 21 November 1925, PCIJ Series B no 12 (1925); *Competence of the International Labour Organization to Regulate, Incidentally, the Personal Work of the Employer*, Advisory Opinion, 23 July 1926, PCIJ Series B no. 13 (1926); *Jurisdiction of the European Commission of the Danube Between Galatz and Braila, (France and others v Romania)*, Advisory Opinion, 8 December 1927, PCIJ Series B no 14 (1927); *Jurisdiction of the Courts of Danzig (Pecuniary Claims of Danzig Railway Officials who have Passed into the Polish Services, against the Polish Railways Administration)*, Advisory Opinion, 3 March 1928, PCIJ Series B no 15 (1928); *Interpretation of the Greco-Turkish Agreement of December 1st, 1926 (Final Protocol, Article IV)*, Advisory Opinion, 28 August 1928, PCIJ Series B no 16 (1926); *Interpretation of the Convention Between Greece and Bulgaria Respecting Reciprocal Emigration, Signed at Neuilly-Sur-Seine on November 27th, 1919 (Questions of the Greco-Bulgarian 'Communities')*, Advisory Opinion, 31 July 1930, PCIJ Series B no 17 (1930); *Free City of Danzig and International Labour Organization*, Advisory Opinion, 26 August 1930, PCIJ Series B no 18 (1930).

I. Advisory Opinions and Legal Scholarship

The Statute of the PCIJ (and its successor the International Court of Justice) provides that the writings of publicists are a source of international law.[32] During the drafting process of this provision, this proved to be one of the contentious issues in the ACJ on which the views of the members differed.[33] Eventually, a compromise was agreed upon. As such, legal writings and teachings are integral to the development of the discipline. The extent to which these were important in the Advisory Opinions of the PCIJ up to 1930 is altogether a different matter, however.

The precise meaning or definition of the type of publicists, writings or teachings the Court could refer to remained unclear. With hindsight, one may surmise that in the modern rendition, the requisite high qualifications include academic appointments as professor, completion of relevant degrees (often a doctorate) and/or having published books or treatises in respected journals. In the early 1920s, the elite cadre that could be regarded as forming part of this group would have been made up of Europeans (in the Grotian tradition), Americans, alongside a few representatives from other 'civilisations' in Asia or Latin America.

Even if in the 1920s, the pool of qualified publicists was still limited, this would hardly have been pressing, or even noticeable, during PCIJ deliberations. With the eyes of the world drawn to the promising new actor in The Hague, the PCIJ was inevitably plagued by a lack of time to develop a comprehensive view on the matter. Moreover, if only due to the booting-up of the Peace Palace Library, the available volume of appropriate publications was limited. There had besides been few writings on such important themes of the era as the extent to which autonomous entities or 'free cities' could become members of alliances or international organisations. It was precisely one such question that the Court was confronted with

---

32 For contemporary purposes, reference is had to the ICJ Statute, Article 38(1)(d) '(...) the teachings of the most highly qualified publicists of the various nations.' Some recent discussions on this include Sondre Torp Helmersen, 'Finding "The Most Highly Qualified Publicists": Lessons from the International Court of Justice' (2019) 30 *European Journal of International Law*, 509; Sandesh Sivakumaran, 'The Influence of Teachings of Publicists on the Development of International Law' (2017) 66 *International and Comparative Law Quarterly*, 1.

33 See Advisory Committee of Jurists, *Procès-Verbaux of the Proceedings of the Committee: June 16th–July 24th 1920*, 334, and other places where terminologies such as 'opinions', 'doctrines' and 'teachings' were often used.

in the Advisory Opinion on the *Free City of Danzig* in 1930.[34] At the end of its deliberations, it concluded that the Free City of Danzig could not join the International Labour Organization (ILO).[35] The PCIJ did not draw on any writings or teachings of publicists to arrive at this conclusion.[36]

The aforementioned dossier did not offer the only occasion in which the affairs and administration of the Free City were referred to the Court. In fact, there were five other instances in which it had to deal with matters concerning this actor, the most famous being *Polish Postal Services*[37] and *Jurisdiction of the Courts of Danzig*,[38] as well as three others after 1931.[39] In light of the Free City's special status, the PCIJ was only required to admit that Polish consent was necessary for it to become an ILO member. By recognising this, the Court avoided the larger question of sovereignty, which was neither an academic issue, nor something the PCIJ had a mandate to address.[40]

In its third pronouncement in this series, *Jurisdiction of the Courts of Danzig*,[41] the Court acknowledged the titles of the (arguably) highly qualified publicists who appeared before it as representatives for the parties. They were sometimes explicitly identified as professors of international

34 *Free City of Danzig and International Labour Organization*, Advisory Opinion, 26 August 1930, PCIJ Series B no 18 (1930).

35 Ibid, 16.

36 In addition to the Majority Opinion, there were two Individual Opinions by Judge Max Huber and Judge Dionisio Anzilotti, neither of which contains any references to legal writings.

37 *Polish Postal Service in Danzig (Poland v High Commissioner of the League of Nations and Free City of Danzig)*, Advisory Opinion, 16 May 1925, PCIJ Series B no 11 (1925).

38 *Jurisdiction of the Courts of Danzig (Pecuniary Claims of Danzig Railway Officials who have Passed into the Polish Services, against the Polish Railways Administration)*, Advisory Opinion, 3 March 1928, PCIJ Series B no 15 (1928).

39 *Access to, or Anchorage in, the Port of Danzig, of Polish War Vessels (Free City of Danzig v Poland)*, Advisory Opinion, 11 December 1931, PCIJ Series A/B no 43, (1931); *Treatment of Polish Nationals and Other Polish Origin or Speech in the Danzig Territory*, Advisory Opinion, 4 February 1932, PCIJ Series A/B no 44 (1932); and, *Consistency of Certain Danzig Legislative Decrees with the Constitution of the Free City, German National Members of the Danzig Popular Assembly and Ors v Senate of the Free City of Danzig*, Advisory Opinion, 4 December 1935, PCIJ Series A/B no 65 (1935).

40 *Free City of Danzig and International Labour Organization*, Advisory Opinion, 26 August 1930, PCIJ Series B no 18 (1930), 15: 'Polish consent would be necessary.'

41 *Jurisdiction of the Courts of Danzig (Pecuniary Claims of Danzig Railway Officials who have Passed into the Polish Services, against the Polish Railways Administration)*, Advisory Opinion, 3 March 1928, PCIJ Series B no 15 (1928).

law.[42] This was for example the case with regard to M.G. Gidel,[43] E. Kaufmann, W. Schucking, A. Cavaglieri and L. Le Fur.[44] The PCIJ identified four legal opinions, signed respectively by the four professors.[45] Their submissions were included in the appeal to the Council of the League of Nations.[46] The eventual Advisory Opinion was accompanied by three annexes which did not include the professorial legal statements.[47] What can be deduced from this however is that their submissions had the aim of influencing the outcome.[48] Perhaps though, it is more important to qualify their submissions in the context of the jurisprudential mode as coming from men who once walked the academic marble halls, especially when they expanded on whether rights or obligations could be created under international agreements.[49]

In its earlier Advisory Opinion, *Polish Postal Service in Danzig*,[50] the PCIJ similarly acknowledged how professors, even if not representing a party, had been playing a consultative role, referring in particular to the Dutch scholar Jan Verzijl.[51] At one stage, the Court pointed out how such

---

42 Ibid, 7.

43 Ibid, 7.

44 Ibid, 12.

45 Ibid, 12.

46 Ibid, 12.

47 *Jurisdiction of the Courts of Danzig (Pecuniary Claims of Danzig Railway Officials who have Passed into the Polish Services, against the Polish Railways Administration)*, Advisory Opinion, 3 March 1928, PCIJ Series B no 15 (1928), 44, Annex 3, however list the documents submitted and this include the legal opinions of the professors.

48 This assumption is based on whether the legal opinions by the professors made references to their own writings or other writings on international law.

49 *Jurisdiction of the Courts of Danzig (Pecuniary Claims of Danzig Railway Officials who have Passed into the Polish Services, against the Polish Railways Administration)*, Advisory Opinion, 3 March 1928, PCIJ Series B no 15 (1928), 26: 'Since the *Beamtenabkommen*, according to its contents, deals precisely with the regime which Poland is bound under international law to grant to its railway officials taken over from Danzig, and since the *Beamtenabkommen* is an agreement to execute, amongst others, the Decision of September 5th, 1921, which established the jurisdiction of the Danzig tribunals, the applicability of the *Beamtenabkommen* by those tribunals must be considered as being in conformity with international law, unless the contrary is proved.'

50 *Polish Postal Service in Danzig (Poland v High Commissioner of the League of Nations and Free City of Danzig)*, Advisory Opinion, 16 May 1925, PCIJ Series B no 11 (1925).

51 *Polish Postal Service in Danzig (Poland v High Commissioner of the League of Nations and Free City of Danzig)*, Advisory Opinion, 16 May 1925, PCIJ Series B no 11 (1925), 30. Jan Hendrik Willem Verzijl (1888–1987) served as Professor of International Law mainly at Utrecht University (1919–1938 and 1947–1958), and would go onto write

individuals were taken in high esteem in their academic capacity, as opposed to mere individuals, acting as counsellor or representative for the parties. Conversely, it is the same position that gave professors of international law an entry point into the inner workings of international tribunals, as they form part of a highly selective group. The aforementioned found themselves in the excellent company of e.g. Jules Basdevant (1887–1968); Charles de Visscher (1884–1973) or Nikolaos Politis (1872–1942) when they wore the hat of counsellor before the PCIJ.

In *Jurisdiction of the Commission of the Danube*, proceedings wherein de Visscher and Politis donned their counsellor hat, the PCIJ opined that the international organisation responsible for the maritime affairs of the eponymous river enjoyed powers 'over the whole of the maritime area'.[52] This Advisory Opinion was exceedingly lengthy and involved a well-covered branch of international law: international waterways law. Interestingly, no academic papers were mentioned, which does not exclude the possibility that the various memorials, letters, and other documents submitted did mention or refer to academic treatises.[53] This almost conveys the impression that scholarship was neglected wholesale, signalling that writings and

influential books such as *International Law in Historical Perspective: International Persons* (Sijthoff, Leiden 1968).

52 *Jurisdiction of the European Commission of the Danube Between Galatz and Braila, (France and others v Romania),* Advisory Opinion, 8 December 1927, PCIJ Series B no 14 (1927), 69; the professors on this occasion were representative of the states, 10. In *Questions Concerning the Acquisition of Polish Nationality,* Advisory Opinion, 15 September 1923, PCIJ Series B no 7 (1923), 8, the PCIJ also identified Michal Jan Rostworowski from the University of Cracow as having made oral statements; see moreover *Delimitation of the Polish-Czechoslovakian Frontier (Question of Jaworzina),* Advisory Opinion, 6 December 1923, PCIJ Series B no 8, (1923), 16, identifying Jan Kremar, University of Prague; *Questions relating to Settlers of German Origin in Poland,* Advisory Opinion, 10 September 1923, PCIJ Series B no 6 (1923), 12, noting the various submissions from professors including letters and observations; *Nationality Decrees Issued in Tunis and Morocco (French Zone) on November 8th, 1921 (Great Britain v France),* Advisory Opinion, 7 February 1923, PCIJ Series B no 4 (1923), 11 identifying 'M.A. de Lapradelle, Professor of International Law, at the University of Paris, on behalf of the French Government'.

53 *Jurisdiction of the European Commission of the Danube Between Galatz and Braila, (France and others v Romania),* Advisory Opinion, 8 December 1927, PCIJ Series B no 14 (1927), Annex, listing the material submitted. The focus here lies on the text of the actual Opinion, regardless of the lists included in Series C of the PCIJ's publications, dedicated to: Acts and Documents Relating to Judgments and Advisory Opinions Given by the Court/Pleadings, Oral Arguments and Documents.

teachings were not a doctrinal form the Court was ready to embrace in Advisory Opinions.

In the *Eastern Carelia* Advisory Opinion however, the PCIJ made an explicit reference to scholarly papers, albeit documents produced by a jurist-scholar who was connected to one of the parties.[54] Rafael Erich (1879–1946) served as professor of international law at the University of Helsinki, and would come to take a seat at the PCIJ in its waning days. He was a prolific author who could claim to fulfil the criterion of being a highly qualified publicist.[55] In 1922 and 1923, Erich published two articles in French, one under the title '*La question de la Carelie orientale*', in a prominent journal.[56] Both of his articles dealt with the contested area between Finland and the Soviet Union in an historical perspective, and the legal issues for the Court to consider. The PCIJ acknowledged his work in its Opinion:

> The Court also heard, at the request of the Finnish Government, the statements of its representative, M. Rafael Erich, and received from him a document containing arguments supplementary to those statements. The Court had informed M. Erich before hearing his statement that it would be glad to have his views as to whether it had competence to give effect to the request for an advisory opinion upon the question of Eastern Carelia, submitted to it by the Council of the League of Nations.[57]

That Erich's papers were known may invite the question whether the Court was enthusiastic to embrace these academic writings and views, or whether the politics surrounding Eastern Carelia proved too intense for the Court. Whatever may explain the outcome, when reviewing the total output from

54 *Status of Eastern Carelia,* Advisory Opinion, 23 July 1923, PCIJ Series B no 5 (1923), 11: 'Furthermore, the Court had before it a certain number of documents transmitted to it on behalf of the Finnish Government, namely: 1. A paper by Erich, called "*La question de la Carelie orientale*." (…) 3. A paper by M. Erich, called '*La question de la Carelie orientale soumise pour avis a la Cour permanente de Justice international*."

55 Erich defended his dissertation written in German in 1907 at the University of Helsinki, see Rafael Erich, *Über Allianzen und Allianzverhältnisse nach heutigem Völkerrecht* (Buchdruckerei-Aktiengesellschaft Sana, Helsingfors 1907).

56 See Rafael Erich, 'La Question de la Carelie Orientale' (1922) 3 *Revue de Droit International et de legislation comparee (1st series)*, 1; Rafael Erich, 'La Question de la Carelie Orientale Soumise pour Avis a la Cour Permanente de Justice Internationale' (1923) 4 *Revue de Droit International et de legislation comparee (3rd Series)*, 227.

57 *Status of Eastern Carelia,* Advisory Opinion, 23 July 1923, PCIJ Series B no 5 (1923), 11-12. Both articles are reproduced in the list of documents in the PCIJ C-Series: Acts and Documents Relating to Judgments, 61.

the 1920s, this Opinion was indeed one of the rare moments where the PCIJ directly referred to legal scholarship.

A further relevant observation from *Eastern Carelia* is that published articles are the only form of doctrinal thinking the Court was ever willing to consider. This suggests that publications in respected international legal periodicals were taken to channel pertinent insight and information on the issues of the day that the Court could reasonably take into account.

One last observation one may make on the basis of the range of Advisory Opinions that saw the light of day is that in the few instances where legal scholarship was referred to, the notion of 'publicists' was habitually equated with 'professors'. Seemingly, the latter constituted the ideal of 'highly qualified' authors. If statements were submitted by others, for example those holding a doctorate, perhaps adhering to a German custom, such a title would be mentioned. This view suggests that there was a significant hierarchal appreciation of publicists employed by universities, possibly reflecting how the ACJ was unable to reach a consensus on the terminology to be used in the Statute, such as 'works', 'opinions', 'teachings', or 'doctrines'.[58] In spite of their paucity though, the findings on the limited role played by legal scholarship in the Court's Advisory Opinions does reveal how ideas, opinions, and teachings were gradually cementing their role as a source of international law, as Article 38(1)(d) of the Statute had presumably intended.

II. The Concept of International Law as 'Principles of International Law'

On some occasions, in the eighteen Advisory Opinions delivered, for the PCIJ the concept of international law appeared to mean a formal reference to the 'principles of international law'. This one may surmise from the fact that in its output, the concept of international law as such would at times only be mentioned within the framework of general principles of international law. In so doing, the Court gives the impression of having embraced a Blackstonian or Oppenheimian understanding of international law. In

58 See Advisory Committee of Jurists, *Procès-Verbaux of the Proceedings of the Committee: June 16th–July 24th 1920.* In *Jurisdiction of the Courts of Danzig (Pecuniary Claims of Danzig Railway Officials who have Passed into the Polish Services, against the Polish Railways Administration)*, Advisory Opinion, 3 March 1928, PCIJ Series B no 15 (1928), 31, Annex I, the role of doctrine was briefly noted.

1905, when Oppenheim published the first volume of his famous treatise on international law, he made it clear that various takes are imaginable:

> Law of Nations or International Law (...) is the name for the body of customary and conventional rules which are considered legally binding by civilised States in their intercourse with each other. Such part of these rules as is binding upon all the civilised States without exception is called *universal* International Law, in contradistinction to *particular* International Law, which is binding on two or a few States only. But it is also necessary to distinguish *general* International Law. This name must be given to the body of such rules as are binding upon a great many States (...).[59]

In some ways, when the PCIJ started to deliver Advisory Opinions, its conceptual approach hinged on whether it was comfortable in discussing general (principles of) international law, customary international law, or to borrow from Oppenheim, universal international law. A closer inspection suggests there has been no uniformity in the application of these terms. Yet, the mentioning of general principles of international law in Advisory Opinions denotes a cautious endorsement of how international law was understood in legal literature in the eyes of leading publicists. As remarked, most of the Advisory Opinions in the 1922–1930 period do not engage with legal scholarship, and therefore avoid linking the discipline of international law as such to a particular teaching.[60] Rather, in the majority of its Opinions, for the PCIJ, international law was *the* argument – the field extended to everything the Court did.[61] Hence, if there was a need to identify specific forms of international law, they were linked to 'principles' those that could be labelled 'customary' or simply 'international law'.[62]

59 Lassa Oppenheim, *International Law: A Treatise, Vol. 1 – Peace* (Longman, Green and Company, London 1905), 1.

60 In *Exchange of Greek and Turkish Populations (Greece v Turkey)*, Advisory Opinion, 21 February 1925, PCIJ Series B no 10 (1925), 17, the Court was close to offer a definition of international law as a concept when it made comparisons with the word 'established': 'In the first place the Court is satisfied that the difference of opinion which has arisen regarding the meaning and scope of the word 'established', is a dispute regarding the interpretation of a treaty and as such involves a question of international law.'

61 Article 38 of the Statute provides that the Court's function 'is to decide in accordance with international law such disputes as are submitted to it.'

62 At the times when the PCIJ invoked 'international law' as a term, it was succinct, for instance in *Questions relating to Settlers of German Origin in Poland*, Advisory

In *Nationality Decrees Issued in Tunis and Morocco*, the question was asked whether the aforementioned decrees, applicable to British subjects, were solely a matter for domestic law pursuant to positive international law.[63] Initially, the PCIJ attempted to clear up any perceived misconceptions regarding international law and domestic jurisdiction:

> It should next be observed that the resolution also differs from the text of the Covenant, in that the latter speaks of 'a matter which by international law is solely within the domestic jurisdiction' – (...) whereas the resolution asks whether the "dispute" between the two Powers is a matter of "domestic jurisdiction" (...). The Court is, however, of opinion that these differences are of no juridical importance. In effect, the question before the Court is whether the dispute mentioned in the Council's resolution relates to a matter which, by international law, is solely within the domestic jurisdiction of France.[64]

The analysis here was Oppenheimian, particularly through its identification of the forms of international law:

> From one point of view, it might well be said that the jurisdiction of a State is *exclusive* within the limits fixed by international law – using this expression in its wider sense, that is to say, embracing both customary law and general as well as particular treaty law. (...) The words "solely within the domestic jurisdiction" seem rather to contemplate certain matters which, though they may very closely concern the interests of more than one State, are not, in principle, regulated by international law. As regards such matters, each State is sole judge.[65]

Opinion, 10 September 1923, PCIJ Series B no 6, (1923), where it noted on p. 36 that: 'Even those who contest the existence in international law of a general principle of State succession do not go so far as to main that private rights including those acquired from the State as the owner of the property are invalid as against a successor in sovereignty.' The term international law on this occasion was linked to general principle, and to the broader question of sovereignty and property.

63 *Nationality Decrees Issued in Tunis and Morocco (French Zone) on November 8th, 1921 (Great Britain v France)*, Advisory Opinion, 7 February 1923, PCIJ Series B no 4 (1923).

64 Ibid, 22.

65 Ibid, 23–24. Italics in original.

Compared to the law of nations, alongside the concept of international law Oppenheim wrote about in 1905,[66] it is clear that some form of jurisprudential mode originating from legal literature loomed large in the minds of the judges. Yet, from *Nationality Decrees Issued in Tunis and Morocco*, it may be inferred too that the Court believed that there was a general concept of international law operating in a wider sense, which included 'customary' international law, 'particular treaty law' or 'principles of international law'.[67] In some way, the PCIJ also appeared to be saying that the concept of international law allowed for 'mutual transactions', given that it was adjudicating a dispute between France and Great Britain. Under these circumstances, mutual transactions rested on the enduring relevance of bilateral treaties as existed between France and Great Britain regarding North Africa, and in a more general sense as well, considering how the Court interpreted these to take into account general principles of international law.[68] The Court proved to be well aware how particular international law such as bilateral treaty law could be useful in resolving disputes. At the same time, the PCIJ acknowledged that it had no authority to interfere in the domestic legislative sovereignty of Great Powers such as France. All in all, the situation was extremely challenging, knowing that on the other side, Great Britain would not accept that its 'subjects' in North Africa would be under the jurisdiction of France.[69] The decree that the French government used to apply to British subjects, the Court concluded, was 'a matter which, by international law, is not solely within the domestic jurisdiction of France'.[70]

---

66 Lassa Oppenheim, *International Law: A Treatise, Vol. 1 – Peace* (Longmans, Green and Company, London 1905).

67 *Nationality Decrees Issued in Tunis and Morocco (French Zone) on November 8th, 1921 (Great Britain v France),* Advisory Opinion, 7 February 1923, PCIJ Series B no 4 (1923), 29, recognizing principles of international law. In other Advisory Opinions, 'principles of public international law' was only mentioned in passing, e.g. *Interpretation of the Greco-Turkish Agreement of December 1st, 1926 (Final Protocol, Article IV),* Advisory Opinion, 28 August 1928, PCIJ Series B no 16 (1926), 14.

68 *Article 3, Paragraph 2, of the Treaty of Lausanne (Frontier between Turkey and Iraq),* Advisory Opinion, 21 November 1925, PCIJ Series B no 12 (1925).

69 *Nationality Decrees Issued in Tunis and Morocco (French Zone) on November 8th, 1921 (Great Britain v France),* Advisory Opinion, 7 February 1923, PCIJ Series B no 4 (1923), 30, pointing out the international character of the legal situation.

70 Ibid, 32. See also Nathaniel Berman, *Passion and Ambivalence: Colonialism, Nationalism, and International Law* (Brill Nijhoff, Leiden 2011), chapter 5, offering an in-depth study of the case.

In later cases such as *Exchange of Greek and Turkish Populations*[71] and *Jurisdiction of the Courts of Danzig*, the PCIJ came close to defining a concept of international law. In the latter Opinion, it essentially stated that international agreements form part of the general principles of international law:

> It may be readily admitted that, according to a well established principle of international law, the *Beamtenabkommen*, being an international agreement, cannot, as such, create direct rights and obligations for private individuals.[72]

In this instance, the Court relied on a previous Opinion to make the point that general principles of international law are so well established that they *inter alia* included its own judicial practices. More importantly for the discussion here, in line with the codification by the ACJ, the Court wished to capture the notion of general principles as forming part of international law's sources.[73] Such principles ought to be seen as being fully recognised by the world's nations, but as such they are broad enough to result equally from 'established' practices in international law. In *Nationality Decrees Issued in Tunis and Morocco*, the PCIJ actually argued that it was impossible to make pronouncements on for example the duration of treaties without engaging with general international law principles.[74]

From this succinct review of Advisory Opinions, we may deduce two tendencies. First, as seen in practice, the concept of international law crops up in situations pertaining to bilateral legal relations of states that conform to the 'mutual transactions' model. Secondly, some of the practice contains

---

71 *Exchange of Greek and Turkish Populations (Greece v Turkey)*, Advisory Opinion, 21 February 1925, PCIJ Series B no 10 (1925), 17.

72 *Jurisdiction of the Courts of Danzig (Pecuniary Claims of Danzig Railway Officials who have Passed into the Polish Services, against the Polish Railways Administration)*, Advisory Opinion, 3 March 1928, PCIJ Series B no 15 (1928), 17, 24.

73 In *Interpretation of the Convention Between Greece and Bulgaria Respecting Reciprocal Emigration, Signed at Neuilly-Sur-Seine on November 27th, 1919 (Questions of the 'Communities')*, Advisory Opinion, 31 July 1930, PCIJ Series B no 17 (1930), 32, the PCIJ also confirmed the existence of general principles of international law; and, similarly, in *Jurisdiction of the European Commission of the Danube*, Dissenting Opinion of Judge Negulesco (31) 92; *Status of Eastern Carelia*, Advisory Opinion, 23 July 1923, PCIJ Series B no 5 (1923), 27.

74 *Nationality Decrees Issued in Tunis and Morocco (French Zone) on November 8th, 1921 (Great Britain v France)*, Advisory Opinion, 7 February 1923, PCIJ Series B no 4 (1923), 29: 'It is clearly not possible to make any pronouncement (...) without recourse to the principles of international law (...).'

elements of the jurisprudential mode, aligning with the conception found in the works of Oppenheim or Bentham. In combination, these analyses capture part of the evolutionary process, which may help to illuminate the Court's philosophy, and in further inquiries, to grasp how it framed its broader concept of international law.

D. Concluding Remarks

The intention of this chapter has been to ascertain how the PCIJ in its Advisory Opinions in the 1922–1930 period approached international law as a concept, and whether legal scholarship had any role to play in this. After an examination of eighteen Advisory Opinions, it was demonstrated above that there was limited use, there were hardly any references to scholarship, nor was the concept of international law subjected to elaborate doctrinal considerations. The latter was rather considered within the general framework of general principles. On other occasions, international law got mentioned in passing to indicate the wider ambit of a particular dispute.

A second finding is that, while the Court was hesitant to embrace scholarship wholeheartedly, it was nevertheless keen to identify the professor of international law as the archetypal scholar-jurist who could inform its sources. This might hypothetically have been an incentive to harness the 'teachings and writings' of the said professors in some of its output – however, it never did so. Only in *Eastern Carelia* were there some vague efforts in this respect, but the eventual Advisory Opinion did not indicate whether the submissions had influenced its conclusions.

A third and last insight relates to the PCIJ's concept of international law, which emerges from the above analysis as essentially being of two types: part of the broader system of international legal relations (mutual transactions), or international law as general principles (jurisprudential mode). In the former, the concept of international law forms part of its general dynamics, serves as a general reference to the discipline, and is devoid of further explanatory value. In the latter, it represents the earlier-established notion of general principles of international law with its historical roots in the law of nations. Traces of both conceptions are observable in the Court's Advisory Opinions of the era, whereby chronologically, the 'jurisprudential mode' may in incremental fashion have been giving way to an adjudicatory approach premised on 'mutual transactions'. It is hoped that the above investigations assist in mapping and explaining the World Court's judicial philosophy as it travelled through the 20th century. They certainly carry the potential to illuminate that old question on whether international law is really law.

'Asking the Right Questions' or 'A Matter of Taste': Subject Matter Preliminary Objections and the Creation of the PCIJ

*Momchil Milanov**

It is difficult – indeed it is well-nigh impossible – to think of a court without at one and the same time having in mind the jurisdiction of the court.
James Brown Scott

We passed hours and hours and days in that committee in discussing subjects where the only difference was not in our discussion or in what we were saying, but in a different set of ideas in the backs of our heads
Elihu Root

A. Introduction

According to Borges, De Quincey once wrote that to discover a new problem was quite as important as discovering the solution to an old one.[1] The problem discussed in this paper is not new. Nor is the solution, or solutions – as will become clear, there is more than one. The paper proposes to discuss the early experiences of the Permanent Court of International Justice with preliminary objections directed against its subject matter jurisdiction in the context of Article 36(1) of the Statute, i.e. where the jurisdiction of the Court is based on a compromissory clause.

It has frequently been argued that from the standpoint of litigant states, jurisdiction is very likely the most important aspect of the work of the ICJ'.[2] With the busier docket and the rising number of applications instituting

* The views expressed are personal and do not necessarily reflect those of the International Court of Justice or the United Nations.

1 Jorge Luis Borges, *This Craft of Verse* (Harvard University Press, Cambridge, Massachussets and London 2000), 2.

2 Juan José Quintana, *Litigation at the International Court of Justice* (Brill Nijhoff, Leiden 2015), 40.

proceedings in the last quarter of a century, there has rarely been a case before the Court where the respondent has not raised preliminary objections *ratione materiae*. In his doctoral thesis on preliminary objections, Georges Abi-Saab wrote that: '*dès le début de l'activité de la Cour internationale, les exceptions préliminaires ont joué un rôle important dans sa procédure, rôle qui ne cesse de s'accroitre*'.[3] In his course given at the Hague Academy in 1938, Mario Scerni observed that '*dans les procès devant la Cour, surtout dans les affaires portées à sa connaissance par requête unilatérale, l'exception d'incompétence joue un rôle bien plus important que dans les procès internes*'.[4] The last edition of *Rosenne's Law and Practice of the International Court*, stated that 'the question whether and to what extent the Court has jurisdiction is frequently of political importance no less than the decision on the merits, if not more'.[5]

In the last one hundred years, the PCIJ and its successor have oscillated between the two diametrically opposed approaches. In some cases, when the respondent argues that that the applicants' claims do not fall in the scope of the treaty, the Permanent Court and its successor have accepted the applicant's allegations on a provisional basis without examining them in detail at the preliminary objections phase. In others, it has done exactly the opposite, explicitly stating that it '[i]t must ascertain whether the violations (...) do or do not fall within the provisions of the Treaty and whether, as a consequence, the dispute is one which the Court has jurisdiction *ratione materiae*'.[6] Scholars,[7] counsel[8] before the Court and even individual

3 Georges Abi-Saab, *Les exceptions préliminaires dans la procédure de la Cour internationale* (Pedone, Paris 1967), 23.

4 Mario Scerni, 'La procédure de la Cour permanente de Justice internationale' (1938) 65 *Recueil des Cours de l'Académie de Droit International de La Haye*, 611.

5 Shabtai Rosenne and Malcolm Nathan Shaw, *Rosenne's Law and Practice of the International Court 1920-2015* (5th edn, Brill Nijhoff, Leiden 2016), 827.

6 *Case concerning Oil Platforms (Islamic Republic of Iran v. United States of America)*, Judgment of 12 December 1996, ICJ Reports (1996), para 16, 810.

7 Marco Dimetto, '"To Fall, or Not to Fall, That Is the (Preliminary) Question": Disputes, Compromissory Clauses and Swinging Jurisdictional Tests at the ICJ' (2022) 21 *The Law and Practice of International Courts and Tribunals*, 5.

8 See e.g. *Case concerning Certain Iranian Assets (Islamic Republic of Iran v. United States of America)* CR 2018/28, at 62, 64 (Kimball); CR 2018/31 (Wordsworth), 10-11, 25; CR 2018/32 (Bethlehem), 25; *Legality of Use of Force (Serbia and Montenegro v. Belgium)* CR 2004/15 (Devadder) 15; *Case concerning Oil Platforms (Islamic Republic of Iran v. United States of America)* CR 96/15 (Crawford) 45-6: 'So the immediate task before the Court is to decide what test it will apply at this jurisdictional stage to determine

judges[9] have referred to this operation as the '*Oil Platforms* test'. However, it has arguably been neglected that this approach was applied more than 70 years before the first *Oil Platforms* judgment and second, the reliance on such a 'test' as if it is an objective, scientific reality cannot be accepted at face value.

Why is this decision so important? If the so-called 'test' is applied and the allegations are analysed at this early stage, part or the entire case may fall before reaching the merits. It is a truism and even a banality that the 'clients' of the Court are states, jealously striving to preserve their sovereignty and it easy to imagine that an applicant can perceive the outcome of this decision as a denial of justice. On the other hand, it is equally possible that if the Court accepts the applicant's allegations *pro tem*, the respondent may complain that the boundaries of its consent have been overstepped. This is the dilemma before the Court.

The tension between the two approaches is visible already in the very first cases submitted to the PCIJ and continues to characterise its case law in its entire existence until today. In this paper I would like to return to the origins of the Permanent Court and take a closer look at the main factors determining the treatment of subject matter preliminary objections. It goes without saying that the discussions within the Advisory Committee of Jurists (ACJ) in the summer of 1920 and the subsequent debates in the Assembly and the Council of the League occupy a central place (Section 2). But the story begins already in the nineteenth century (Section 1). That is why the paper will first present the historical antecedents of such objections, before briefly turning to the projects of an international court preceding the ACJ. In Sections 3 and 4 I will try to analyse the first experiences of the PCIJ with preliminary objections and show the two earliest instances of the competing approaches. The last section offers some brief concluding observations.

---

whether the dispute involves, or concerns, the Treaty of Amity within the meaning of the compromissory clause'.

9 *Case concerning Oil Platforms (Islamic Republic of Iran v. United States of America)*, Judgment of 12 December 1996, ICJ Reports (1996), 854, Separate Opinion of Judge Higgins; *Case concerning Oil Platforms (Islamic Republic of Iran v. United States of America)*, Judgment of 12 December 1996, ICJ Reports (1996), 822-824, 826, Separate Opinion of Judge Shahabuddeen.

B. Preliminary Objections prior to 1920

Any history of the emergence of preliminary objections *ratione materiae* is also a history of how compromissory clauses gradually became the default instrument of international (judicial) dispute settlement. Such clauses appeared well before the establishment of the Permanent Court. They hark back to the 1870-1880s[10], a period traditionally associated with the birth of international law as a professional discipline mainly due to the creation of the *Institut de droit international* and the *Alabama* arbitration.

In 1875, very soon after its establishment, the *Institut* adopted Draft Regulations for International Arbitral Procedure.[11] They are significant in two respects: first, in admitting the possibility for objections on the competence of the arbitral tribunal and second, on the recognition of the *compétence de la compétence* rule.[12] In 1877, the *Institut* adopted a resolution at the Zurich session in which it recommended the inclusion of a compromissory clause in the treaties,[13] thus showing that the arbitration is compatible with the respect for the sovereignty of the states.

10 See *Case concerning Oil Platforms (Islamic Republic of Iran v. United States of America)*, Judgment of 12 December 1996, ICJ Reports (1996), 823, Separate Opinion of Judge Shahabuddeen referring to PCIJ, *Factory at Chorzbw* (Series C, No. 13 (I)), "Réponse du Gouvernement allemand à l'exception préliminaire du Gouvernement polonais", pp. 174-176, and John Bassett Moore, *History and Digest of the International Arbitrations to Which the United States Has Been a Party, Vol. V* (U.S. Government Printing Office, Washington 1986), 5057. But there are even earlier examples. Already in 1874, such a clause appeared in multilateral postal conventions. See Treaty concerning the formation of a General Postal Union, Bern, 9 October 1874, Article 16, Edward Hertslet, *A Complete Collection of the Treaties and Conventions between Great Britain and Foreign Powers* (1880), 67, at 72. See also Convention for a Universal Postal Union, Paris, 1 June 1878, Article 17.

11 An English translation made by James Brown Scott is available online at https://www.idi-iil.org/app/uploads/2016/01/1875-Session-of-The-Hague-Arbitral-Procedure-translated-Scott.pdf. See also *Revue de droit international et legislation comparée 1874*, 589ff. See also Advisory Committee of Jurists, *Procès-Verbaux of the Proceedings of the Committee: June 16th–July 24th 1920*, 14 (Descamps): 'En ce qui concerne la procédure arbitrale, il n'existait pas, avant la Conference de 1899, de règles juridiques générales acceptées de concert par les Etats. Un projet de réglement concernant cette matière avait été élaboré par l'Institut de Droit International, et complété par d'autres travaux de jurisconsultes éminents'.

12 See in particular Article 14.

13 l'Institut de Droit International, *Arbitrage international: clause compromissoire à insérer dans les traités*, https://www.idi-iil.org/app/uploads/2017/06/1877_zur_01_fr.pdf

This brief *rappel historique* would be incomplete without mentioning the two peace conferences in The Hague in 1899 and 1907. The members of the 1920 Advisory Committee of Jurists evaluated the success of their endeavour against the background of these conferences and in that sense, they served as important benchmarks. While the conferences failed to create a 'real' court of justice, the outcome of their work shows the first timid beginnings of some key principles in the nascent international procedural law. Article 53 of the 1907 Convention for the Peaceful Settlement of International Disputes is particularly interesting in that it recognises the competence of the PCA to 'settle the compromis' (l'établissement du compromis'). According to this provision, the PCA is competent (even if the request is made only by one of the parties!) when negotiations have failed, in the case of a dispute 'covered by a general Treaty of Arbitration providing for a "Compromis" in all disputes and not either explicitly or implicitly excluding the settlement of the "Compromis" from the competence of the Court.' On the other hand, the PCA is not competent, if the other party declares that in its opinion the dispute does not belong to the category of disputes which can be submitted to compulsory arbitration, unless the Treaty of Arbitration confers upon the Arbitration Tribunal the power of deciding this preliminary question. Article 71 provides that parties to the case can raise 'objections and points'. Article 73 authorises the Tribunal 'to declare its competence in interpreting the 'Compromis', as well as the other Treaties which may be invoked, *and in applying the principles of law*'.[14] Thus, we see how on the one hand the competence-competence principle begins to make its way and on the other, there is no automatic acceptance for the idea that the tribunal can decide whether a certain claim falls or not in the scope of the treaty. However, the competence - competence principle was not unlimited. At the time, clauses exempting disputes related to the national honour and vital interests (the so-called 'vital interests' reservation) of states from the jurisdiction of tribunals were considered to be too closely related to the sovereignty of the parties and consequently, their self-judging character preserved the ultimate appreciation to the states concerned.[15] Arthur Eyffinger beautifully encapsulated the

14 Emphasis added. See Article 48 of the 1899 Convention.

15 The issue was discussed at the Advisory Committee of Jurists, see Advisory Committee of Jurists, *Procès-Verbaux of the Proceedings of the Committee: June 16th–July 24th 1920*, Draft agenda submitted by the Secretariat at 34, 229 (Root), 243 (Descamps), 246 (Ricci-Busatti)

gradual transformation from The Hague to Versailles: 'There is a huge gap of thought between 1899 and 1919, between the Salle d'Orange at Huis Ten Bosch and the Salle de l'Horloge at Quai d'Orsay. Still, in essence the issue was the same. It was the Rule of Law battering the walls of Power Politics'.[16] Throughout the summer of 1920, numerous references were made justifying the immediate links existing between the outcome of the 1907 conference and the work of the ACJ aiming to legitimise the acceptance of compulsory jurisdiction.[17]

Around the turn of the century, there were at least a couple of cases, in which the arbitrators had to decide whether the claims were related to the interpretation or the application of the treaty in question, i.e. whether the dispute actually was within the scope of the compromissory clause.[18] A Spanish tax law, enacted in 1888, was considered by the United Kingdom of Sweden and Norway as contrary to the 1883 Treaty of commerce (which contained a compromissory clause). The Spanish Government agreed to submit to arbitration the question whether the new tax on alcoholic beverages was a question of domestic jurisdiction or a question within the scope of the 1883 treaty. The arbitrator, the Portuguese envoy to Madrid Count Casal Ribeiro, found that the Spanish law was a matter of internal administration.[19] Another example: in 1911, France and Switzerland submitted a dispute whether French legislation enacted in 1910, which treated steam turbines for customs purposes differently from stationary steam engines with pistons, was contrary to the 1906 bilateral treaty of commerce.[20] The tribunal held that the French government could change the tariffs only within the limits agreed in the treaty, thus implicitly rejecting the argument based on *domaine réservé*.

In the decade preceding the creation of the Court, several projects for a permanent international court were discussed in various fora. The American Society of Judicial Settlement of International Disputes was particularly active in this regard. One of the key questions featured in several projects

16 Arthur Eyffinger, 'Tobias Asser's Legacy: The Pertinence of the Institut de droit international to The Hague' (2019) 66 *Netherlands International Law Review*, 313.

17 See *Procès-Verbaux of the Proceedings of the Committee: June 16th–July 24th 1920*, 231 (Root), 754 (Descamps).

18 See Louis B. Sohn, 'Settlement of disputes relating to the interpretation and application of treaties' (1976) 150 *Recueil des Cours de l'Académie de Droit International de La Haye*, 230ff.

19 Ibid, 230, 242.

20 Ibid, 231-232.

presented before the Society concerned the scope of the Court's jurisdiction. Some influential lawyers, such as James Brown Scott, deemed it 'indispensable that any international court of justice ... must be one of limited jurisdiction. We cannot ask the nations to create overnight an international court with the extensive jurisdiction that national courts possess. We must be content to wait upon experience, not to anticipate it'.[21] Unlike national courts, the new court could not be automatically competent to hear any case submitted to it.

This section has tried to briefly set the context and demonstrate that the drafters of the Statute could rely on a rich trove of expertise and ideas. All these factors, projects and considerations help to understand better the context in which the jurisdiction of the new Court was brought to bear.

C. The Work of the Advisory Committee of Jurists in 1920

There was something utopian in the idea to gather ten (initially twelve nominees were invited, but half of them turned down the invitation) very different personalities tasked with the elaboration of the Statute of the very first permanent international court of justice. However, in order to pass the ultimate test – the agreement of the members of the newly created League of Nations, the drafters of the Statute had to demonstrate pragmatism. Also, while some of the members were adamant on their capacity as independent experts,[22] others, like Adachi and Ricci-Busatti, considered themselves as representing their country.[23] In any case, despite their different backgrounds and views, those who gathered in the summer of 1920 in The Hague belonged to the same networks of lawyers and diplomats, scholars and practitioners and believed in the need to create the figure of the international judge.[24]

---

21 James Brown Scott, Project of an International Court of Justice to and Approved by the American Institute of International Law at its Session in Havana, January, 1917 (1917) 29 *Judicial Settlement of International Disputes*, 8.

22 Advisory Committee of Jurists, *Procès-Verbaux of the Proceedings of the Committee: June 16th–July 24th 1920*, 22 (Hagerup): "The members of the Committee were not representatives of individual countries: they were independent jurists; their countries had complete liberty of derision on the proposal which would be the outcome of the work of the Committee. The committee was not a diplomatic conference."

23 See Arthur Eyffinger, 'The Hope of Ages', in this volume, sub F.I.

24 Arthur Eyffinger, 'Tobias Asser's Legacy: The Pertinence of the Institut de droit international to The Hague' (2019) 66 *Netherlands International Law Review*, 313.

During their discussions, the issue of preliminary objections appeared only incidentally (pun unintended); it was understood that even though the Court would have a very broad jurisdiction, the respondent would still be able to contest its competence in the particular case.[25]

Most of the key themes that were discussed by the ACJ, e.g. the composition and the procedure for the nomination of judges, the use of judges *ad hoc*, the nature of the court's jurisdiction and the applicable law, the cases involving states that are not members of the League, the issue of non-appearance and unilateral seisin were interrelated. This is particularly visible in the context of the relationship between jurisdiction and applicable law.

However, the single most important decision taken by the Committee was the (almost unanimous) choice to opt for a broad compulsory subject matter jurisdiction and its members were aware of it.[26] It is unquestionably at the core of the draft scheme and the most significant proof of the willingness of the committee members to present the League with a project establishing 'a real court of justice' whose jurisdiction and applicable law are closer to those of domestic courts, in particular the US Supreme Court.[27] This was not a unanimous choice. Mineichirō Adachi expressed a vigorous dissent, supported by Ricci-Busatti. The proponents of a broad jurisdiction and their colleagues holding opposing views, relied on diametrically opposed interpretations of Article 14 of the Covenant. The debate on the nature of the court's jurisdiction is revelatory of the sharp divisions within the committee both on the freedom to interpret this provision and to go beyond what was perceived by some as a restrictive interpretation.[28]

---

25 See e.g. the final Report drafted by Albert De Lapradelle, Advisory Committee of Jurists, *Procès-Verbaux of the Proceedings of the Committee: June 16th–July 24th 1920*, 726, 739

26 See e.g. Advisory Committee of Jurists, *Procès-Verbaux of the Proceedings of the Committee: June 16th–July 24th 1920*, 229 (Altamira). See also Manley Ottmer Hudson, *The Permanent Court of International Justice, 1920-1942* (The MacMillan Company, New York 1943), 191. Compulsory jurisdiction 'was the outstanding feature of the draft-scheme to occupy the attention of the Council and the Assembly'.

27 The tension between the common law/continental law can be observed also in the discussions on the future Article 38 of the Statute, where the term 'general principles of law recognised by civilised states' was accepted by Root only because the expression was used by the US Supreme Court.

28 Advisory Committee of Jurists, *Procès-Verbaux of the Proceedings of the Committee: June 16th–July 24th 1920*, 225-232. See also 233, 234 (Descamps). Ole Spiermann, '"Who Attempts Too Much Does Nothing Well": The 1920 Advisory Committee of Ju-

The role of Elihu Root and Robert Phillimore was crucial in both downplaying the importance of a narrow interpretation of the Covenant and accepting compulsory jurisdiction as a governing principle.[29] Phillimore was the first to put a proposal in which the Permanent Court should have compulsory jurisdiction in respect of the four categories of disputes that according to Article 13(2) of the Covenant were 'generally suitable for submission to arbitration'.[30] In a key moment in the debate on compulsory jurisdiction, Root pointed out that progress could only be made a step at a time: 'Has the time come to take a new step in advance?' He unambiguously expressed his preference. 'The hopes of the world rested upon the realisation of *the rule of law*'.[31] He also insisted that the Committee 'should also take into consideration the work of the two Hague Conferences, *which so strangely was forgotten in the drafting of the Covenant at Paris*'.[32] For Loder, 'the Covenant was intended to mark a step forward. This step was to consist in making it unnecessary to have a previous agreement between the contesting parties'.[33] He stressed that '[i]t was only the institution of the League of Nations that made possible a real Court of Justice',[34] and the intention of the Covenant was not to abolish arbitration, 'but to place

---

rists and the Statute of the Permanent Court of International Justice' (2002) 73 *British Yearbook of International Law*, 187 (210-211): 'As made clear in Hammarskjöld's draft report, the prevailing view reflected notions of a court of justice taken from national legal systems. According to Hammarskjöld, the majority position was that the Advisory Committee 'was at liberty to make all suggestions which it found necessary to ensure the creation of a Court that might be able to fulfil its purpose, irrespective of the wording of the Covenant'.

29 Advisory Committee of Jurists, *Procès-Verbaux of the Proceedings of the Committee: June 16th–July 24th 1920*, 229ff, 235, 240 and 252.

30 Advisory Committee of Jurists, *Procès-Verbaux of the Proceedings of the Committee: June 16th–July 24th 1920*, 252. The list of legal disputes had been based on Articles 16 (1899) and 38 (1907) of the Hague Conventions on Pacific Settlement and on a declaration adopted at the 1907 Peace Conference, according to which 'certain disputes, in particular those relating to the interpretation and application of the provisions of international agreements, may be submitted to obligatory arbitration without any restriction'. See Ole Spiermann, '"Who attempts too much does nothing well: The 1920 Advisory Committee of Jurists and the Statute of the Permanent Court of International Justice' (2002) 73 *British Yearbook of International Law*, 187 (210).

31 Advisory Committee of Jurists, *Procès-Verbaux of the Proceedings of the Committee: June 16th–July 24th 1920*, 230. Emphasis added.

32 Ibid, 243. Emphasis added.

33 Ibid, 235.

34 Ibid, 250-251, memorandum by M. Loder on unilateral summons or previous agreement.

beside it a Court of Justice'.[35] Any other solution would place the plaintiff in the (old) unenviable position to wait for the good will of its opponent.[36]

That compulsory jurisdiction won the day was certainly at least in part, the result of the idea that the new court must be 'a real court of justice'[37] capable to adjudicate disputes which gradually made its way among the group members, such as the President Descamps, Hagerup,[38] Root[39] and Phillimore who presented the first project and contributed most significantly to the *cause commune.*[40] The majority took the view that it was not necessary to focus too much on the Covenant and that the Permanent Court would only have jurisdiction as provided for in treaties, but that the Statute of the Permanent Court should be such a treaty.[41]

As already mentioned, the provision on subject matter jurisdiction was the fruit of a collective effort. The majority's decision to support this

35 Ibid, 250.

36 Ibid, 251.

37 See also the interventions of Loder who went even further in his belief that Court should have a compulsory jurisdiction without the consent of both parties (except if the applicant was not a member of the League). Advisory Committee of Jurists, *Procès-Verbaux of the Proceedings of the Committee: June 16th–July 24th 1920*, 224, 229, 249-51.

38 Michalsen, op.cit., 102.

39 Ross, op.cit., 124-5: Root strongly supported the committee's agreement that the court should have the power to adjudicate cases rather than merely to arbitrate disputes. Root believed that adjudication would enable the court to make the legally correct decision rather than merely to reach the kind of compromise that characterizes arbitration (...) [A]rbitrators (...) tend to act under a sense of diplomatic obligation rather than under a sense of judicial obligation.

40 Ole Spiermann, 'The History of Article 38 of the Statute of the International Court of Justice' in Jean d'Aspremont and Samantha Besson (eds), *The Oxford Handbook of the Sources of International Law* (Oxford University Press, Oxford 2017), 169. Advisory Committee of Jurists, *Procès-Verbaux of the Proceedings of the Committee: June 16th–July 24th 1920*, 104 (Phillimore): "(...) [T]he Committee's task is to prepare plans for the establishment of a Permanent Court of Justice which should be a Court of Justice in the true sense of the word, a Court before which it should be possible to call States having broken the law of Nations, without having to obtain their consent in advance."

41 Advisory Committee of Jurists, *Procès-Verbaux of the Proceedings of the Committee: June 16th–July 24th 1920*, 224-32. Also ibid, 727, 728: 'In this case the convention establishing compulsory arbitration is the constituent Statute of the Court'. See also Ole Spiermann, '"Who Attempts Too Much Does Nothing Well": The 1920 Advisory Committee of Jurists and the Statute of the Permanent Court of International Justice' (2002) 73 *British Yearbook of International Law*, 210. Walter Phillimore, 'Scheme for the Permanent Court of International Justice' (1920) 6 *Transactions of the Grotius Society*, 93.

bold step was the result of an alliance between the representatives of Anglo-American and continental traditions,[42] based on a less formalist interpretation of the Covenant. It reflected the vision of a permanent court modelled after and comprising the main features of domestic courts, in particular the US Supreme Court.[43] It was the decisive moment in which international adjudication parted ways with international arbitration understood as a temporary, i.e. *ad hoc* dispute settlement controlled by the parties in which considerations of political expediency prevail over the strict application of legal rules.[44]

In his opening speech before the Committee, Léon Bourgeois drew a similar analogy and also gave special attention to the limits of the court's competence.[45] He stressed that *'[l]a Cour de Justice doit être une véritable Cour Permanente (...) Cette Cour Permanente ne sera pas, nous l'avons dit, une Cour d'arbitrage, mais une Cour de justice'.*[46] Becoming a party to the Statute was not sufficient to bring just any dispute.[47] De Lapradelle even used a key paragraph from the opening speech of Bourgeois in order to turn it upside down and use it as an argument for its decision to opt for compulsory jurisdiction.[48] While the committee and its president Descamps succeeded in adopting the principle of compulsory jurisdiction, Bourgeois ultimately triumphed in the Council and the Assembly. Sir Ronald Graham thought the project 'represent[ed] a complete victory for the Anglo-American point of view'.[49] However, questions of legal tradition and foreign policy did not necessarily overlap in the work of the Commit-

42 See Advisory Committee of Jurists, *Procès-Verbaux of the Proceedings of the Committee: June 16th–July 24th 1920*, 582.

43 Ole Spiermann, '"Who Attempts Too Much Does Nothing Well": The 1920 Advisory Committee of Jurists and the Statute of the Permanent Court of International Justice' (2002) 73 *British Yearbook of International Law*, 187 (198, 217, 257-58).

44 Ibid, 189.

45 Ibid, 196-197.

46 Advisory Committee of Jurists, *Procès-Verbaux of the Proceedings of the Committee: June 16th–July 24th 1920*, 7, 8.

47 Ole Spiermann, '"Who Attempts Too Much Does Nothing Well": The 1920 Advisory Committee of Jurists and the Statute of the Permanent Court of International Justice' (2002) 73 *British Yearbook of International Law*, 187 (197).

48 Ibid.

49 Graham's despatch, 24 July 1920, *Public Record Office* F0371 General 209523/203188. See also Phillips' despatch, 23 July 1920, *National Archives and Records Administration* 500CI 14/32: 'I think it may be said that the success of the meeting has been largely through the close cooperation between Mr. Root and Lord Phillimore'. Cited in Ole Spiermann, '"Who Attempts Too Much Does Nothing Well": The 1920 Advi-

tee.[50] The Foreign Secretary Lord Curzon observed wryly observed: '[i]t would seem (...) that Lord Phillimore or whoever represented us in framing this scheme must have been singularly oblivious to British interests'[51].

Another important point was the exclusion of objections based on honour and vital interests from the subject-matter jurisdiction of the Court. During the debate on the nomination of judges, Altamira stated that: 'It is essential, at the present time, to avoid all uncertainty, it must be recognised that no political questions are outside the scope of justice; all questions, whether political or economic, are in their final analysis questions of law.'[52] Referring to the 1907 Hague Convention, Root also insisted that there was unanimity that 'certain disputes, especially those relative to the interpretation and application of international contractual provisions, may be submitted to compulsory arbitration *without reservation*'.[53] This essentially should be understood as disqualifying the objection based on independence, honour and vital interests.

Article 29 of the Root-Phillimore project provided that '[i]n the event of a dispute as to whether a case does or does not come within one of the categories mentioned in this article,[54] the Permanent Court shall decide the point as an interlocutory question.[55] The provision is important in

---

sory Committee of Jurists and the Statute of the Permanent Court of International Justice' (2002) 73 *British Yearbook of International Law*, 187 (253).

50 Suffice it to recall the statement made by the Foreign Secretary Lord Curzon: '[i]t would seem (...) that Lord Phillimore or whoever represented us in framing this scheme must have been singularly oblivious to British interests'. Curzon's minutes October 1920, *Public Record Office* F0371 W512/241/98 and also F0371 W6943/22/98; see also Lorna Lloyd, *Peace Through Law: Britain and the International Court in the 1920s* (1997) 9-12 cited in Ole Spiermann, '"Who Attempts Too Much Does Nothing Well": The 1920 Advisory Committee of Jurists and the Statute of the Permanent Court of International Justice' (2002) 73 *British Yearbook of International Law*, 187 (255).

51 Curzon's minutes October 1920, *Public Record Office* F0371 W512/241/98 and also F0371.

52 Advisory Committee of Jurists, *Procès-Verbaux of the Proceedings of the Committee: June 16th–July 24th 1920*, 102 (Altamira)

53 Advisory Committee of Jurists, *Procès-Verbaux of the Proceedings of the Committee: June 16th–July 24th 1920*, 243 (Root). Emphasis added.

54 a) the interpretation of a treaty; b) any question of international law; c) the existence of any fact which, if established, would constitute a breach of an international obligation d) the extent or nature of reparation due for the breach of an international obligation; e) the interpretation of a sentence passed by the Court.

55 Advisory Committee of Jurists, *Procès-Verbaux of the Proceedings of the Committee: June 16th–July 24th 1920*, 547.

three respects. First, it clarifies that the subject-matter jurisdiction of the Court is very broad but not unlimited and the respondent can contest its existence. Second, the Court has the power to decide by virtue of the *competence-competence* principle. Third, its pronouncement takes the form of an interlocutory decision. In the subsequent versions of the provision, the 'interlocutory' qualifier disappeared.[56]

In his report, De Lapradelle cited one of his colleagues that the grant of powers regulating the jurisdiction of the Court 'though perhaps not strictly in accordance with the letter of the Covenant, follows its spirit so exactly that it would seem a great pity, now that the Court is being definitely organised, not to complete the progress made by this last provision'.[57] Minor issues should be disregarded in favour of the grand objective – to have the compulsory jurisdiction of the Court accepted by states,[58] because 'there is an immutable law, in the evolution of legal institutions, which shows that an optional jurisdiction has always sooner or later been followed by a definite compulsory jurisdiction'.[59] At the end, adjudication and arbitration are both instances of judicial dispute settlement, 'the administration of justice between sovereign States'.[60] The 1907 conference prepared the ground for the acceptance of compulsory jurisdiction and in that sense, the Committee could be said to have remained loyal to its spirit.[61]

---

56 See Advisory Committee of Jurists, *Procès-Verbaux of the Proceedings of the Committee: June 16th–July 24th 1920*, 566. See also ibid, 616 (Fernandes). The provision was eventually deleted (see ibid, 628). See also 618 (Hagerup) and 619 (Ricci-Busatti and Root) and 655 (De Lapradelle)

57 Advisory Committee of Jurists, *Procès-Verbaux of the Proceedings of the Committee: June 16th–July 24th 1920*, 728. See also the letter of Anzilotti to Drummond, cited Ole Spiermann, '"Who Attempts Too Much Does Nothing Well": The 1920 Advisory Committee of Jurists and the Statute of the Permanent Court of International Justice' (2002) 73 *British Yearbook of International Law*, 187 (241): 'Later, when referring to 'the opinion which has prevailed' in the Advisory Committee, namely 'that a compulsory judicature must be admitted', Anzilotti noted that 'I am not sure if the members who have agreed to this opinion thought that the Covenant admits such a compulsory judicature or that it is a forwarding step allowed if not imposed by the Covenant'.

58 Advisory Committee of Jurists, *Procès-Verbaux of the Proceedings of the Committee: June 16th–July 24th 1920*, 538 (Root).

59 Ibid, 694-5 (report by De Lapradelle)

60 Ibid, 696 (report by De Lapradelle). The relevant provisions of the Covenant containing the term 'arbitration', must therefore, be interpreted accordingly as 'as implying "Judicial Settlement of International Disputes"'.

61 Advisory Committee of Jurists, *Procès-Verbaux of the Proceedings of the Committee: June 16th–July 24th 1920*, 727 (report by De Lapradelle)

In conclusion of this section, the drafting of a Statute was a compromise between radically opposed views. According to Arthur Eyffinger, '[i]t bears the grim scars of battle and an inconclusive encounter. Both in its merits and its shortcomings the document bespeaks the strategy of either camp in 1907 to wrongfoot and outwit its foe, of sallies made and losses taken. It was an agreement on compromise, never mistaken for the optimum. It was, above all, unfinished business. In some respects it still is. For this Statute still governs the wheelings and dealings of the International Judiciary in our times'.[62] The majority of the ACJ members who voted in favour of compulsory jurisdiction did not anticipate that the core principle in their scheme could be undone. Yet, as it is well known, this is precisely what happened in the autumn of 1920 during the meetings of the Council and the Assembly.[63] The position defended by Adachi and Ricci-Busatti which viewed the draft scheme for compulsory jurisdiction as a modification of the Covenant prevailed. This rather deferential approach to sovereignty was the price that had to be paid for the success of the entire project. Lord Robert Cecil's words at the Assembly 'that if the Court was established, made up, as it would be, of members of worldwide repute, its jurisdiction would gradually expand. A great institution like the Court must be allowed to develop organically' reflect the same tension between hope and caution that is still visible today. Once created with certain default settings, the institution continues to operate in the frames and within the paradigm that was engrafted on it at its inception. Respect for sovereignty and compulsory jurisdiction are not mutually incompatible but the judicial policy of the institution dictates that this tension should be avoided to be portrayed as a zero-sum game. This requires the Court to adopt a case-by-case approach to preliminary objections and to maintain a degree of constructive ambiguity and unpredictability. If the outcome of a decision can be predicted on the basis of law, potential applicants would be dissuaded from filing an application if the case law of the Court shows an insignificant chance for success, and states would be equally reluctant to file declarations under Article 36(2) or to appear as respondents. All these general remarks serve to emphasise that the fundamental premises for the functioning of the Court were forged in 1920 and are still valid today.

62 Eyffinger, op.cit, 332.

63 On the discussions at the Council and the Assembly, see Ole Spiermann, 'Who attempts too much does nothing well: The 1920 Advisory Committee of Jurists and the Statute of the Permanent Court of International Justice' (2002) 73 *British Yearbook of International Law*, 187 (242ff.).

The following two sections discuss the first two cases in which subject matter preliminary objections were raised by the respondent. They demonstrate the two diametrically opposed approaches of the Court, namely the 'provisional conclusion' and the so-called jurisdictional test which continue to characterise the judicial policy of the Court until the present day.

D. Nationality Decrees *and the Birth of the 'Provisional Conclusion'*

Curiously, the first case in which such an objection was raised was is not in the context of contentious proceedings. It was an advisory opinion, a rather unusual situation, in which the two governments involved, namely Great Britain and France, 'merely wanted an advisory opinion, but they treated the case as a contentious proceeding instituted by a special agreement' which 'had encouraged the Permanent Court to assimilate its advisory and contentious jurisdictions'[64].

In November 1922, the Council of the League requested an advisory opinion concerning a dispute between France and Great Britain on the application of some nationality decrees to British subjects.[65] The dispute arose from France's concern about the growing number of non-French Europeans in Tunis and Morocco and decided to impose French nationality on most second generation Europeans in those territories under its jurisdiction. Great Britain protested against the application of the decrees to its subjects born in Tunis and in the French zone of the Moroccan protectorate and declared that it would not recognise their application to the persons in question. After the French refusal to submit the matter to arbitration,[66] Great Britain seized the Council of the League following the procedure provided by Article 15 of the Covenant.[67] France objected

64 Ole Spiermann, *International Legal Argument in the Permanent Court of International Justice* (Cambridge University Press, Cambridge 2005), 168 citing the French argument exposed by De Lapradelle, Series C, No. 2, 52-54.

65 For a summary of the facts, see Nathaniel Berman, 'The Nationality Decrees case, or, of Intimacy and Consent' (2000) 13 *Leiden Journal of International Law*, 265.

66 The British proposal was based on the 1903 bilateral Convention for the settlement by arbitration of certain classes of disputes Series C, No. 2, App. 22, 214.

67 "If there should arise between Members of the League any dispute likely to lead to a rupture, which is not submitted to arbitration or judicial settlement in accordance with Article 13, the Members of the League agree that they will submit the matter to the Council. Any party to the dispute may effect such submission by giving notice

that pursuant to Article 15(8),[68] the matter was solely within its domestic jurisdiction ('*compétence exclusive*' in the French text) and therefore, the Council was not competent.[69] At the oral pleadings before the Court, the French argument (exposed by none other than Albert De Lapradelle) based on Article 15(8) can be assimilated to a preliminary objection *ratione materiae.*

Usually the case is mentioned in the context of the pronouncement of the Court that the scope of *domaine réservé* is essentially a relative question which depends upon the development of international relations.[70] It was portrayed as a victory of the 'growing internationalisation over of the life of the peoples of the world, involving a corresponding constant loss of ground by the concept of absolute sovereignty'.[71] States could not claim that a certain issue fell in their domestic jurisdiction if that state had undertaken treaty obligations. But for the purposes of the present paper the interpretation of Article 15(8) has to be understood in connection with two other elements – first, the interpretation of a treaty provision which was contingent on a particular conception of the state and its jurisdiction and second – the competence of the Council.[72]

At the core of the case was the possibility for a state to remove a certain matter from the Council's competence by merely asserting that the matter in question was solely (*exclusivement* in the French version) within its jurisdiction.[73] While the refusal of the Court to apply 'extensive interpretation'

---

of the existence of the dispute to the Secretary General, who will make all necessary arrangements for a full investigation and consideration thereof."

68 'If the dispute between the parties is claimed by one of them, and is found by the Council, to arise out of a matter which by international law is solely within the domestic jurisdiction of that party, the Council shall so report, and shall make no recommendation as to its settlement'.

69 Robert Kolb has pointed out that the objection cannot be raised *ex officio* by the Council. It has to be invoked by the respondent. Robert Kolb, 'Article 15' in Robert Kolb (ed), *Commentaire du Pacte de la SDN* (Bruylant, Bruxelles 2014), 655.

70 PCIJ, *Nationality Decrees Issued in Tunis and Morocco*, Advisory Opinion of 7 February 1923 (Series B, No. 4), 24.

71 *Barcelona Traction, Light and Power Company, Limited (Belgium v. Spain)*, Judgment of 5 February 1970, ICJ Reports (1970), 286 (313), Separate Opinion of Judge Ammoun.

72 Ole Spiermann, *International Legal Argument in the Permanent Court of International Justice* (Cambridge University Press, Cambridge 2005), 150ff.

73 PCIJ, *Nationality Decrees Issued in Tunis and Morocco*, Advisory Opinion of 7 February 1923 (Series B, No.4), 23-24.

due to the exceptional character of the provision is certainly notable,[74] the case is important because the Court was confronted with an objection to its jurisdiction which was also related to the merits of the dispute. And these merits were reserved for another body – the Council of the League. There were two diametrically opposed possibilities – either to reach a provisional conclusion as to its jurisdiction or to make a definitive interpretation of the provisions in question potentially affecting the merits. The latter was clearly excluded:

> If, in order to reply to a question regarding exclusive jurisdiction, raised under paragraph 8, it were necessary to give an opinion upon the merits of the legal grounds (titres) invoked by the Parties in this respect, this would hardly be in conformity with the system established by the Covenant for the pacific settlement of international disputes.[75]

Thus, the Court limited itself to interpreting Article 15(8) while reserving the application of the provision to the facts for the Council.

After an analysis published in the *American Journal of International Law* infuriated Huber and Anzilotti,[76] Åke Hammarskjöld wrote an article under the pen-name Paul de Vineuil, published in the *Revue de droit international et legislation comparée*, in which he explained the rationale behind the decision: the fact that the invocation of international obligations was not sufficient to release a dispute from the exclusive jurisdiction of a state to which it otherwise belonged. The Court's role was strictly circumscribed by the Covenant and the question put before it by the Council. It did not have a free hand in deciding on the entire dispute. It merely accepted provisionally Great Britain's claim. It was necessary that 'ces engagements soient de nature à permettre la conclusion provisoire qu'ils peuvent avoir une importance juridique pour le différend. D'autre part, cette conclusion *provisoire* suffit'.[77] Hammarskjöld did not miss to point out that by reach-

74 Ibid, 25.
75 Ibid, 26.
76 Ole Spiermann, *International Legal Argument in the Permanent Court of International Justice* (Cambridge University Press, Cambridge 2005), 159.
77 Paul De Vineuil, 'Actualités: Les Leçons du Quatrième Avis Consultatif de la Cour Permanente de Justice Internationale', (1923) 4 *Revue de Droit International et de Législation Comparée*, 297.

ing this provisional conclusion, the Court in a way substituted itself for the Council which was the competent organ pursuant to Article 15.[78]

In *The Function of Law*, Lauterpacht criticised the 'provisional conclusion' and argued in favour of a pronouncement on the merits. In his view, 'the argument that the Court may declare itself competent in a matter claimed by the defendant state to be within its exclusive jurisdiction, but that this need not necessarily result in a final judgment in favour of the plaintiff state, is to a large extent fallacious'.[79] Lauterpacht was certainly correct that there was no matter belonging to the exclusive state jurisdiction which cannot become the object of an international obligation. But his analysis neglected one key element: the merits were reserved for the Council and not for the Court.[80] The provisional conclusion was justified at least to a certain extent by the lack of compulsory jurisdiction in the Covenant.[81]

The Permanent Court and its successor have always been very careful when the merits of a case have been reserved for another body, legal or political.[82] In that sense, the political nature of the Council has no decisive importance over the distinction between questions of jurisdiction and questions of merits. By delivering the advisory opinion, the Court fulfilled its duty to the dispute settlement system.[83]

There are additional reasons why the Court opted for a provisional conclusion. Knowing that the case may return once again to it in another form, basic considerations of prudence militated against a clear decision on

---

78 Ibid, 300. This was noted in a letter by Judge Moore to Judge Finlay, cited in Ole Spiermann, *International Legal Argument in the Permanent Court of International Justice* (Cambridge University Press, Cambridge 2005), 158.

79 Hersch Lauterpacht, *The Function of Law in the International Community* (Oxford University Press, Oxford 1933), 362.

80 Ole Spiermann, *International Legal Argument in the Permanent Court of International Justice* (Cambridge University Press, Cambridge 2005), 156.

81 Ibid, 159.

82 See eg *Ambatielos (Greece v. United Kingdom)* and the 1972 *ICAO (India v. Pakistan)* case. See also Hersch Lauterpacht, *The Development of International Law by the International Court* (Cambridge University Press, Cambridge 1982), 238-239.

83 However, it was agreed that if the Court gave a negative answer to the request made by the Council, the entire case had to be submitted either to arbitration, or to 'judicial settlement'. Paul De Vineuil, 'Actualités: Les Leçons du Quatrième Avis Consultatif de la Cour Permanente de Justice Internationale', (1923) 4 *Revue de Droit International et Legislation Comparée*, 292, 294.

the merits.[84] A stricter test would have meant precisely getting deeper into the merits and could have led to accusations that the Court had acted *ultra vires.*[85] In addition, a stricter test would mean that Article 15(8) could be turned against the State relying on it which was arguably not the rationale behind the provision.[86] Yet another reason for rejecting a stricter test was that the dispute was not submitted in contentious proceedings, let alone those under the 'optional clause'. In other words, context mattered.[87]

The *Nationality Decrees* stands out as the closest to what a contentious case in the guise of an advisory opinion could look like. It may seem unusual that the very first case which deals with the subject matter preliminary objections is in the context of advisory proceedings. As explained by Ole Spiermann, the Court was put in a rather delicate position by the parties and the fact that it was in the context of a request for an advisory opinion further complicated the matter, as the Court has not dealt with such a problem before and its individual members held differing views on the extent and proper exercise of its advisory function. The uncertainty stemming from the novelty of the advisory proceedings (which has no equivalent in domestic law) perhaps prompted the members of the Court to search for common ground and to opt for assimilating the two types of proceedings – contentious and advisory.[88]

E. The So-called 'jurisdictional test' in Mavrommatis

The jurisdiction *ratione materiae* of the Court was disputed for the first time in the second contentious case – *Mavrommatis Palestine Concessions.* Just like the *Nationality Decrees* opinion, was product of the Huber-Anzilotti tandem.

84 Paul De Vineuil, 'Actualités: Les Leçons du Quatrième Avis Consultatif de la Cour Permanente de Justice Internationale', (1923) 4 *Revue de Droit International et Legislation Comparée*, 300.

85 See Ole Spiermann, *International Legal Argument in the Permanent Court of International Justice* (Cambridge University Press, Cambridge 2005), 159-160.

86 Paul De Vineuil, 'Actualités: Les Leçons du Quatrième Avis Consultatif de la Cour Permanente de Justice Internationale', (1923) 4 *Revue de Droit International et Legislation Comparée*, 299.

87 Ole Spiermann, *International Legal Argument in the Permanent Court of International Justice* (Cambridge University Press, Cambridge 2005), 157.

88 Ibid, 174.

The dispute concerned concessions[89] for the supply of water and electricity in Palestine, a sensitive issue with political repercussions.[90] Without entering into a long presentation of the facts[91] it suffices to mention that the dispute concerned two sets of concessions in Jaffa and Jerusalem.[92] Greece relied on the compromissory clause of Article 26 in the Mandate for Palestine[93] which contained the established formula 'dispute ... relating to the interpretation or the application'. The respondent raised three preliminary objections. According to the third one, the dispute did not concern the interpretation or the application of a provision of the Mandate. The Court refused to characterise the preliminary objections and use particular national categorisation.[94] It stated that the parties' arguments have indicated 'the extremely wide bearing of the objection upon which, before the case can be argued on its merits, the Court has to take a decision (without, however, in so doing, in any way prejudging the final outcome of such argument) (...)'[95] It also stated that in the absence of any rules in the Statute or the Rules of the Court to be followed in case of an objection *in limine litis*, '[t]he Court therefore is at liberty to adopt the principle which it considers best calculated to ensure the administration of justice, most suited to procedure before an international tribunal and most in conformity with the fundamental principles of international law'.[96] As pointed out by

89 The Court found that it had no jurisdiction over the Jaffa claims. Greece did not pursue the third concession in Jordan.

90 See M. Waibel, 'Mavrommatis Palestine Concessions (Greece v Great Britain) (1924–27)' in Eirik Bjorge and Cameron Miles (eds), *Landmark Cases in Public International Law* (Hart Publishing, Oxford and Portland, 2017), 33.

91 See ibid, 34ff.

92 The third set of concessions, relating to the irrigation of the Jordan valley, lacked any kind of definitive contract. The Ottoman Parliament, which had adjourned once the war began, had yet to approve this set.

93 The Mandatory agrees that, if any dispute whatever should arise between the Mandatory and another Member of the League of Nations relating to the interpretation or the application of the provisions of the Mandate, such dispute, if it cannot be settled by negotiation, shall be submitted to the Permanent Court of International Justice provided for by Article 14 of the Covenant of the League of Nations.

94 PCIJ, *Mavrommatis Palestine Concessions (Objection to the Jurisdiction of the Court)*, Judgment of 30 August 1924 (Series A, No. 2), 10.

95 Ibid.

96 PCIJ, *Mavrommatis Palestine Concessions (Objection to the Jurisdiction of the Court)*, Judgment of 30 August 1924 (Series A, No. 2), 16. Anzilotti called the passage 'a very accurate statement of the principles of international law which govern the Court's jurisdiction' PCIJ, *Case concerning Certain German Interests in Polish Upper Silesia*, Judgment of 25 August 1925 (Series A No. 6), at 30; see also PCIJ, *Acts and Documents*

Spiermann, this triple justification may be seen as an expression of the different views of the members of the drafting committee[97] and serves a couple of objectives. First, it asserts the autonomy of the Court as opposed to an arbitral tribunal. The parties to the dispute are free to raise preliminary objections, but they are not masters of the procedure. Second, this autonomy does not mean arbitrariness. The good administration of justice serves precisely to express the Court's intention to act in conformity with the general principles of (the nascent) international procedural law. Third and following from the previous two considerations, this is the earliest and among the strongest assertions of the freedom of the Court to adopt a judicial policy which best corresponds to its perception of the proper discharge of the judicial function.

This was the first time when the Court was divided in two almost equally strong groups, as demonstrated by the diaries of Max Huber.[98] A first version of the judgment was circulated which was heavily influenced by civil law concepts and which was subsequently redrafted by Huber, Anzilotti and Hammarskjöld.[99] The letters exchanged between Anzilotti and the common law judges Moore and Finlay reveal Anzilotti's concern that the judgment reflects the disproportionate influence of the continental system of procedure. He was convinced that the Court needed to approach the question not through the lenses of a particular national system. At the same time he was aware that 'international law will not help us very much, as the question, as far as I know, never presented itself in international courts or relations'.[100] Anzilotti asked Moore whether in the common law there could be found a similar case, where the Court had to adopt a definitive construction of the relevant provision of the Mandate or only a provisional one and second, whether it was possible for the Court, once affirmed its competence in a preliminary judgment, to recognise that it was not competent in the judgment on the merits.[101]

Indeed, international law at the time had little to offer. The few arbitration cases where such a preliminary objection was raised did not provide

concerning the Organization of the Court (Series D, No. 2, Add., 1926), at 83 (Judge Anzilotti) and 88-89 (Judge Huber); as well as Anzilotti, 119.

97 Ole Spiermann, *International Legal Argument in the Permanent Court of International Justice* (Cambridge University Press, Cambridge 2005), 205.

98 Ibid, 193.

99 Ibid, 194.

100 Ibid.

101 Ibid.

sufficient guidance and national law could not be of help either, since the question of consent did not exist in the same way. Judge Moore's reply made it clear that such a rule, providing for the dismissal of a preliminary objection was unknown in the United States.[102] The following paragraph of the judgment is important and deserves to be quoted *in toto*:

> For this reason the Court, bearing in mind the fact that its jurisdiction is limited, that it is invariably based on the consent of the respondent and only exists in so far as this consent has been given, cannot content itself with the provisional conclusion that the dispute falls or not within the terms of the Mandate. The Court, before giving judgment on the merits of the case, will satisfy itself that the suit before it, in the form in which it has been submitted and on the basis of the facts hitherto established, falls to be decided by application of the clauses of the Mandate. For the Mandatory has only accepted the Court's jurisdiction for such disputes.[103]

The same provisional conclusion, which had been accepted a year ago in *Nationality Decrees*, now was rejected categorically. The contrast between the two approaches is clear. In an attempt to mitigate this radical reversal, the Court felt compelled to distinguish the current case from the advisory opinion and explained that while in *Nationality Decrees* the jurisdiction of the Council under Article 15(1) (to which paragraph 8 was an exception) was extremely broad, in the present case the jurisdiction of the Court was limited to some categories of legal disputes and it was thus conditioned by the discretion of States.[104]

---

102 He added: 'No one can be more desirous than I am always to make the greatest possible progress with our business, but we should not permit ourselves to be hurried into taking decisions the purport of which even those who propose them apparently do not understand.' Cited in Ole Spiermann, *International Legal Argument in the Permanent Court of International Justice* (Cambridge University Press, Cambridge 2005), 195. But cf. with Article 12 of the federal rules of civil procedure. The motion to dismiss figured in the first Federal Rules of Civil Procedure adopted in 1938. https://www.uscourts.gov/sites/default/files/fr_import/CV04-1937.pdf (at p.31) However, motions to dismiss were introduced in equity rule 29 https://www.jstor.org/stable/1064311?seq=1#metadata_info_tab_contents.

103 PCIJ, *Mavrommatis Palestine Concessions (Objection to the Jurisdiction of the Court),* Judgment of 30 August 1924 (Series A, No. 2), 16.

104 PCIJ, *Mavrommatis Palestine Concessions (Objection to the Jurisdiction of the Court),* Judgment of 30 August 1924 (Series A, No. 2), 16-17. See Hersch Lauterpacht, *The Development of International Law by the International Court* (Cambridge University Press, Cambridge 1982), 10.

Then the case turned on the interpretation of Article 11 of the Mandate, a rather lengthy provision on the powers of the Administration of Palestine in regards to public ownership or control of the natural resources of the country and other issues related to land and natural resources.[105] The question was whether the granting of the Rutenberg concessions 'which cover[ed] at least a part of the same ground – British authorities have breached their international obligations, by which Greece is entitled to benefit'.[106] If the Rutenberg concessions were found to be 'within the scope of Article 11, the dispute undoubtedly relates to that article', hence the crucial importance of the phrase 'public control'.[107] Applying a mixture of textual, linguistic, and effective interpretation, the Court reached the conclusion that the Rutenberg concessions constituted an application by the administration of Palestine of the system of 'public control' as regards to the object of developing the natural resources of the country and as such, these concessions may fall within the scope of Article 11 of the Mandate.[108] The dispute would fall within the compromissory clause 'if the international obligations mentioned in Article 11 affect the merits'[109] or affect the Mavrommatis concessions.[110] The Court had no jurisdiction over those claims which had no connection with Article 11 of the Mandate. Spiermann captured the main problem with the approach of the 'definite construction': 'Hammarskjöld found that the Permanent Court's result had been unforeseeable'.[111] The jurisdictional test was not exactly a test. It was an exercise in treaty interpretation whose outcome was unpredictable in legal terms.

In an article published in the *Revue de Droit International et de Legislation Comparée* in 1925, again under the pen-name Paul de Vineuil, the

105 "The Administration of Palestine shall take all necessary measures to safeguard the interests of the community in connection with the development of the country, *and, subject to any international obligations accepted by the Mandatory*, shall have full power to provide *for public ownership or control* of any of the natural resources of the country or of the public works, services and utilities established or to be established therein." Emphasis added.

106 Ibid.

107 Ibid.

108 Ibid, 19-20.

109 Ibid, 23.

110 Ibid, 26.

111 Hammarskjöld to Hjalmar Hammarskjöld, 19 August 1924, Hammarskjöld papers 30. Cited in Ole Spiermann, *International Legal Argument in the Permanent Court of International Justice* (Cambridge University Press, Cambridge 2005), 199.

Registrar observed that the question how to approach such preliminary objections was 'd'une importance capitale'.[112] Unlike national courts, the Permanent Court could not benefit from a presumption in favour of the existence of jurisdiction. The restrictions imposed by the compromissory clause implied the limited nature of the Court's jurisdiction and militated in favour of a definitive interpretation[113], hence the need for an in-depth analysis.

In the 'provisional conclusion' approach, the Court generally approaches the dispute as defined by the applicant and it is decided only at the merits. Inversely, the 'definitive interpretation', where the respondent's consent is of primary importance, implies an early determination. In *Mavrommatis*, the Court explained that 'at the present stage of the proceedings the question whether there *really* has been a breach of these obligations [those contained in Article 11 of the Mandate] can clearly not be gone into; to do so would involve a decision as to the responsibility of the respondent, a thing which the two Governments concerned do not at the moment ask the Court to do'.[114] 'But', the Court continued, 'in accordance with the principles set out above [the three considerations mentioned on page 16 of the judgment], the Court is constrained at once to ascertain whether the international obligations mentioned in Article 11 affect the merits of the case and whether any breach of them would involve a breach of the provisions of this article'.[115] Unlike the 'provisional conclusion' approach, the Court did not rely on the definition of the dispute provided by the applicant. It used the compromissory clause as a smokescreen and stated that it '*feels* that the present judgment should be based principally on the first part of paragraph I of Article 11'.[116]

Some conclusions can be drawn from this move. The determination of the existence and the definition of the dispute, being part of the inherent powers of the Court, may have a significant impact on the outlook of

112 Paul de Vineuil, 'Décisions de la Cinquième Session Ordinaire de la Cour Permanente de Justice Internationale' (1925) 6 *Revue de Droit International et de Legislation Comparée*, 108.

113 Ibid.

114 PCIJ, *Mavrommatis Palestine Concessions (Objection to the Jurisdiction of the Court)*, Judgment of 30 August 1924 (Series A, No. 2), 23.

115 Ibid.

116 Ibid, 18. Emphasis added. See the dissenting opinion of Judge Nyholm, Ser A, No.11, p. 28-29.

the judgment. In this case, the dispute was defined not by the applicant[117] but by the Court operating an interpretation of the compromissory clause and Article 11 of the mandate, which focused on the meaning of 'public control' and 'international obligations'. Great Britain argued for a restrictive interpretation of the latter, while Greece favoured an extremely broad construction encompassing 'all international obligations in general'.[118] While initially the Court stated that it would abstain from giving an opinion on the opposing contentions, at the end of the same paragraph it expressed a preference towards an intermediate interpretation which included 'obligations contracted having some relation to the powers granted to the Palestine Administration under the same article'.[119]

Second and following directly from the first point, this Court's approach demonstrates how the 'existence of a legal dispute' requirement can be used as a malleable filter mechanism, that can vary according to the context and the particular circumstances of the case and can serve the judicial policy of the Court.[120]

Third, the reference in Article 11 of the Mandate to 'any international obligations was used to extend the Court's jurisdiction beyond the Mandate and the compromissory clause in Article 26.[121] It was the first judgment

117 The Greek government's application 'relates to the question whether the Government of Palestine and consequently also the British Government have, since 1921, wrongfully refused to recognise to their full extent the rights acquired by M. Mavrommatis under the contracts and agreements concluded by him with the Ottoman authorities in regard to certain public works' PCIJ, *Mavrommatis Palestine Concessions (Objection to the Jurisdiction of the Court),* Judgment of 30 August 1924 (Series A, No. 2), 17.

118 PCIJ, *Mavrommatis Palestine Concessions (Objection to the Jurisdiction of the Court),* Judgment of 30 August 1924 (Series A, No. 2), 24.

119 Ibid.

120 Cf Christian J. Tams, 'The Contentious Jurisdiction of the Permanent Court' in Christian J. Tams and Malgosia Fitzmaurice (eds), *Legacies of the Permanent Court of International Justice* (Martinus Nijhoff, Leiden/Boston 2013), 34.

121 Ole Spiermann, *International Legal Argument in the Permanent Court of International Justice* (Cambridge University Press, Cambridge 2005), 200-202. The Court held that (at 26): 'The Court considers that the reservation made in Article 11 regarding international obligations *is not a mere statement of fact devoid of immediate legal value*, but that, on the contrary, it is intended to afford these obligations within the limits fixed in the article, the same measure of protection as all other provisions of the Mandate.' Emphasis added. Spiermann notes that 'the majority did not refer to 'legal value' but to 'immediate legal value'. It was only when relied upon before the Permanent Court that obligations got a 'legal value' that was 'immediate'. Ibid, 202.

where the Court sought to expand its jurisdiction iresembling the maxim *boni judicis ampliare est jurisdictionem.*[122] The Court incorporated Protocol XII to its jurisdiction and demonstrated its intention to act as a court of justice as opposed to an arbitral tribunal created to accommodate the will of States.[123] Three of the dissenting judges, Finlay, Moore and Oda, paid particular attention to this issue.[124]

By focusing on the compromissory clause and the provisions invoked by the applicant, the Court demonstrated that it was in full control of the case and created the impression of an objective determination as to the issues which would be decided on the merits. Spiermann's conclusion reflects the unpredictable nature of the approach.

> Whether the Permanent Court selected the questions to be answered already when deciding on the preliminary objection, instead of in the following judgment on the merits, might more than anything else have been *a matter of taste.*[125]

Fourth, the outcome of the judgment opposed European continental lawyers and the rest of the world. All the five dissenting judges were representatives either of civil law systems outside Europe or of common law. Judge Moore considered that the majority did not grasp the third jurisdictional objection, because some of them 'seemed to think that, if

122 Cf. Åke Hammarskjöld, 'The Permanent Court of International Justice and the Development of International Law', (1935) 14 *International Affairs (Royal Institute of International Affairs 1931-1939)*, 801. 'It is not, however, to be inferred from this that the Court has adopted the maxim *boni judicis est ampliare jurisdictionem.* On the contrary, it has emphasised over and over again, that, as its jurisdiction is limited and exists only in so far as it has been accepted by the parties, its existence cannot be presumed but must be clearly established'. See also the pleading of Sir Douglas Hogg in PCIJ, *Mavrommatis Jerusalem Concessions (Readaptation)*, 8/9/10 September 1927 (Series C, No. 13-III), at 20.

123 Ole Spiermann, *International Legal Argument in the Permanent Court of International Justice* (Cambridge University Press, Cambridge 2005), 202-203: 'It may have seemed unsatisfactory that the Permanent Court could entertain disputes if a violation of 'international obligations accepted by the Mandatory' had been determined, while it had no jurisdiction to make that determination itself... The reasoning in the motifs leading to the opposite conclusion looked like the epitome of analogical interpretation, holding that the better law was the law guarded by a court of justice.'

124 PCIJ, *Mavrommatis Palestine Concessions (Objection to the Jurisdiction of the Court)*, Judgment of 30 August 1924 (Series A, No. 2), at 42, 60 and 85, respectively.

125 Ole Spiermann, *International Legal Argument in the Permanent Court of International Justice* (Cambridge University Press, Cambridge 2005), 201. Emphasis added.

the plea was allowed, the claim could never under any circumstances be renewed'.[126]

Fifth, the tandem Huber-Anzilotti had a decisive influence over the foundational period of the Court, in particular as regards to the exposition of the reasoning. In 1925, Huber replaced Loder as President of the Court. This change inaugurated a new period in the construction of the institution. First, it was during the presidency of Huber that the Rules of the Court were amended for the first time and a provision on preliminary objections was finally included. Second, jurisdictional issues remained of paramount importance. Third, the role of the president was further strengthened as he became *ex officio* member of each drafting committee.

On the merits, Mr Mavrommatis achieved a rather Pyrrhic victory because, although the Court ruled in his favour, it was merely a declaratory relief, his claim for pecuniary compensation being rejected. However, a larger majority within the Court considered that he was entitled to re-adaptation of his concession in light of the new economic conditions (Article 4 of the Mandate)[127].

F. Conclusion

The present paper traced the origins of the preliminary objections *ratione materiae* and the first experiences of the Permanent Court which very early in its existence was confronted with them. A couple of conclusions can be drawn from the two examples discussed above.

First, since the very beginning, the Court exercised '[g]reat caution and restraint (...) when ascertaining [its] own jurisdiction'.[128] Its function has always been conditioned by two diametrically opposed factors: respect for sovereignty and the temptation to expand its jurisdiction pursuant to the *boni judicis* principle. This oscillation has not disappeared and continues

126 See Anzilotti to Hammarskjöld, 25 November 1922, Hammarskjöld papers 478 in Ole Spiermann, *International Legal Argument in the Permanent Court of International Justice* (Cambridge University Press, Cambridge 2005), 203-204.

127 Waibel, *op.cit.*, 48-9.

128 *ICAO Council (India v Pakistan)*, Judgment of 18 August 1972, Judge Lachs' declaration, ICJ Reports (1972), 73. He also cites Lauterpacht: 'Nothing should be done which creates the impression that the Court, in an excess of zeal, has assumed jurisdiction where none has been conferred upon it.' (Hersch Lauterpacht, *The Development of International Law by the International Court* (Cambridge University Press, Cambridge 1982), 91).

to characterise the judicial policy. The unpredictability sensed by Hammarskjöld in respect of the so-called 'jurisdictional text' was not merely 'a matter of taste'. Or at least, not exactly. The Court's judicial policy was not elaborated in the abstract. It has gradually developed as a response to concrete situations. This does not mean that the main factors (legal and extra-legal) behind it cannot be gleaned (the paramount role of consent, deference where the merits are reserved for another organ, the role of the Court in the UN system, etc.). These predetermine the use of effective or restrictive interpretation in each particular case.

Second, the early experiences of the Permanent Court attest to the confusion persisting as to the exact nature of preliminary objections. For a long time, it was not clear whether 'preliminary' had to be understood as related to the time of the filing of the objection or materially, i.e. which issues can and have to be decided by the Court before the merits. At the present day the answer is clear – both are relevant. The perspective has changed and the question is rather how far it is permissible to enter into the merits. The 'what' and the 'when' are intrinsically related. The PCIJ quickly realised that the preliminary objections are a powerful tool with the potential to alter the course of the proceedings. The absence of rules on preliminary objections between 1922 and 1926 and the brevity of the first provision on preliminary objections in the Rules was a conscious choice (for instance the absence of any mention of joinder to the merits which appeared only in the 1930s). expressing a preference for flexibility and unwillingness to tie its hands with a particular approach without having accumulated some experience first.

Third, while the birth of international procedural law was influenced by the search of common ground between and the blending of continental and common law traditions, as evidenced from the discussions on jurisdiction within the ACJ in 1920, another line of division which played an equally important, if not more important, role. This was the need to distinguish the new Court from the concept of international justice based on arbitration understood as process controlled by the parties and to model it after domestic courts of justice, in particular the US Supreme Court. If we compare the early PCIJ with the ICJ in the *Oil Platforms* case (generally considered as an example of the jurisdictional test), the difference there was not between common law judges and those representing the continental tradition but between different approaches toward the judicial function. In that sense, the tension between the two schools of law may have been more apparent than real even at the time of the drafting of the Statute and the first years of the Court.[129]

The struggle for a permanent international court of justice and the procedural rules applied by it was essentially a struggle against some powerful ideas and concepts in the legal imaginary (in the first place sovereignty and the self-judgment associated with it). Only when it was demonstrated that first, these ideas do not need to be interpreted in the most deferential way to sovereignty and second, their most radical forms are incompatible with the very idea of an international rule of law, that the ground was prepared for 'a real court of justice'. However, 'the idols of sovereignty and unanimity'[130] have not disappeared completely. The struggle for the international rule of law is not over. And the treatment of preliminary objections, which may appear *prima facie* as a technical and thus not so essential activity, is a fundamental part of it.

129 This is precisely what was argued by Lauterpacht in an early article: Hersch Lauterpacht, 'The So-Called Anglo-American and Continental Schools of Thought in International Law' (1931) 12 *British Yearbook of International Law*, 31.

130 See Arthur Eyffinger, 'The Hope of Ages', in this volume, sub H.I.

'Not Courts of the Same Character': The Permanent Court of International Justice and the Mixed Arbitral Tribunals

Michel Erpelding

A. Introduction

The Permanent Court of International Justice ('PCIJ') has been rightly described as a 'culmination' of decades-long efforts at institutionalizing third-party peaceful settlement of international disputes.[1] Its permanent, prestigious, and large bench, its relatively broad jurisdiction (which, at least potentially, was open to all states and all kinds of disputes subject to international law), its formal designation as a 'judicial' forum, and, symbolically, its location within the Great Hall of Justice at the Hague Peace Palace, gave it an unrivalled prestige in the world of international adjudication. This prestige has outlived the institution itself. While the PCIJ's close association with the League of Nations eventually caused its dissolution in 1946, its successor, the International Court of Justice, formally characterised as 'the principal judicial organ of the United Nations', has – in sharp contrast to the UN itself – never attempted to distance itself from its interwar predecessor.[2] Sharing the same premises and seal, and a nearly-identical Statute, both the PCIJ and the ICJ have been invariably referred to, especially in non-academic contexts, as the 'World Court'. While this designation does testify to the unique international position of both institutions, it should not be seen as establishing a single reference for what international adjudication can and should be.

---

1 Ole Spiermann, *International Legal argument in the PCIJ; the Rise of the International Judiciary* (Cambridge University Press, Cambridge 2005), 3; Christian Tams, 'Peace Through International Adjudication: The Permanent Court of International Justice and the Post-war Order' in Michel Erpelding, Burkhard Hess and Hélène Ruiz Fabri (eds), *Peace Through Law: The Versailles Peace Treaty and Dispute Settlement After World War I* (Nomos, Baden-Baden 2019), 219.

2 Christian J. Tams and Malgosia Fitzmaurice, 'Introduction' in Christian J. Tams and Malgosia Fitzmaurice (eds), *Legacies of the Permanent Court of International Justice* (Martinus Nijhoff, Leiden/Boston 2013), 1–4.

Neither the PCIJ nor the ICJ have ever existed in isolation. Today, with the multiplication of often politically momentous international legal disputes, the broader public is not only rediscovering the World Court, but also realizing that it is only one of many fora dedicated to the peaceful settlement of international disputes by third parties. Conversely, informed by new historical research, scholars of international law are increasingly regaining awareness of the PCIJ's embeddedness into a context characterised by the simultaneous existence of numerous other international courts and tribunals.[3] This context was not limited to the institution of interstate arbitration that had preceded – and, indeed, because of its limitations, led to – the establishment of the PCIJ. Admittedly, the advent of a 'World Court' did have a major impact on interstate arbitration – and notably on the Permanent Court of Arbitration (PCA), which experienced somewhat of a loss of prestige,[4] symbolically driven home by its having to make way to the PCIJ and move to the Peace Palace's Small Hall of Justice.[5] Nevertheless, the establishment of the PCIJ was not the only major innovation in international adjudication of the interwar period. As well as paving the way for the World Court, the post-World War I peace treaties and related agreements established numerous other forms of third-party international dispute settlement.[6] Among these, the most prolific were the Mixed Arbitral Tribunals.[7]

3 On the relation of the PCIJ with other contemporary international bodies, see Ian Scobbie, 'The Permanent Court of International Justice, Arbitration, and Claims Commissions of the Interwar Period' in Christian J. Tams and Malgosia Fitzmaurice (eds), *Legacies of the Permanent Court of International Justice* (Martinus Nijhoff, Leiden/Boston 2013), 203–220.

4 Anneliese Quast Mertsch, 'The Relationship between the Permanent Court of Arbitration and the Permanent Court of International Justice, and Their Significance for international law' in Christian J. Tams and Malgosia Fitzmaurice (eds), *Legacies of the Permanent Court of International Justice* (Martinus Nijhoff, Leiden/Boston 2013), 253–255.

5 Shabtai Rosenne, 'Permanent Court of International Justice (PCIJ)' in Rüdiger Wolfrum (ed), *Max Planck Encyclopedia of International Law* (Oxford University Press 2006), para. 23.

6 Michel Erpelding, 'Introduction: Versailles and the Broadening of "Peace through Law"' in Michel Erpelding, Burkhard Hess and Hélène Ruiz Fabri (eds), *Peace Through Law: The Versailles Peace Treaty and Dispute Settlement After World War I* (Nomos, Baden-Baden 2019), 11–17.

7 On the Mixed Arbitral Tribunals, see Marta Requejo Isidro and Burkhard Hess, 'International Adjudication of Private Rights: The Mixed Arbitral Tribunals in the Peace Treaties of 1919–1922' in Michel Erpelding, Burkhard Hess and Hélène Ruiz Fabri (eds), *Peace Through Law: The Versailles Peace Treaty and Dispute Settlement After*

The Mixed Arbitral Tribunals (MATs) were established pursuant to the Treaties of Versailles, Saint-Germain, Neuilly (all three concluded in 1919), Trianon (1920), and Lausanne (1923) between various Allied and Associated Powers on the one hand and the former Central Powers of Germany, Austria, Bulgaria, Hungary, and Turkey on the other hand. Their mission was very different from that of the PCIJ. Whereas the latter was established in order to resolve disputes between 'States or members of the League of Nations' and provide advisory opinions at the request of the Council or the Assembly of the League of Nations,[8] the MATs were entirely dedicated to the protection of private interests, notably examining private claims regarding pre-war debts and outstanding contractual obligations, intellectual property rights, as well as damages or injuries inflicted by states upon the 'property, rights and interests' of individuals. The latter type of claims was especially sensitive, as it would lead the MATs to examine the legality of 'exceptional war measures' against Allied (and Turkish) nationals and, in the case of Romania and the 'new States' (Poland, Czechoslovakia, and Yugoslavia), postwar measures against property owned by nationals of the former Central Powers.[9] Numerically, the MATs were by far the busiest international courts of the interwar period. All in all, 39 MATs were established, handling some 90,000-100,000 cases between the entry into force of the peace treaties and the Second World War, during which the last MATs wound down their activities.[10] Although the precise number of decisions actually handed down by the MATs remains unknown, it is safe to say that, at least from this point of view, their activity by far dwarfed that

---

World War I (Nomos, Baden-Baden 2019), 239–276; Jakob Zollmann, 'Mixed Arbitral Tribunals: Post-First World War Peace Treaties' in Hélène Ruiz Fabri, *Max Planck Encyclopedia for International Procedural Law* (Oxford University Press 2022); Hélène Ruiz Fabri and Michel Erpelding (eds), *The Mixed Arbitral Tribunals, 1919–1939: An Experiment in the International Adjudication of Private Rights* (Baden-Baden, Nomos 2023).

8 Art. 14 Covenant of the League of Nations.

9 Jakob Zollmann, 'Mixed Arbitral Tribunals: Post-First World War Peace Treaties' in Hélène Ruiz Fabri, *Max Planck Encyclopedia for International Procedural Law* (Oxford University Press 2022), paras 34–39. In the case of Romania, the jurisdiction of the MATs over compensation claims for such measures was based on Art 250 Trianon Treaty.

10 Michel Erpelding and Hélène Ruiz Fabri, 'Introduction: International adjudication and the legacy of the Mixed Arbitral Tribunals' in Hélène Ruiz Fabri and Michel Erpelding (eds), *The Mixed Arbitral Tribunals, 1919–1939: An Experiment in the International Adjudication of Private Rights* (Nomos, Baden-Baden 2023), 12–13.

of the PCIJ, which between 1922 and 1939 handled 63 cases,[11] resulting in 32 judgments, 27 advisory opinions, 6 orders indicating provisional measures of protection, and over 100 procedural orders.[12] Bearing in mind these staggering figures, it seems hardly surprising that the PCIJ would occasionally mention the MATs. Indeed, one of the Court's advisory opinions engaged in some way with an MAT,[13] as did seven of its judgments[14] – two of which, handed down respectively in 1933 and in 1936, were effectively given on appeal from MAT decisions. From a political perspective, the decisions of the MATs, which could have major financial consequences for states, could hardly be ignored. While some of their cases, like that of the Belgian deportees in 1924, elicited international media coverage,[15] others, like the series of cases known as the 'Hungarian optants dispute', also led to heated doctrinal debates.[16] During their heydays in the 1920s, which coincided

11 *The Permanent Court of International Justice, 1922–2012* (International Court of Justice, The Hague 2012), 55–67.

12 Shabtai Rosenne, 'Permanent Court of International Justice (PCIJ)' in Rüdiger Wolfrum (ed), *Max Planck Encyclopedia of International Law* (Oxford University Press 2006), para. 36.

13 *Interpretation of the Greco-Turkish Agreement of December 1st, 1926*, Advisory Opinion, 28 August 1928, PCIJ Series B no 16 (1928).

14 *Interpretation of Para. 4 of the Annex following Article 179 of the Treaty of Neuilly*, Judgment, 12 September 1924, PCIJ series B no 16 (1924); *Case Concerning Certain German Interests in Polish Upper Silesia*, Preliminary Objections Judgment, 25 August 1925, PCIJ Series A no 6 (1925); *Factory at Chorzów*, Jurisdiction Judgment, 26 July 1927, PCIJ Series A no 9 (1927); *Factory at Chorzów*, Merits Judgment, 13 September 1928, PCIJ Series A no 17 (1928); *Appeal from a Judgment of the Hungaro-Czecoslovak Mixed Arbitral Tribunal (The Peter Pázmány University)*, Judgment, 15 December 1933, PCIJ Series A/B no 61 (1933); *Pajzs, Czáky, Esterházy*, Judgment, 6 December 1936, PCIJ Series A/B no 68 (1936); *Electricity Company of Sofia and Bulgaria*, Preliminary Objection Judgment, 4 April 1939, PCIJ Series A/B no 77 (1939).

15 Michel Erpelding, 'An Example of International Legal Mobilisation: The German-Belgian Mixed Arbitral Tribunal and the Case of the Belgian Deportees' in Hélène Ruiz Fabri and Michel Erpelding (eds), *The Mixed Arbitral Tribunals, 1919–1939: An Experiment in the International Adjudication of Private Rights* (Nomos, Baden-Baden 2023), 309–362.

16 Antal Berkes, 'The League of Nations and the Optants' Dispute in the Hungarian Borderlands: Romania, Yugoslavia, and Czechoslovakia' in Peter Becker and Natasha Wheatley (eds), *Remaking Central Europe: The League of Nations and the Former Habsburg Lands* (Oxford University Press 2020), 283–314; Marilena Papadaki, 'The Hungarian Optants Cases before the Romanian-Hungarian Mixed Arbitration Tribunal: International Lawyers, the League of Nations and the Judicialization of International Relations' in Hélène Ruiz Fabri and Michel Erpelding (eds), *The Mixed Arbitral Tribunals, 1919–1939: An Experiment in the International Adjudication of Private Rights* (Nomos, Baden-Baden 2023), 363–380.

with the PCIJ's original bench, the MATs disseminated their case-law via a semi-official collection edited by the Clearing Office for Private Property and Interests (*Office des Biens et Intérêts Privés*), a French administration established pursuant to the peace treaties.[17] And yet, apart from general references, such as 'the interpretations which may have been placed by the Mixed Arbitral Tribunals',[18] 'the decisions of arbitral tribunals'[19] or, perhaps more graciously, 'the consistent practice of the Mixed Arbitral Tribunals',[20] the PCIJ refrained from any deep engagement with the practice of the MATs.[21] To be fair, something similar could be said about the latter, since the roughly 10,000 pages of their published decisions include less than half a dozen references to PCIJ case-law – although these references are usually much more precise and used to back up the relevant MAT's own decision.[22] All in all, the 'dialogue' between the two most important international judicial institutions of the interwar period seems to have been almost non-existent. But does this mean that they had no impact whatsoever on each other?

This chapter contends that the Permanent Court of International Justice and the Mixed Arbitral Tribunals did mutually impact each other in ways

17 *Recueil des décisions des tribunaux arbitraux mixtes institués par les traités de paix* (Librairie de la Société du Recueil Sirey, Paris 1922–1930), hereafter Recueil TAM.

18 *Interpretation of Para. 4 of the Annex following Article 179 of the Treaty of Neuilly*, Judgment, 12 September 1924, PCIJ series B no 16 (1924), 7.

19 *Factory at Chorzów*, Jurisdiction Judgment, 26 July 1927, PCIJ Series A no 9 (1927), 47.

20 *Appeal from a Judgment of the Hungaro-Czecoslovak Mixed Arbitral Tribunal (The Peter Pázmány University)*, Judgment, 15 December 1933, PCIJ Series A/B no 61 (1933), 243.

21 Ian Scobbie, 'The Permanent Court of International Justice, Arbitration, and Claims Commissions of the Interwar Period' in Christian J. Tams and Malgosia Fitzmaurice (eds), *Legacies of the Permanent Court of International Justice* (Martinus Nijhoff, Leiden/Boston 2013), 214.

22 See, most notably: Romanian-German MAT, 'Weitzenhoffer v German State' (18 January 1926) 5 *Recueil TAM*, 935 (939) (on the concurring interpretation of Art 297(e) Treaty of Versailles by the Court and the MATs); Romanian-Hungarian MAT, 'Archduke Frederick of Habsburg-Lorraine v Romanian State' (10 January 1927) 7 *Recueil TAM*, 128 (136-37) (reference to the PCIJ's preliminary objections judgment in the *Certain German Interests* case); Czechoslovakian-Hungarian MAT, 'Alexandre Pallavicini v Czechoslovakian State' (31 January 1929) 9 *Recueil TAM*, 713 (718) (same reference); Romanian-Austrian MAT, 'Aron Kahane successor v Francesco Parisi and Austrian State' (19 March 1929) 8 *Recueil TAM*, 943 (962) (citing the PCIJ's advisory opinion on *the Competence of the ILO in regard to International Regulation of the Conditions of the Labour of Persons Employed in Agriculture* with regard to principles of treaty interpretation).

that cannot be inferred from their respective case-law alone. However, as the chapter's two sections will show, this mutual impact did not take the form of a dialogue among equals, but reflected the fundamental inequality between both institutions. The first section will show how the hybrid nature of the MATs, which combined features that contemporaries considered typical of 'international adjudication' with characteristics traditionally associated either with bilateral arbitration or domestic adjudication, resulted in an unequal relationship with the PCIJ. Whereas the MATs would try to establish themselves as a bona fide example of 'international adjudication' by emulating certain features of the Court, the latter's 'modest brief'[23] prevented it from imitating the most innovative features of the MATs, which it did, however, eventually recognise as truly 'international' institutions. The second section of this chapter will further develop this point by looking at the connections that existed between several members of the PCIJ and the Mixed Arbitral Tribunals and their relevance for both institutions. It will point out that while these connections might have been a source of prestige for the MATs, they could also be considered by some members of the Permanent Court as a potential liability for their institution's reputation of impartiality.

B. A Fundamentally Unequal Relationship: the Permanent Court, the MATs, and the Debate on the Distinction between International Arbitration and Adjudication

When the Advisory Committee of Jurists met in June-July 1920 to '[prepare] plans for the establishment of the Permanent Court of International Justice',[24] the first MATs were already in operation.[25] And yet, this brand-new form of third-party international dispute settlement went totally unmen-

---

23 Christian Tams, 'Peace Through International Adjudication: The Permanent Court of International Justice and the Post-war Order' in Michel Erpelding, Burkhard Hess and Hélène Ruiz Fabri (eds), *Peace Through Law: The Versailles Peace Treaty and Dispute Settlement After World War I* (Nomos, Baden-Baden 2019), 221.

24 Advisory Committee of Jurists, *Procès-Verbaux of the Proceedings of the Committee: June 16th–July 24th 1920,* III.

25 Notably, the French-German MAT had had its first meeting on 10 March 1920 and adopted its Rules of Procedure on 2 April 1920. Otto Göppert, *Zur Geschichte der auf Grund des Vertrags von Versailles eingesetzten Gemischten Schiedsgerichte und Schiedsinstanzen für Neutralitätsansprüche* (unpublished typoscript, Berlin March 1931), 43.

tioned in the discussions of the Committee. This contrasted markedly with the attention given to two other precedents. Most notably, the members of the Committee referred several times to the stillborn International Prize Court,[26] whose 1907 Convention was mentioned as a possible inspiration for the Statute of the future PCIJ.[27] Somewhat more predictably, the Committee made frequent mention of the Permanent Court of Arbitration, whose shortcomings the new Permanent Court of International Justice was supposed to remedy and whose continuing existence was in fact guaranteed in Article 1 of the Draft Statute adopted by the Committee.[28] This might seem somewhat surprising, as the MATs had been specifically mentioned by the memorandum drafted by the Secretariat of the League of Nations to help prepare the Committee's discussions, albeit only in relation to the Court's composition[29] and, much more briefly, its subject-matter jurisdiction.[30] However, the MATs were not the only precedent that the Committee of Jurists chose to ignore. Even more blatantly perhaps, the members of the Committee failed to make any mention of the Central American Court of Justice (1907–1918), arguably the first permanent international court,[31] despite the fact that the convention establishing that court had been included within the volume of documents presented to them prior to their meeting.[32] As far as the the MATs are concerned, the Committee's negligence has a straightforward explanation: the tribunals simply did not correspond to the idea that most contemporary jurists had of international adjudication.

26 On this precedent, see Natalino Ronzitti, 'International Prize Court (IPC)' in Rüdiger Wolfrum (ed), *Max Planck Encyclopedia of International Law* (Oxford University Press 2006).

27 See e.g.: Advisory Committee of Jurists, *Procès-Verbaux of the Proceedings of the Committee: June 16th–July 24th 1920*, 317, 347–350.

28 The relevant part of this provision went as follows: '[The PCIJ] shall be in addition to the Court of Arbitration organised by the Hague Convention of of 1899 and 1907, and to the special Tribunals of Arbitration to which States are always at liberty to submit their disputes for settlement.' Ibid, 699.

29 *Documents presented to the Committee relating to existing plans for the establishment of a Permanent Court of International Justice* (The Hague 1920), 65.

30 Ibid, 17.

31 On this Court, see Rosa Riquelme Cortado, 'Central American Court of Justice' in Rüdiger Wolfrum (ed), *Max Planck Encyclopedia of International Law* (Oxford University Press 2013); Freya Baetens, 'First to rise and first to fall: the Court of Cartago (1907-1918)' in Ignacio de la Rasilla and Jorge E Viñuales (eds), *Experiments in International Adjudication: Historical Accounts* (Cambridge University Press, Cambridge 2019), 211.

32 *Documents presented to the Committee relating to existing plans for the establishment of a Permanent Court of International Justice* (The Hague 1920), 141.

More precisely, from the perspective of these jurists, they were prima facie at odds with two main features of the Court, namely its judicial and its international character.

Embodying the difference between international 'adjudication' and international 'arbitration' was one of the defining aims set for the PCIJ by its creators.[33] In a memorandum presented to the Committee of Jurists and written by Åke Hammarskjöld,[34] who would later become the PCIJ's first Registrar, the Secretariat of the League of Nations specified that

> arbitration is distinguished from judicial procedure in the strict sense of the word by three features: the nomination of the arbitrators by the parties concerned, the selection by these parties of the principles on which the tribunal should base its findings, and finally its character of voluntary jurisdiction. But there are transactional methods of procedure, where only one or two of the factors are in evidence.[35]

Acknowledging the 'ambiguity' of the term 'arbitration', the memorandum further specified that the essential features of the future PCIJ should be defined in response to the criticisms directed against the Permanent Court of Arbitration. Thus, the Court should not only be truly permanent, i.e. 'accessible at all times', but also constitute a real court 'of justice' by 'applying the law' just like 'the Courts of Justice of the different countries.'[36] This implied that it would also develop a proper case law, as Léon Bourgeois, speaking as a delegate of the League Council, would later stress in his inaugural speech before the Committee of Jurists.[37] Given the importance of this distinction, it is hardly surprising that the Committee would neglect to take a closer look at the MATs, whose 'arbitral' nature could be inferred not only from their denomination, but also from their tripartite composition. Reminiscent of that of most interstate arbitral tribunals of the time, this composition

33 Ole Spiermann, *International Legal Argument in the Permanent Court of International Justice* (Cambridge University Press, Cambridge 2005), 3–4.

34 Ibid, 7.

35 *Documents presented to the Committee relating to existing Plans for the Establishment of a Permanent Court of International Justice* (The Hague 1920), 113.

36 Ibid.

37 Advisory Committee of Jurists, *Procès-Verbaux of the Proceedings of the Committee: June 16th–July 24th 1920*, 8.

was later often criticised for exacerbating tensions within the MATs.[38] The only exception to this principle would take place pursuant to the Paris Accords of 28 April 1930,[39] by which Hungary and the members of the Little Entente (Czechoslovakia, Romania, and Yugoslavia) agreed to let the PCIJ appoint two additional neutral members to their mutual MATs.[40] That said, going back to the criteria presented to the Committee of Jurists, the MATs were not necessarily less 'judicial' than the PCIJ. First and foremost, whereas the League Council eventually rejected the Committee of Jurists' suggestion to confer compulsory jurisdiction to the PCIJ in favour of voluntary jurisdiction,[41] the jurisdiction of the MATs was premised only on the ratification of the relevant peace treaty. Second, once they were operational, the MATs went to great lengths to expand their 'judicial' features. As already mentioned, this included the publication of a semi-official collection of its case law, whose relevance the Permanent Court eventually recognized.[42] As specified by their Rules of Procedure, hearings before the MATs were public.[43] In practice, members of a Mixed Arbitral Tribunal would be referred to[44] and sign as[45] 'judges' rather than 'arbitrators'. In some MATs, they would wear judges' robes.[46] However, these efforts could not hide the

38 Jakob Zollmann, 'Mixed Arbitral Tribunals: Post-First World War Peace Treaties' in Hélène Ruiz Fabri, *Max Planck Encyclopedia for International Procedural Law* (Oxford University Press 2022), para. 19.

39 Agreements (I to IV) relating to the Obligations Resulting from the Treaty of Trianon of 4 June 1920, with Annexes (signed 28 April 1930, entered into force 9 April 1931) 121 *LNTS*, 69.

40 7 *PCIJ Annual Report* (1930–31), 188–89. On this process, see Maja Stanivuković and Sanja Djajić, 'Something Old, Something New: The 1930 Reform of the Trianon Mixed Arbitral Tribunals and the Contemporary Discussion of the Appeal Mechanism in Investment Arbitration' in Hélène Ruiz Fabri and Michel Erpelding, (eds), *The Mixed Arbitral Tribunals, 1919–1939: An Experiment in the International Adjudication of Private Rights* (Nomos, Baden-Baden 2023), 459–523.

41 Christian J. Tams, 'The Contentious Jurisdiction of the Permanent Court' in Christian J. Tams and Malgosia Fitzmaurice (eds), *Legacies of the Permanent Court of International Justice* (Martinus Nijhoff, Leiden/Boston 2013), 19–21.

42 *Appeal from a Judgment of the Hungaro-Czecoslovak Mixed Arbitral Tribunal (The Peter Pázmány University)*, Judgment, 15 December 1933, PCIJ Series A/B no 61 (1933), 243.

43 See e.g. the Rules of Procedure of the French-German (Art. 46), the Belgian-German (Art. 60), the Anglo-German (Art. 30), and the French-Turkish (Art. 45) MATs.

44 See e.g.: 1 *Recueil TAM*, 541.

45 See e.g.: 5 *Recueil TAM*, 1012.

46 Marta Requejo Isidro and Burkhard Hess, 'International Adjudication of Private Rights: The Mixed Arbitral Tribunals in the Peace Treaties of 1919–1922' in Michel

fact that although the MATs were, just like the PCIJ, 'accessible at all times', their existence was limited to the time it would take to terminate (whether by judicial decision or by settlement) the disputes brought before them. The undetermined duration of their existence led some participants in the MATs system to characterise them as 'quasi-permanent', advocating their transformation into permanent institutions.[47] However, the interest this project had raised with certain governments eventually fizzled out in the late 1930s.[48] In combination with their small benches, the precariousness of the MATs certainly led the PCIJ to refuse them the status of truly 'judicial' institutions. It is with this context in mind that one should read the PCIJ's statement in the *Certain German Interests* case that there could be no litispendence between the Court and the Polish-German MAT, since 'the Mixed Arbitral Tribunals and the Permanent Court of International Justice are not courts of the same character'.[49]

Another factor that would have discouraged the Committee of Jurists from referring to the MATs as a useful precedent for the future PCIJ was their respective personal jurisdiction. Since the MAT's jurisdiction essentially revolved around suits by private persons against each other or against sovereign states, discussing these institutions would only have been meaningful in the eventuality that the Committee of Jurists would have advocated for a Permanent Court with jurisdiction over private suits. However, at that time only the Dutch and the German Governments had pronounced themselves in favour of such a solution, which would have combined the jurisdiction over interstate disputes with the kinds of private

Erpelding, Burkhard Hess and Hélène Ruiz Fabri (eds), *Peace Through Law: The Versailles Peace Treaty and Dispute Settlement After World War I* (Nomos, Baden-Baden 2019), 255.

47 'Procédure arbitrale : Rapport présenté par MM. F. L. de la Barra et A. Mercier' (1927) 33 *Annuaire IDI*, 565 (575); 'Le rapport de l'accès des particuliers à des juridictions internationales : Rapport de M. Séfériadès' (1929) 35 *Annuaire IDI*, 505 (510). Francisco de la Barra was a member of six MATs, five of which he presided; Stelios Seferiades was agent-general of his government before three MATs.

48 Michel Erpelding and Jakob Zollmann, 'Epilogue: The Early and Long End of the Mixed Arbitral Tribunals, 1920–1930' in Hélène Ruiz-Fabri and Michel Erpelding (eds), *The Mixed Arbitral Tribunals, 1919-1939: An Experiment in the International Adjudication of Private Rights* (Nomos, Baden-Baden 2023), 537–540.

49 *Case Concerning Certain German Interests in Polish Upper Silesia*, Preliminary Objections Judgment, 25 August 1925, PCIJ Series A no 6 (1925), 20.

suits dealt with by the MATs.[50] Within the Committee, Albert Geouffre De Lapradelle and Bernard Loder tried to defend this idea, both noting the insufficiency of diplomatic protection to protect private interests.[51] However, the Committee ultimately rejected their arguments, Elihu Root noting on his part that to him the word 'international' used to describe the PCIJ necessarily referred to the interstate character of the disputes to be brought before it.[52] While the ensuing state-centrism of the Court made it less inclusive than the clearly 'judicial' precedents of the International Prize Court and the Central American Court of Justice,[53] the PCIJ would eventually recognise the 'international' character of the MATs. This was by no means a foregone conclusion, as the international or domestic nature of the MATs was constantly debated during the interwar period,[54] with one of the Court's most prominent publicists, Dionisio Anzilotti, characterizing them in 1929 as 'common organs of the parties'.[55] By contrast, the PCIJ's characterisation of the MATs as 'arbitral tribunals of a special international character' in its 1928 judgment on the merits in the *Chorzów Factory* case[56] amounted to a relatively early recognition of their role within the new international institutional framework established by the post-World War I peace treaties.

---

50 Advisory Committee of Jurists, *Procès-Verbaux of the Proceedings of the Committee: June 16th–July 24th 1920*, 78-80.

51 Ibid, 205–206, 209–211.

52 Ibid, 207.

53 Christian J. Tams, 'The Contentious Jurisdiction of the Permanent Court' in Christian J. Tams and Malgosia Fitzmaurice (eds), *Legacies of the Permanent Court of International Justice* (Martinus Nijhoff, Leiden/Boston 2013), 14–15.

54 Marta Requejo Isidro and Burkhard Hess, 'International Adjudication of Private Rights: The Mixed Arbitral Tribunals in the Peace Treaties of 1919–1922' in Michel Erpelding, Burkhard Hess and Hélène Ruiz Fabri (eds), *Peace Through Law: The Versailles Peace Treaty and Dispute Settlement After World War I* (Nomos, Baden-Baden 2019), 263-64.

55 Dionisio Anzilotti, *Cours de droit international* (re-edition, Paris Editions Panthéon-Assas 1999), 135–136.

56 *Factory at Chorzów*, Merits Judgment, 13 September 1928, PCIJ Series A no 17 (1928), 27.

C. A Controversial Reference and Source of Experience for International Judges: the MATs and the Bench of the Permanent Court

While their respective case-law would suggest that the Permanent Court and the Mixed Arbitral Tribunals mostly tended to ignore each other, a look at their respective benches[57] shows that a non-negligible number of judges who sat on the PCIJ's bench actually knew the MATs from personal experience. The existence of these overlaps, but also their limited character, reflected contemporary debates about the qualities of international judges, both with regard to their training and their reputation of impartiality.

Looking at the Court's permanent members, such an overlap existed only within its first generation of judges (ca. 1922-1930), whose terms in the Hague coincided with the period of greatest activity of the MATs. Out of the 12 individuals appointed during that period as judges to the Court's bench (not counting the four deputy-judges), two also sat as members of MATs, namely the PCIJ's first President, the Dutchman Bernard Loder, and his Danish colleague Dïdrik Galtrup Gjedde Nyholm. Both had qualities that were very much sought after by the MATs. To begin with, Loder as well as Nyholm were not only well-versed in international affairs, but also accomplished practitioners in the field of civil procedure and private international law, which corresponded to the MATs' subject-matter jurisdiction and their reliance on extremely detailed Rules of Procedure, once described as 'miniature civil procedure codes'.[58] Before being appointed to the PCIJ in 1921, Loder, who had been a member of the Dutch Supreme Court *(Hoge Road)* since 1908, had established a reputation in maritime law, advised his government on issues of international law, and represented it at various international conferences, including, crucially, the Paris Peace Conference. He was also a member of the Advisory Committee of Jurists

57 For a list of the members of the PCIJ, see *The Permanent Court of International Justice, 1922–2012* (International Court of Justice, The Hague 2012), 206–217. For a list of the members of all 39 MATs, see Michel Erpelding, 'Appendix: Alphabetical list of the Mixed Arbitral Tribunals and their members' in Hélène Ruiz Fabri and Michel Erpelding (eds), *The Mixed Arbitral Tribunals, 1919-1939: An Experiment in the International Adjudication of Private Rights* (Nomos, Baden-Baden 2023), 547–581.

58 Piero Calamandrei, 'Il Tribunale arbitrale misto italo-germanico e il suo regola mento processuale' (1922) *Rivista del diritto commerciale*, 293.

that helped establish the PCIJ.[59] In comparison, Nyholm's experience was more strongly turned toward judicial practice, with a particular expertise in private international law and government liability, as he had been a member of the Mixed Courts of Egypt (which shared several features with both the PCIJ and the MATs),[60] first in Mansura (1896-1902), later in Cairo (1902-1921).[61] In that capacity, which he combined with that of a member of the Permanent Court of Arbitration, Nyholm had taken the initiative of submitting a plan for a 'World Court' ('*Tribunal mondial*') to the League Secretariat,[62] which was repeatedly mentioned in the documents submitted to the Committee of Jurists.[63] Conversely, neither Loder nor Nyholm had published any major doctrinal work. In addition to their technical - and decidedly practical - expertise, both were nationals of countries that had remained neutral during World War I - a status that could only be enhanced by their quality as members of the World Court. Their careers as MAT members were relatively short-lived, but not devoid of significance for the relations between both institutions. In Loder's case, his appointment to the PCIJ more or less coincided with his presidency of the London-based Anglo-Austrian, Anglo-Bulgarian, and Anglo-Hungarian MATs, which like the Court started their work in 1922. Although Loder resigned from these three positions already in 1923[64] after deciding several major cases,[65] this did not diminish his public support for the MATs. Until

59 Freya Baetens and Veronica Lavista, '"Where is your Tribunal?" Bernard Loder (1849-1935) and the Quest for International Justice' in P. Sean Morris (ed), *The League of Nations and the Development of International Law: A New Intellectual History of the Advisory Committee of Jurists* (Routledge, Oxon 2022), 199.

60 On these courts, see Jasper Yeates Brinton, *The Mixed Courts of Egypt* (revised edition, Yale University Press, New Haven/London 1968); Mark S. Hoyle, *Mixed Courts of Egypt* (Graham & Trotman, London/Dordrecht/Boston 1991); Michel Erpelding, 'Mixed Courts of Egypt' in Hélène Ruiz Fabri (ed), *Max Planck Encyclopedia of International Procedural Law* (Oxford University Press 2020).

61 Frantz Dahl, 'Dommer D. G. Nyholm' (1931) 2 *Nordisk Tidsskrift for International Ret*, 147 (148).

62 Didrik Nyholm, *Le Tribunal mondial* (Whitehead, Morris & Co., Cairo 1918), United Nations Archives at Geneva, R1300/21/859/859.

63 *Documents presented to the Committee relating to existing plans for the establishment of a Permanent Court of International Justice* (The Hague 1920), 26, 74–77, 80–87.

64 3 *Recueil TAM*, 215.

65 See e.g. Anglo-Bulgarian MAT, 'George Stevenson & Co Ltd v National Bank of Bulgaria' (25 and 26 May 1922) 2 *Recueil TAM*, 77; Anglo-Austrian MAT, "Vulkan' Maschinenfabrik AG of Vienna v John I Thornycroft & Co Ldt' (7 and 12 December 1922) 2 *Recueil TAM*, 711; Anglo-Austrian MAT, 'Victor Rubens v Austrian State' (26 April and 2 May 1923) 3 *Recueil TAM*, 37.

they were discontinued in 1931, the MATs' official case-law collection was published under his (and other active and former MAT Presidents') 'high patronage' – in Loder's case, with the additional mention of his functions as PCIJ President.[66] As for Nyholm, his experience of the MATs resulted from exceptional circumstances. When France and Belgium occupied the Ruhr region in January 1923 in response to Germany's failure to meet its reparation payments, Germany reacted amongst others by suspending its participation in the MATs with both countries. Based on its interpretation of Article 304 Versailles Treaty and its Annex,[67] France submitted to the Council of the League of Nations the names of four neutral nationals as replacements for the German members of the French-German MAT's four sections. Following their appointment by the League Council on 3rd February 1923, the neutrals – which included Nyholm – began their work on 3rd March 1923.[68] These appointments were not entirely unproblematic – as noted by a German commentator, the Swiss President of the Belgian-German MAT protested and successfully thwarted the appointment of a neutral on his tribunal, whereas the League Council later rejected a similar initiative by Romania when Hungary suspended its participation in the two countries' MAT.[69] Generally speaking, the MATs were often criticised

66 See the front covers of all 10 volumes of the *Recueil TAM*.

67 Art 304 Versailles Treaty ran as follows: '(a) Within three months from the date of the coming into force of the present Treaty, a Mixed Arbitral Tribunal shall be established between each of the Allied and Associated Powers on the one hand and Germany on the other hand. Each such Tribunal shall consist of three members. Each of the Governments concerned shall appoint one of these members. The President shall be chosen by agreement between the two Governments concerned.
In case of failure to reach agreement, the President of the Tribunal and two other persons either of whom may in case of need take his place, shall be chosen by the Council of the League of Nations, or, until this is set up, by M. Gustave Ador if he is willing. These persons shall be nationals of Powers that have remained neutral during the war.
If any Government does not proceed within a period of one month in case there is a vacancy to appoint a member of the Tribunal, such member shall be chosen by the other Government from the two persons mentioned above other than the President.
The decision of the majority of the members of the Tribunal shall be the decision of the Tribunal. (...)'.
Annex: '1. Should one of the members of the Tribunal either die, retire, or be unable for any reason whatever to discharge his functions, the same procedure will be followed for filling the vacancy as was followed for appointing him. (...)'.

68 2 *Recueil TAM*, 872.

69 Walter Schätzel, *Das deutsch-französische Schiedsgericht, seine Geschichte, Rechtsprechung und Ergebnisse* (Georg Stilke, Berlin 1930), 36–37.

by contemporary commentators for being structurally biased against the former Central Powers, chiefly because of their selective jurisdiction, which usually favoured Allied nationals, but also because they mostly convened in Allied territory and exclusively operated in the languages of Allied states.[70] However, Nyholm seems to have remained unfazed by such considerations. Just like the other neutrals, he not only ignored Germany's legal arguments against their appointment,[71] but refused to give up his position after Germany resumed its participation in November 1923,[72] only handing it over to his German counterpart in May 1925.[73] Others considered the close relations established by Loder and Nyholm with the MATs problematic, notably their colleague Max Huber. Having already identified Loder and Nyholm as his main antagonists on the Court, notably because they were eager to resolve problems by recourse to rules of civil procedure, Huber noted in his memoirs that in 1924 he flatly refused the presidency of an MAT offered to him by Hungary on grounds of 'strict neutrality'.[74] His assessment of the whole system of the MATs as 'a very sophisticated legal system exclusively turned against one party' (*'ein ganz raffiniertes, nur gegen die eine Partei gerichtetes Rechtssystem'*)[75] may therefore also be understood as an implicit criticism of his Dutch and Danish colleagues, whose participation in that system he might have viewed as potentially detrimental to the Court's reputation as an impartial judicial body. That said, the PCIJ's reputation of impartiality had remained solid enough for the Turkish Government agreeing to Article 92 of the Lausanne Treaty. Pursuant to that provision, in 1924 it fell upon the Court's president – by then none other than Max Huber – to appoint the presidents of Turkey's MATs with Britain, Greece, Italy, and Romania, after the relevant governments had failed to reach an agreement to this effect.[76] Similarly, Nyholm's role as a replacement judge in the French-German MAT did not prevent the Court from appointing

70 Marta Requejo Isidro and Burkhard Hess, 'International Adjudication of Private Rights: The Mixed Arbitral Tribunals in the Peace Treaties of 1919–1922' in Michel Erpelding, Burkhard Hess and Hélène Ruiz Fabri (eds), *Peace Through Law: The Versailles Peace Treaty and Dispute Settlement After World War I* (Nomos, Baden-Baden 2019), 256–258.

71 Göppert, op. cit. (fn 25) 54–55.

72 *Ibidem*, 62–63.

73 5 *Recueil TAM*, 384.

74 Max Huber, *Denkwürdigkeiten, 1907–1924* (Orell Füssli, Zürich 1974), 272.

75 Ibid, 296.

76 5 *Recueil TAM*, 1.

him as one of two additional members of the Yugoslavian-Hungarian MAT in 1930.[77]

The overlap between the benches of the PCIJ and the MATs was even more pronounced in the case of the judges ad hoc appointed to the Court by individual states engaged in a dispute before it. Of 23 judges ad hoc, five also sat as 'national' members of various MATs. Three of them joined the bench of the PCIJ in cases engaging at some point with MAT decisions. Ernst Rabel, who was a member of the Italian-German and French-German MATs in the 1920s, was appointed by Germany in the *Certain German Interests* and *Chorzów Factory* cases, whose subject-matter had also been examined by the Polish-German MAT. Theohar Papazoff, who sat as an arbitrator on five out of six MATs with Bulgaria,[78] also joined the bench of the PCIJ for the *Electricity Company of Sofia and Bulgaria* case.[79] In this case, which concerned the implementation by Bulgaria of a decision of the Belgian-Bulgarian MAT taken with Papazoff's participation, the Bulgarian judge ad hoc issued a dissenting opinion endorsing his government's position that the mere decision of the MAT, and not Bulgaria's subsequent implementation of the latter (as held by the PCIJ),[80] had given rise to the dispute.[81] An even more transparently partisan judge ad hoc appointment was that of Vilmos Pál Tomcsányi, who sat for Hungary on the PCIJ in two cases regarding the appeal against MAT decisions,[82] had participated in similar decisions of the Yugoslavian-Hungarian MAT[83] and wrote a dissenting opinion criticizing the Court's choice to confirm the decisions made by that Tribunal.[84] The two remaining ad hoc judges had also a history of defending their government's interests within the MAT system. Stelios

77 7 *PCIJ Annual Report* (1930-31), 188–189.

78 Namely, the Anglo-Bulgarian, Belgian-Bulgarian, French-Bulgarian, Greek-Bulgarian, and Yugoslavian-Bulgarian MATs.

79 He also sat in the *Greco-Bulgarian 'Communities'* and the *Interpretation of the Greco-Bulgarian Agreement of 9 December 1927* cases, which were unrelated to any MAT decisions.

80 At 81–82.

81 *Electricity Company of Sofia and Bulgaria*, Judgment, 4 April 1939, PCIJ Series A/B no 77 (1939), dissenting opinion by judge ad hoc Papazoff, 146.

82 Namely, the *Peter Pázmány University* (1933) and the *Pajzs, Czáky, Esterházy* (1936) cases.

83 *Pajzs, Czáky, Esterházy*, Application and Documents of the Written Proceedings, PCIJ Series C no 79 (1935), 19, 21, 22.

84 *Pajzs, Czáky, Esterházy*, Judgment, 16 December 1936, PCIJ Series A/B no 68 (1936), separate opinion of M. de Tomcsányi, 99.

Seferiades, appointed by Greece in the *Lighthouses case between France and Greece* before the PCIJ,[85] had been his country's Agent-General before its MATs with Austria, Bulgaria, and Germany.[86] As for Victor Bruns, judge ad hoc for Danzig in three advisory opinion proceedings related to the Free City,[87] he also served as judge for Germany on the Czechoslovakian-German and Polish-German MATs. Both types of appointments could be seen as complementary to his position as founding Director of the (Kaiser Wilhelm) Institute for Comparative Public Law and International Law.[88] Just like Ernst Rabel's (Kaiser Wilhelm) Institute for Comparative and International Private Law, it owed much of its existence to its role in helping the German Government fight the adverse consequences of the peace treaties before international courts, notably the MATs.[89] This function is further backed up by Bruns' recently rediscovered correspondence as member of the Polish-German MAT, which also sheds additional light on the partisan and unequally prestigious nature of national appointments to the MATs and the PCIJ. The correspondence shows for instance that after Bruns was appointed in 1927 to the Polish-German MAT, he regularly updated his government on his efforts to sway the Tribunal in Germany's interest.[90] It also reveals that he saw his role in the Hague in a similar light. When in late 1931 he received the news of his appointment as judge ad hoc for Danzig, he immediately informed the President of the MAT that he would prioritise

85 *Lighthouses Case between France and Greece*, 17 March 1933, Judgment, PCIJ Series A/B no 62 (1934).

86 He assumed this position from 1922 to 1923. Thomas Skouteris, 'The vocabulary of progress in interwar international law: an intellectual portrait of Stelios Seferiades' (2006) 16 *European Journal of International Law*, 823 (847).

87 Namely *in the Jurisdiction of the Courts of Danzig* (1928), the *Access to, or Anchorage in, the Port of Danzig, of Polish War Vessels* (1931), and the *Treatment of Polish Nationals and Other Persons of Polish Origin or Speech in the Danzig Territory* (1932) advisory opinions.

88 Rüdiger Hachtmann, 'The Kaiser Wilhelm Institute for Comparative Public Law and International Law 1924 to 1945' (15 December 2023), DOI: 10.17176/20240403-184342-0.

89 Jakob Zollmann, 'Mixed Arbitral Tribunals: Post-First World War Peace Treaties' in Hélène Ruiz Fabri, *Max Planck Encyclopedia for International Procedural Law* (Oxford University Press 2022), para. 32.

90 The papers of Victor Bruns preserved at the Max Planck Institute for Comparative Public and International Law (hereafter 'Bruns MPIL Papers'), include more than 400 pages of correspondence between Bruns and both the German Ministry of Foreign Affairs and the German State Agents before the MAT between 1927 and 1932. I would like to thank Philipp Glahé, who rediscovered these files, for sharing them with me.

these new functions over those within the Tribunal. Invoking the overtly partisan motive that he 'could not leave unheeded the call of a German city that has been in a difficult situation for a long time', he declared that he would not participate in the MAT's last session, instead devoting his time to the (clearly more important) PCIJ proceedings.[91] As becomes clear from these profiles, prior participation in the MAT system was a guarantee of concrete technical expertise and loyalty – qualities that were also required from judges ad hoc at the PCIJ – more than of a general commitment to the ideal of impartial international adjudication.

D. Conclusion

While they were both the result of the new international order established by the post-World War I peace treaties, the Permanent Court of International Justice and the Mixed Arbitral Tribunals were indeed 'not courts of the same character'.[92] During the entirety of their existence, which roughly coincided, the relationship between the two institutions was one of inequality.

From an institutional point of view, the MATs would (sometimes successfully) seek validation from the PCIJ, and not the other way around. On the part of the Permanent Court, this was not only due to its relatively restrictive conception of what could constitute an international 'judiciary', but also to its jurisdiction, which – being restricted to disputes between states – could make little use of the elaborate procedural rules entirely tailored toward suits involving private parties, as established by the MATs. From the latters' perspective, the Permanent Court was less a source of inspiration for their own case law (which mostly revolved around economic provisions of the peace treaties that were only occasionally discussed in the Hague), than an authority that could bolster the tribunals' legitimacy as bona fide examples of international adjudication. The PCIJ only partly offered the required support: it recognised the 'international' character of the MATs, but rather than acknowledging their deeply innovative (and

91 Bruns to President Lachenal (28 October 1931), Bruns MPIL Papers. French original: *'je n'ai pu me soustraire à l'appel d'une ville allemande se trouvant depuis longtemps dans une situation difficile'*.

92 *Case Concerning Certain German Interests in Polish Upper Silesia*, Preliminary Objections Judgment, 25 August 1925, PCIJ Series A no 6 (1925), 20.

arguably 'judicial') features, always characterised them just as another form of arbitration.

From a personal point of view, a look at the respective benches of the PCIJ and the MATs confirms the unequal character of the relations between both institutions. Whereas the MATs' official collection of case law would proudly advertise the support given to it by the PCIJ's first President, the Permanent Court could only have little interest in using the MATs as a recruiting ground or a source of additional experience for its own members. The two permanent members of the PCIJ that had any direct experience as members of the MATs were representatives of a particular current within the Court which held that only individuals with a background in a domestic judiciary could make good international judges. Conversely, PCIJ judges that wanted the Court to represent abstract conceptions of impartial international adjudication could only be critical of any association of their institution with the structurally biased MATs system. The fact that the MATs more frequently served as a recruiting pool for ad hoc judges – which were themselves a controversial institution, often described as a regrettable relict from interstate arbitration –, would hardly have altered these views.The fundamentally unequal character of the relations between the Permanent Court and the Mixed Arbitral Tribunals would outlive the institutions themselves. At the termination of the various MATs, the question of the conservation of their archives arose. Whereas the archives of several MATs were left with, or even divided between, individual states, others were promised to a more 'internationalist' fate. At the initiative of the Belgian and French Agents-General, who held that the international character of the MATs made them improper for conservation by domestic institutions, the archives of several Paris- and Geneva-based MATs – including the 22,000 case files of the French-German MAT[93] – were sent to the Peace Palace Library at The Hague, both before the outbreak and after the end of World War II, where they were supposed to inspire future generations of international lawyers. However, contrary to the legacy of the Permanent Court, which continued to be cherished by the International Court of Justice and the Carnegie Foundation, the archives of the Mixed

93 Letter of the French Agent-General to the Head of the French Clearing Office (5 July 1938), French Diplomatic Archives, OBIP11/BIP.

Arbitral Tribunals were eventually discarded by the Peace Palace Library in the 1970s–80s.[94]

94 Michel Erpelding and Jakob Zollmann, 'Epilogue: The Early and Long End of the Mixed Arbitral Tribunals, 1920–1930' in Hélène Ruiz-Fabri and Michel Erpelding (eds), *The Mixed Arbitral Tribunals, 1919-1939: An Experiment in the International Adjudication of Private Rights* (Nomos, Baden-Baden 2023), 543–545.

Epilogue: Two Hague Icons, Three Surprises, and the Virtue of Looking Again

Christian J. Tams

A. Introduction

Despite its Protestant tradition and some Dutch fondness for austerity, The Hague is not short on icons. Johannes Vermeer's *Girl with a Pearl Earring* is one of them. Since 1902, it has been on display in the Mauritshuis, a lovely museum in the heart of the city, close to the centres of Dutch political power, and visited there by hundreds of thousands of visitors every year. Even those who have not visited the Mauritshuis are likely to feel that they know the *'Girl'*. Vermeer's depiction, sometimes referred to as the 'Mona Lisa of the North', has become iconic. It is omnipresent in popular culture, including in novels, in a Hollywood movie starring Scarlett Johansson, and as an image reproduced on countless tote bags and fridge magnets around the world. While some questions will never be answered (notably 'who was she?'), everyone is familiar with the *'Girl'*, and everything that can usefully be said about her seems to have been said.

But how much do we really know? Work by museum experts over the past decades suggest that despite her omnipresence, the *Girl with a Pearl Earring* continues to surprise. Amongst other things, recent restorations have revealed that the famous second highlight on the pearl (which had – as *Forbes* magazine had speculated – "no doubt been the subject of countless undergraduate art history papers") was in fact "just a fleck of paint that had chipped off".[1] By contrast, new research has shown that the girl not only had but one highlight on her earring initially; Vermeer also painted her with eyelashes, which later faded from view: as a result, much learned speculation about the implications of the apparent *absence*

1 David Alm, 'Peeling Back The Layers Of "Girl With A Pearl Earring" With Medical Technology', *Forbes* (28 February 2018), https://www.forbes.com/sites/davidalm/2018/02/28/peeling-back-the-layers-of-girl-with-a-pearl-earring-with-medical-technology.

of eyelashes was, as we now know, based on insufficient knowledge.[2] New research has opened up novel perspectives. It made sense to look again.

***

The Permanent Court of International Justice (PCIJ) is another icon of The Hague. At least international lawyers will see in it some of the qualities of the *Girl with a Pearl Earring.* Everyone knows (of) it. The PCIJ comes from another era, but as with Vermeer's paintings, its historicity is tempered with more than a dose of timelessness. This timelessness keeps current generations interested, who feel that, despite its age, the PCIJ experience still speaks to us and who look for traces of the PCIJ in subsequent incarnations (such as the ICJ). As a result, the PCIJ icon is omnipresent in international legal literature. In fact, it has been a favourite topic of international legal writing for a century. Everything that can be said about the PCIJ seems to have been said.

But just as the *Girl with a Pearl Earring,* the PCIJ has the odd surprise in store for us. There is room for novel perspectives. It does make sense to look again. This is what this book is about.

Henri de Waele's Introduction identifies central contributions made in the book's individual chapters. In this epilogue, I propose to synthesise these central contributions into three questions, which reflect my own surprise at what the contributors' further look has revealed. I should admit that my questions not only synthesise and simplify, but purposefully overstate matters, at least a little, with a view to encouraging debate. More specifically, the preceding contributions in my view encourage reflection and debate around three questions: (i) A European World Court?; (ii) Unhurried Justice?; (iii) The Hague, Capital of Peace? I address these in the following, before offering some brief final reflections.

B. A European World Court?

The first question takes us into the well-known terrain of Eurocentrism. The PCIJ in many ways was a Court, not only *based in* Europe, but also *for* Europe. Its main clients were European States - only in four of the

2 The Mauritshuis website offers a useful overview: see https://www.mauritshuis.nl/en/our-collection/restoration-and-research/closer-to-vermeer-and-the-girl.

33 contentious cases did non-European States appear at all, and of these four, only one – *Brazilian Loans* – was really shaped by a non-European party (Brazil).[3] The legal issues raised before the PCIJ were predominantly European in nature or origin: proceedings addressed problems of minority protection in Central and Eastern Europe and many of the legacies of the Paris post-war settlement. Where disputes were set elsewhere (such as *Oscar Chinn* or the *Concessions* cases), they were usually triggered by European States' meddling abroad. All this gave the first 'World Court' a strong European touch. Georges Abi-Saab's remark captures the gist of this perspective: the PCIJ, as he noted in the mid-1990s, "faithfully reflected in its stance and its jurisprudence the legal outlook of [its] Eurocentric community".[4]

The preceding chapters do not fundamentally challenge this general assessment. In fact, many contributors affirm aspects of it. The significance of European disputes in the day-to-day practice of the Court, for example, is noted by many.[5] Beyond affirming it, contributors in fact accentuate the conventional wisdoms in relevant respects. Artur Eyffinger perceptively notes that the Court's workload could simply not be dealt with in the course of one annual session (as had been assumed); as a result, non-European judges "never coped with the tight schedule" and often failed to attend important meetings during the regular and extraordinary sessions. Statistics are indeed "telling": "De Bustamante missed out on 24 out of the 35 Sessions up to 1935; Pessõa attended 6 out of the 16 Sessions up to 1931; judge Moore attended 6 out of 14 Sessions, judge Kellogg a mere 3 out

3 See *Brazilian Loans*, PCIJ Series A, No 18. Other non-European states participating in contentious proceedings were Japan (as joint applicant in *SS 'Wimbledon'*, PCIJ Series A, No 1, and *Statute of Memel*, PCIJ Series AB, No. 47) and China (in *Denunciation of the Sino-Belgian Treaty of 2 November 1865*, PCIJ Series, No 8). For more see. C. Wilfred Jenks, *The Prospects of International Adjudication* (Stevens & Sons, London 1964), 75-76.

4 Georges Abi-Saab, 'The International Court as a World Court', in Malgosia Fitzmaurice and Vaughan Lowe (eds), *Fifty Years of the International Court of Justice. Essays in Honour of Sir Robert Jennings* (Cambridge University Press, Cambridge 1996), 3, at 4. In his contribution to this volume, Apter agrees that "[t]he idea of establishing a system of international adjudication to resolve global disputes reflected a Euro-centric approach which can be traced to the 1899 and 1907 Hague Peace conferences" (at 164) – but then goes on to offer significant qualifications, as indicated below.

5 Eyffinger notes forcefully: "Barring a single exception, [cases] exclusively touched the dismal legacy of Versailles and the self-inflicted wounds of the European Powers" (in this volume, at 79).

of 14".[6] The basic point is straightforward: non-European part-time judges struggled to shape debates taking place in Europe, a growing pain only soothed when the Court moved to permanent annual sessions.

Yet participants from outside Europe did leave their mark on the Court. In fact, chapters to the book highlight two absolutely crucial contributions that can be traced back to interventions from outside Europe and that risk being overlooked in general statements about the PCIJ's 'European' nature. These interventions go to the heart of the Court's competence, namely its regime of jurisdiction, as devised in the debates of 1920–1922. The first concerns the fundamental decision against compulsory jurisdiction: it has come to define the parameters of the PCIJ's and ICJ's operation to this day, which remains premised on the "fundamental principle of consent".[7] As is well known (and as noted by contributors[8]), the Advisory Committee of Jurists (ACJ) had initially favoured a different course, proposing to invest the new Court with compulsory jurisdiction.[9] This proposal, set out in Article 34 of the Committee's text, was not unanimous. Arturo Ricci-Busatti from Italy argued against it. However, the most sustained critique of the proposed Article 34 was offered by a non-European, namely the Japanese member Mineichirō Adachi who – as Itar Apter recalls in his contribution – "strongly objected to [compulsory jurisdiction]" and instead "advocated for a consent requirement".[10] Noting that "who attempts too much does nothing well", Adachi placed on record his strong "reservation (...) concerning the whole compulsory jurisdiction", and recommended the "Committee (...) go gently with the infant" it had brought into being.[11] But the Committee felt that "any concession (...) made to chi's idea" would require "a complete re-drafting of the whole scheme, which is implicitly based on the

6 Eyffinger, 79; and further Ollivier (in this volume), at 171-172.

7 See ICJ, *Case concerning Application of the International Convention on the Elimination of All Forms of Racial Discrimination* ICJ Reports (2011), para. 131.

8 See e.g. the comments by Apter, at 156 and Milanov, at 218-219..

9 According to Momchil Milanov, this was "the single most important decision taken by the Committee" (at 218).

10 See Apter, at 162. Eyffinger concurs, noting that "Adachi spoke up against compulsory jurisdiction as politically unfeasible" (his fn. 87).

11 See Adachi's remarks in Advisory Committee of Jurists, *Procès-Verbaux of the Proceedings of the Committee: June 16th–July 24th 1920*, 542-543; and Hammarskjöld's assessment cited by Ole Spiermann, '"Who Attempts Too Much Does Nothing Well": The 1920 Advisory Committee of Jurists and the Statute of the Permanent Court of International Justice' (2002) 73 *British Yearbook of International Law*, (210), 239.

conception of the new Court as a real court of justice, with a compulsory jurisdiction with very wide limits".[12]

In the end, the whole scheme was to be re-drafted. Adachi's approach, outvoted in the Committee, was to win the day (and the argument) in the next stage of the drafting process, when matters had moved on to the political organs of the League. Adopted in July 1920, Article 34 was not to survive the autumn debates, as the Council "uprooted the core concept of the Committee's draft" and "[i]n a single strike (...) fatally struck the entire proposition out of balance".[13] As Adachi had predicted, there was simply no political support to invest the Court with compulsory jurisdiction. As far as the jurisdictional parameters were concerned, reform (Adachi's "going gently") was favoured over revolution. Looking back with the benefit of a century of hindsight, one cannot help but wonder at the ACJ's approach. Were its (mostly European) members naive when proposing to set up a Court with compulsory, automatic jurisdiction, to be seised unilaterally by any State? Was this a form of bravery?[14] Adachi's position – if we adapt those terms – was neither 'brave' not 'naïve', but informed by sound political judgment. It articulated concerns that remain very live to this day. Where European and Western lawyers on the ACJ may have got carried away, a century ago Mineichirō Adachi was the voice of reason – as Apter notes, his interventions pointed the way to an 'age of international courts' shaped, and limited, by State consent.[15] It is difficult to think of a more fundamental contribution.

So, how was consent to the expressed? Once the Committee's proposed Article 34 was out of the way, this became the key question. And as with the principle of consensualism, an intervention from outside Europe proved

---

12 Hammarskjöld, cited in Spiermann (ibid.), 233

13 Eyffinger, at 49. On this "uprooting", see van Leeuwen, at 119-121. According to Manley O. Hudson, the jurisdictional scheme of the Court eventually reflected in Article 36 of the Statute had been "the result of the greatest contest waged in the creation of the Court": see *The Permanent Court of International Justice. A Treatise* (2nd edn., 1943), 190.

14 Eyffinger seems to lean towards 'bravery', this is at least suggested by his comment on futile attempts to defend the principle of automatic (compulsory) jurisdiction: "a last truly brave and desperate stand in favour of 'the real thing' – untrammelled compulsory jurisdiction – was made (...) in the Plenary of the Assembly, in electrifying speeches by the First Delegates of the neutral Powers and the Latin American nations" (at 50).

15 See Apter, at 164, noting that "the need for consent[-based] jurisdiction (...) originated almost exclusively from Adachi's views".

crucial. The PCIJ, of course, was to be able to exercise jurisdiction on the basis of a *compromis* and compromissory clauses. Yet to these two standard modes of conferring jurisdiction, which continue to shape binding dispute settlement to this day,[16] the drafters added a third, which was particular to the PCIJ (and would remain particular to the ICJ): Under Article 36 of the Statute, the PCIJ could hear cases brought on the basis of matching optional clause declarations, where the parties had agreed to accept the Court's jurisdiction "as compulsory ipso facto and without special agreement"[17] – a third path to the World Court. This in itself is well-known, as is the fact that the "ingenious compromise"[18] on the optional clause proved a useful way to mend fences after the bruising debate about compulsory jurisdiction. How that compromise was reached is briefly recounted in contributions to this volume.[19] Yet these contributions also highlight a further element: they show that the 'third path' to the World Court was mapped out by another non-European participant, namely Raul Fernandes from Brazil. As Lucas Lima notes in his chapter, Fernandes "coined the well-known 'optional clause of compulsory jurisdiction' attributing jurisdiction to the Court". This (as Lima goes on to observe) was indeed a "highlight" of "his intervention at the Council of the League of Nations".[20] Looking at the importance of the optional clause to the entire jurisdictional scheme, we can perhaps go further. It was a decisive intervention; one which is properly recognised in the Latin American literature,[21] though perhaps not sufficiently elsewhere. As this is so, it is worth stating that the "ingenious compromise"[22] shaping the PCIJ's jurisdictional regime, finds its roots in

16 For more on this see Christian J. Tams, 'Controlling Consent. Insights from Binding Dispute Settlement', in Samantha Besson (ed), *Consenting to International Law* (Cambridge University Press, Cambridge 2023), 72.

17 See Article 36(2) of the PCIJ's Statute.

18 Ram Prakash Anand, *Compulsory Jurisdiction of the International Court of Justice* (Asia Publishing House, London 1961), 35. Jörg Kammerhofer calls it "a stroke of genius": see his 'Introduction', in Advisory Committee of Jurists, *Procès-Verbaux of the Proceedings of the Committee: June 16th–July 24th 1920* (re-issue, New Jersey, Lawbook Exchange 2006).

19 See e.g. the comments by Eyffinger, at 49-50; Lima, at 136-137.

20 Lima, at 126.

21 See Lima, at 126-127; and the account offered in Judge Cançado Trindade's dissenting opinion in *Case concerning Application of the International Convention on the Elimination of All Forms of Racial Discrimination* (Judgment) [2011] ICJ Rep. 239, at paras. 16, 26, 36.

22 Anand (n. 18), 35.

a 'Brazilian' intervention.[23] Taking up Lima's point, perhaps the optional clause should indeed be called the "Raul Fernandes clause".[24]

Stepping back from these debates, it seems to me that this book invites some further reflection on the 'European' character of the World Court. This further reflection does not prompt a complete re-think, as the data on the Court's usage and focus areas so clearly points to Europe. But there is merit in recalling how significantly two non-European participants intervened in the PCIJ's formative period, insisting on the virtue of jurisdictional reform over revolution and mapping out a third path The Hague. The World Court, as created in 1922, was at least partly shaped by powerful interventions that reflected the legal outlook of non-European participants, and these have continued to define it over the course of the past century.

C. Unhurried Justice?

The second question takes us away from the influences shaping the Court; it looks at the handling of cases by the PCIJ. How did the Court go about its business, how did it strike the balance between the competing demands of 'Respecting Sovereign States and Running a Tight Courtroom'?[25] The issues arising in this respect are manifold, and as they have been studied for decades, it is not easy to make out clearly-articulated positions of the Abi-Saab type. However, a glance at the standard works reveals patterns in our retrospective assessment of the first World Court: It is commonly seen as a Court that (like the ICJ for most of its time) had "only a modest caseload", and that took time to administer justice, prioritising the "unhurried consideration of the issues brought before it".[26] Viewed from this vantage-point, one might be tempted to think that 'running a tight courtroom' would have been a non-issue for the PCIJ. Recent inquiries into the ICJ's attempt to improve its working methods affirm that perspective: they tend to view the ICJ's desire to modernise its business as something

23 For details see PCIJ, *Documents Concerning the Action Taken by the Council of the League of Nations under Article 14 of the Covenant* (Geneva 1921), at 107, 168 and 222.

24 Lima, at 126.

25 Cf. Rosalyn Higgins, 'Respecting Sovereign States and Running a Tight Courtroom', (2001) 50 *The International and Comparative Law Quarterly*, 121.

26 See, respectively, Gary Born, 'A New Generation of International Adjudication', (2012) 61 *Duke Law Journal*, 775, 802; and Terry Gill, *Rosenne's The World Court: What It Is and How It Works* (Martinus Nijhoff, The Hague 2003), 14.

new, which requires a break with a century-old tradition of deference to sovereign litigants. In that conventional perspective, the PCIJ is seen as belonging to an early era of international adjudication when the disputes were not that pressing and when justice was dispensed not only "unhurried[ly]", but also "dispassionate[ly]".[27] That the Court's first bench included "far too many professors (...) and too few judges"[28] perhaps adds to this common perception of a charming, yet slightly stuffy, institution.

The PCIJ as depicted in the preceding chapters can appear a bit stuffy (and perhaps charming). But professorial it is not, rather we are presented with a Court that is surprisingly hands-on and at times interventionist.

This is true first of all in respect of its handling of cases. The chapters by Milanov, Morris and, above all, Ollivier, point readers to forms of case-management that do not easily fit the image of an unduly deferential Court keen not to upset its sovereign clients. Momchil Milanov duly notes that, "since the very beginning, the Court exercised '[g]reat caution and restraint' (...) when ascertaining [its] own jurisdiction".[29] But his detailed examination of the PCIJ's approach to preliminary objections suggests that a rival consideration was more influential, viz. "the need to distinguish the new Court from the concept of international justice based on arbitration understood as process controlled by the parties".[30] The 'real court of justice' that the Advisory Committee envisaged had to grapple, like the arbitral tribunals of old, with the problem of consent. But it would grapple with them from a position of permanence. And even during the PCIJ's early years, when the bench was said to be too professorial, the Court was guided by a sense of pragmatism that "developed as a response to concrete situations"[31] and that (as Sean Morris notes based on his discussion of advisory opinions) avoided theorising on abstract questions as much as "references to scholarship".[32] The professors were quickly adjusting to their new role.

In fact, Ollivier's account suggests that especially during its early (allegedly professorial) decade, the PCIJ was effective in controlling proceedings: "the written phase of the proceedings [was organised] in relatively

27 Gill (n. 26), 14.

28 As famously claimed by Sir Cecil Hurst: see his remarks quoted in Ole Spiermann, *International Legal Argument in the Permanent Court of International Justice* (Cambridge University Press, Cambridge 2005), 140.

29 Milanov, at 238 (citing Judge Lachs' Declaration in the *ICAO Council case*).

30 Milanov, at 239.

31 Milanov, at 238.

32 Morris, at 208.

short timeframes, generally not exceeding a few months", with extensions (if granted) "usually limited to a few days or weeks at most".[33] Not much time was spent on oral hearings either: "usually held (...) shortly after the closure of the written procedure", these hearings, "did not, at least in the early practice of the Court, last more than eight days".[34] (Contrast this to handling of oral proceedings in *South West Africa*, when the ICJ and its clients had reached 'peak inefficiency': merits hearings stretched out, with inter-sessional breaks, from 15 March to 29 November 1965 – and ended up being irrelevant as the Court decided the case on a point not put to the parties (...). But it was not just a question of timing; the PCIJ also was keen to make sure that the oral proceedings were used meaningfully. Many judges "complained of the practice of 'reading of prepared written statements' which was 'contrary to the principle underlying oral proceedings'"[35] – a principle since given up, as the ICJ insists on prepared written statements, which counsel are to read out. And at least in individual instances, the PCIJ's judges did use their power to direct parties to particular aspects of the proceedings, something now increasingly asked of the current ICJ. In his chapter, Sean Morris points to the *Eastern Carelia* opinion, where the PCIJ had informed Finland's representative (and former prime minister, later PCIJ judge and published Carelian expert), Rafael Erich "before hearing his statement that [the Court] would be glad to have his views as to whether it had competence to give effect to the request for an advisory opinion upon the question of Eastern Carelia, submitted to it by the Council of the League of Nations".[36]

As with the earlier point on Eurocentrism, these assessments and vignettes do not require history books to be rewritten. However, they accentuate our understanding of the PCIJ's approach to the handling of cases. In some passages at least, the PCIJ emerges as quite an astute manager of its case-load – focused, pragmatically, on getting things done, and perhaps benefiting (as Erpelding's chapter seems to suggest) from the experience of those of its members who had sat as arbitrators on the inter-war mixed

33 Ollivier, at 182.
34 Ollivier, at 184.
35 Ollivier, at 183.
36 Morris, 9, citing PCIJ, *Status of Eastern Carelia*, Advisory Opinion, 23 July 1923, PCIJ Series B no 5 (1923), 11-12.

arbitral tribunals.[37] Numbers bear out this impression, and they are worth restating:

> On average, the length of the proceedings on the merits of a case, from the institution of the proceedings to the reading of the judgment, lasted between one and one and a half year, which also often included preliminary or other incidental proceedings. Several requests for advisory opinions, often submitted as urgent by the Council of the League of Nations, were even dealt with within a few months, and for the very first requests, within a few weeks. Over its first decade of existence (1922-1931), the PCIJ delivered between three to seven judgments or advisory opinions every year.[38]

If this was "unhurried" justice, it was dispensed efficiently.

D. The Hague, Capital of Peace?

The final question looks at the locus of the project of international justice, the city of The Hague. Hailed as the global "city of peace" and "legal capital of the world",[39] the choice of The Hague as a seat of the World Court may seem obvious from today's perspective. It was a choice strongly recommended by the Advisory Committee: Whereas Article 14 of the Covenant had left the matter open, the Committee, reflecting on the seat of the future Court, settled on The Hague. As is clear from the debates, and recalled by contributors, this recommendation was based on two factors: a desire "to separate the political functions of the League of Nations [to be based in Geneva] from its judicial functions";[40] and respect for the 'Hague tradition' shaped by the Peace Conferences. As regards the latter, Baron

37 As Erpelding notes in his chapter (at 251-258), there was significant overlap between the benches of the mixed arbitral tribunals and those of the PCIJ. As indicated below, in section D of this Epilogue, this resulted in frictions, but it may have provided the PCIJ with experience in case-management.

38 Ollivier, at 182.

39 See Peter van den Dungen, 'Idee und Geschichte der neuzeitlichen Friedensstadt', in Reiner Steinweg et al. (eds), *Kommunale Friedensarbeit* (Magistrat der Landeshauptstadt Linz, Linz 2009), 59, at 62-63. The Hague's city government now seems to have settled on 'city of peace and justice', sometimes adding 'security': see <https://www.denhaag.nl/en/international-the-hague/international-city-of-peace-and-justice>.

40 See Baron Descamps' remarks in Advisory Committee of Jurists, *Procès-Verbaux of the Proceedings of the Committee: June 16th–July 24th 1920*, 202.

Descamps underlined the beneficial link with the Hague-based PCA, while Mineichiro Adachi found words that would likely make the city's marketing department beam with pride: "In Japan, when the Hague is mentioned, it means Peace and Justice".[41]

All this is recalled in the preceding contributions, notably those by Karin van Leuwen and Henri de Waele, which help us retrace The Hague's rise to its present 'capital' status. But the chapters highlight another aspect as well, which later generations may have forgotten: that the new Court would take its seat in The Hague was by no means a preordained conclusion. In fact, as Henri de Waele poignantly notes, at least initially, "the odds were actually stacked heavily against this location [The Hague]".[42] Stacked against, because, as Karin van Leeuwen demonstrates, the Dutch government was not among the early sponsors of a permanent world court. Quite to the contrary, at the second Peace Conference of 1907, its attitude was one of "restraint", not least out of fear that a new court would harm or even "wreck" an already existing Hague institution, viz. the PCA.[43] But stacked against the Hague also because during the late 1910s, the Netherlands had placed itself in a "dire corner indeed":[44] neutrality during the Great War was not a popular choice with the Allied and Associated powers, as Belgium and France suffered destruction. And by granting exile to the Kaiser and refusing extradition requests, the Dutch government did not endear itself to the leading powers of the post-war era either.[45]

As is clear, the decision in favour of The Hague required a clever exercise in "Repositioning The Hague",[46] and much skillful lobbying from key players such as Bernard Loder (who became the voice of the neutral powers on the Advisory Committee and then continued his work in the League Assembly) and his nephew, Joost van Hamel (who had secured for Loder a place on the Committee). As the contributions illustrate, the repositioning exercise (intriguingly referred to as "the sly manoeuvring of the van Hamel-Loder tandem"[47]) was as effective as it was swift. Dutch persuasion ensured that the Advisory Committee would meet in The Hague (and not

---

41 See statements by Baron Descamps and Adachi, ibid., 202.

42 De Waele, at 21.

43 Van Leeuwen, at 104; and see also Erpelding, at 242.

44 De Waele, at 22.

45 See also Eyffinger, at 54, who mentions Queen Wilhelmina's "swooning" ("SCHWÄRMEN") over "the German military and Junkertum".

46 Van Leeuwen, at 109.

47 De Waele, at 27.

in Brussels, as had been suggested) and recommend the same place for the future Court. Following the Committee's recommendation, by mid-1920, the seat was The Hague's to lose; in December 1920, Loder could declare that his country "'gladly and with deep emotion' accepted the Court on its soil".[48] Enshrined by Article 22 of the Statute, the World Court in its two incarnations has stayed there for over century, and mostly without second thoughts.[49] But it was a close-run thing, much closer than the mantra-esque references to The Hague as the 'legal capital of the world' and 'city of peace' might suggest.

The latter epitaph is misleading in a further respect, as the preceding chapters illustrate. Put simply, things were not that peaceful in The Hague and in its newly-establishment Court. Of course, judges were often guided by (in Rosenne's much-cited phrase) "high standards of personal integrity, professional competence, and worldly wisdom".[50] But saints they were not – and the contributions to this volume are an antidote to romanticising retrospection. To illustrate, in his discussion of the PCIJ's "growing pains", Arthur Eyffinger mentions the Court's "keen rivalry with the three other institutes on the premises, the PCA, the Peace Palace Library, and that other newcomer, the Hague Academy of International Law".[51] Michel Erpelding highlights the Court's dismissive attitude *vis-à-vis* the mixed arbitral tribunals of the inter-war era, which the Court clearly saw as inferior.[52] Going beyond the inter-institutional squabbles, many contributions note tensions playing out within the Court, especially during its first decade, as personalities and different visions of the judicial function clashed. The "Huber-Anzilotti tandem"[53] assumes particular prominence, perhaps not least because both of its members left to the world observations of refresh-

48 Loder, 'Twentieth plenary meeting (13 December 1920)', in League of Nations, *Records of the First Assembly I* (Geneva 1920) 443-446 (adding that the Netherlands would look after the Court "as a mother protects her child".

49 But see the ICJ's Memorandum of 1969, in which the Court proposed to amend Article 22, so to facilitate a move away from The Hague and the Peace Palace, which "was totally unsuitable to the [then] needs of the Court": see *ICJ Yearbook 1968-1969*, 108 et seq. The General Assembly did not act upon this proposal. By the late 1970s, a new building was added to the Peace Palace. Shaw has details: see 'Article 22', in Andreas Zimmermann and Christian J. Tams (eds), *The Statute of the International Court of Justice. A Commentary* (Oxford University Press, Oxford 2019), MN 11-14.

50 See Gill (n. 26), 14.

51 Eyffinger, at 78-79.

52 For details on this "fundamentally unequal relationship", see Erpelding, at 246-251.

53 Milanov, at 230.

ing candour.[54] As Momchil Milanov notes, the tandem palpably shaped the PCIJ's understanding of the preliminary objections procedure, to the chagrin of other judges who felt misunderstood in the debates.[55] Michel Erpelding draws attention to disputes about judicial propriety, resulting from the involvement of Judges Loder and Nyholm with mixed arbitral tribunals: an involvement that undoubtedly gave both judges significant practical experience in case-management, but that Huber and Anzilotti viewed with much scepticism.[56] Arthur Eyffinger, for his part, reflects on the impact of the "[k]een personal frictions" between judges and their outlook on proceedings. Personal rivalries between Loder and Huber – culminating in the latter's last-minute candidature for the presidency in late 1924 – are brought out clearly, and Huber's and Anzilotti's exasperation at their colleagues' limitations (only half of whom they considered to understand international law) becomes very tangible.[57]

These manifold observations do not seek to discredit the Court, nor are they offered with the primary aim of elucidating the 'inner workings' of the PCIJ. But they do cast light on the judicial institution and its members, as they were acting in their professional habitats of a century ago. Taken together, chapters by Erpelding, de Waele, van Leeuwen, Milanov and Eyffinger add texture to the often hagiographic and bland official accounts of the PCIJ. They affirm that, even in the peaceful and stately The Hague of the 1920s, "beneath the smooth surface of the law, international judicial processes bubble[d] with socio-professional struggles [and] clashing worldviews".[58] And precisely because of that, renewed engagement with the PCIJ, from a century's distance, surprisingly often is a "captivating spectacle".[59]

---

54 Huber's memoirs remain a wonderful source of PCIJ gossip: see Max Huber, *Denkwürdigkeiten* (Orell Füssli Verlag, Zürich 1972).

55 Milanov at 234-237.

56 See Huber's remarks referred to by Erpelding, at 255 ; and Anzilotti's reference to the mixed arbitral tribunals as "common organs of the parties" (i.e. not proper courts), cited ibid., at 251.

57 For more on this, including references, see Eyffinger, at 80-83.

58 To bring out as much is the central aim of Tommaso Soave, *The Everyday Makers of International Law* (Cambridge University Press, Cambridge 2022) (from whose preface the quote is taken [ix]).

59 Eyffinger, at 83.

E. The Virtue of Looking Again

A European 'World Court' whose jurisdictional regime was shaped by Japanese and Brazilian drafters. The Dutch in a dire corner, relying on 'sly manoeuvring' to bring the Court, against all odds, to The Hague. The PCIJ as a case-manager, administering justice efficiently, and all this despite significant factional infighting on the bench, and in the Peace Palace ...

None of these findings require the history of the PCIJ to be rewritten. But then again – to return to The Hague's other icon – the history of Vermeer's *Girl with the Pearl Earring* did not need to be rewritten after the restoration of the 1990s and late 2010s. The painting retained its immediacy, mystery and exotic touches; new research carried out by experts did not affect those timeless qualities. But new research, and the researchers' willingness to look again, did correct some misunderstandings, and perhaps opened up novel perspectives for admirers. "[W]e got to know (...) [the *Girl*] a little better", said the director of the Mauritshuis at the end of the most recent restoration works.[60]

Perhaps the same could be said of the PCIJ at the end of this book?

60 As cited in Mark Brown, 'Dutch Researchers coax Secrets from Girl with a Pearl Earring', at https://www.theguardian.com/artanddesign/2020/apr/28/dutch-researchers-coax-secrets-from-girl-with-a-pearl-earring.